A REBIRTH FOR CHRISTIANITY

A Rebirth for
Christianity

Alvin Boyd Kuhn

Quest Books
Theosophical Publishing House

Wheaton, Illinois ♦ Chennai (Madras), India

Quest Books
The Theosophical Publishing House
PO Box 270
Wheaton, IL 60189-0270

www.questbooks.net

"Tol'doth Yeshu" or "The Generations of Yeshu" reprinted with permission of The Macmillan Company from *Jesus of Nazareth* by Joseph Klausner, translated by Herbert Danby. Copyright 1925 by The Macmillan Company, renewed 1953 by Herbert Danby.

Cover design, book design, and typesetting by Kirsten Hansen
Cover image: Photodisc Green/Andrew Ward/Life File
    courtesy Getty Images

ISBN-13: 978-0-8356-0838-1
ISBN-10: 0-8356-0838-7

First edition (hardcover):
ISBN: 0-8356-0015-7

Library of Congress Cataloging-in-Publication Data
Kuhn, Alvin Boyd, 1880-1963.
A rebirth for Christianity / Alvin Boyd Kuhn.--2nd ed.
      p.   cm.
Includes index.
ISBN 0-8356-0838-7
1. Theosophy.   2. Christianity.   I. Title

BP567.K8 2005
299'.934--dc22   2004060132
        5 4 3 2 1 * 05 06 07 08 09 10

Printed in the United States of America

CONTENTS

FOREWORD

This is a prophetic book. When the late Dr. Alvin Boyd
Kuhn finished it in 1963, very few, if any, would have
foreseen the remarkable developments that came to influence
the spirituality of the late twentieth and early twenty-first centuries. Our author notes the discovery of The Gospel According to Thomas in 1945 and of the Dead Sea Scrolls two years
later, both but small waves of a floodtide of revelations to come.
Several years after that discovery, the entirety of the now well-
known Nag Hammadi Library was published, followed by
Elaine Pagels's pioneering classic, *The Gnostic Gospels*. A large
number of books of academic scholarship as well as those of
a popular nature ensued. The prophecy implicit in Kuhn's title
has come true: what Elaine Pagels in one of her later works
(Beyond Belief, 2003) aptly called "Alternative" Christianity has
indeed been reborn.

Moreover, the consequences and implications of Kuhn's
work cannot be seen as in any way negligible. His thesis that the
sacred scriptures of Judaism and Christianity for the most part
do not portray historical truths, but symbolic and mystical
metaphors, represents the very cornerstone of the approach of

Gnostic, or alternative, Christianity. Myth and symbol have always been the primary means whereby mystics and Gnostics have attempted to document their own ineffable experiences of transcendental realities. The mystical Jewish milieu of the centuries BC and AD wherein the Christian tradition originated had a keen sense of myth, symbol, and metaphor. The late pioneering scholar of Jewish mysticism, Gershom G. Scholem, expressed this sense in unmistakable terms:

> The historical aspects of religion have a meaning for the mystic chiefly as symbols of facts which he conceives as being divorced from time, or constantly repeated in the soul of every man. Thus the exodus from Egypt . . . cannot, according to the mystic, have come to pass once only in a place: it must correspond to an event, which takes place in ourselves, an exodus from the inner Egypt in which we are all slaves. Only thus conceived does the Exodus cease to be an object of learning and acquire the dignity of immediate religious experience.[1]

Today it is becoming increasingly evident that early Christianity abounded in writers and teachers of Gnostic orientation. Many of these persons were partakers of nonordinary states of consciousness and seemed to possess first-hand knowledge of the spiritual realities they proclaimed. The literary genre they employed was appropriate to their experiences; it consisted of myth, metaphor, poetry, and symbol. It was not until the second and third centuries that the mounting influence of certain prosaically disposed church fathers suppressed this literature and the spiritual orientation it embodies. Gospels such as The Gospel According to Thomas were replaced by The Gospel of John and the synoptic Gospels. Alternative Christianity ceased its open existence; it became a "lost light," as Alvin Boyd Kuhn named it.

The author of *A Rebirth for Christianity* has devoted much of his life to the task of assembling scholarly data and adding to it his outstanding interpretive insight. His was a transcendental and transhistorical vision that pointed beyond physical history to a timeless land of inexhaustible inspiration and wonder. This keynote runs like a golden thread through all his works, including *The Lost Light*, *Who is This King of Glory?*, *The Shadow of the Third Century*, *Sex as Symbol*, and *India's True Voice*. Regrettably, with the passage of time and the author's death, all of these remarkable books have gone out of print and are found now only in some libraries. It is thus doubly felicitous that his very last book, *A Rebirth for Christianity*, is now reappearing in a new edition.

Finally, a concluding word about Alvin Boyd Kuhn. I consider it one of the major blessings of my life that I met him in the early 1950s and that I maintained close contact with him until his death in 1963. He listed among his rare distinctions the fact that in the early 1930s he received his Ph.D. from Columbia University by writing a thesis on Theosophy. (This currently flourishing academic field of the study of esoteric movements was nonexistent at that time.) Dr. Kuhn was an accomplished student of Egyptian hieroglyphics and thus was able to trace many elements in Jewish and Christian scriptures to Egyptian sources. Inspired as he was by nineteenth-century esoteric spirituality, he was keenly aware of the trends of scholarship and the culture in the twentieth century. It was thus that he discerned the coming of a certain rebirth of the once lost, but now rediscovered, alternative or Gnostic Christianity. Today, even as he did several decades ago, he has much to say to us. It is to be hoped that many will be listening!

Stephan A. Hoeller
Los Angeles, 2005

PREFACE

I n the domain of religion and theology, the present age is
witnessing a phenomenon of extraordinary character and
significance. It is now being demonstrated that scholarly research in the field of Christian history and exegesis is at last
beginning to be motivated by the spirit of truth-seeking. The
amazing discovery in recent times of the Dead Sea Scrolls, and
other documents such as the Gospel of Thomas, has lifted a cur-
tain of secrecy from the studies and counsels of Christian theology, and has brought out into the open the questions of biblical
history and interpretation. It is a happy circumstance that a
scholar can speak out today and publish things relevant to the
history, the doctrines, and the scriptures of the Christian faith
that would have brought upon him the sternest reprobation
only a few years ago. It heralds the dawn of a fresh, clear conscience in the mind of Western man.

The most striking manifestation of this new orientation is
the sharp, sudden about-face of the Roman Catholic hierarchy
regarding Bible interpretation. Some leading Catholic universi-
ties and biblical institutes have scheduled courses in such previously banned subjects as Neoplatonic philosophy, Gnostic and

Hermetic systems, and movements of theosophic esotericism. Individual Catholic scholars and Catholic journals are publishing *pronunciamentos* hailing the advent of a new era in scriptural exegesis, in which, so to say, the Catholic cleric and lay mind alike may find themselves liberated from the shackles of a literal and historical dogmatism in searching the scriptures for a message of blessed truth, and may range freely through the whole gamut of mystico-spiritual values to be appropriated from the scriptural context.

It is now becoming apparent that ancient religionists held a knowledge of many recondite truths: They commanded an expansive synthetic view of the principles of a science that related the life of consciousness on being's subjective side harmoniously with the life of nature on being's objective side, in something like Kant's predicated "synthetic unity of apperception." This comes close to saying that the sages of old had a clear picture of life as an organic whole in a synthesis of all its component parts. Modern philosophy has always regarded such a comprehensive view as a possibility and a goal of human intellectual attainment, but has been skeptical about its actual realization.

The recognition is dawning that the so-named sacred scriptures or Holy Writ of past ages were the products of an effort to embody in terms and modes of expression this precious structure of understanding. A thing of such exalted revelation could be expounded only through the medium of poetic imagery, the forms and archetypes of which could be found in and drawn from an objective world that itself was the manifest expression of that soul of the universe in its creational effort. The burden of the message thus delivered was the endeavor to acquaint man with the basic principles of a universal science that would enable him to relate his life commodiously and harmoniously to the demands upon his intelligence and his will. The history of man's efforts to utilize this code of cryptic wisdom in the ordering of his life activity is the saga of world religion. And this story turns to tragedy when the posterity to which the heritage of arcane wisdom was transmitted proved obtuse to the divine message embodied in archetypal imagery, as well as to the perception of the underlying unity of the whole structure of truth. Thus there followed a general disintegration of this delicate structure, resulting in the weakening and the derationalization of religion, with the fateful results that humanity has been experiencing ever since.

The present break with two thousand years of a literal reading of the cryptograms of arcane wisdom is in every respect momentous. It points to a revival of the effort to recapture the esoteric significance of our scriptural heritage. Science has largely restored to the world the basic knowledge of the constitution of real being, the fiery core of universal life. Now, to accompany this illumination there must come the restoration of the structure of an equally scientific synthesis of truth in the domain of religion and philosophy, revealing the ultimate unity of all knowledge.

The transition now in progress will push the human mind far ahead in its march toward illumination. It will be a stride toward the attainment of a stable balance between the realism of common experience and the fantasy with which man inevitably tends to apostatize the realities of the world conceived to be lying above the range of rational meaning. Man's happiness, his weal or bodily woe, hinges upon his ability to maintain a steady balance between the world of his bodily existence and the one he pictures so irrationally as enticing him into its glories.

Chapter One

RELIGHTING AN
ANCIENT LAMP

From many quarters of the religious field, there is resounding today the cry of a new age in Bible interpretation. There are substantial grounds for asserting that we are beholding the dawn of a brilliant new day in scriptural scholarship that does indeed harbinger the bright promise of a new enlightenment. All down the years there have been men individually or in groups who have spoken out in strong dissent from accepted orthodox codes of interpretation. Jesus challenged the strict legalism and formalism in Jewish religion and incurred the hostility of the Sanhedrin for his courage. Then in Christianity itself there arose dissenters, both in the early years and in later times. In the fifth century, Scotus Erigena made a strong case for using the Platonic philosophy as the elucidative key to the scriptures, and the seed he planted has borne fruit. Dionysius the Areopagite sounded a similar note. St. Paul's contribution is described as a widely variant approach to Bible meaning, stressing subjectivism and pure spirituality rather than the historical element in Christianity. Clement, Origen, and even Augustine emphasized the allegorical nature of the writings and doctrines, taking their cue from the Jewish Philo. Even the climactic reconstruction of Christian systematization by the great Aquinas and the schoolmen in medieval times represented, in many respects, a departure from former codes and standards. Many of these movements, however, merely exchanged old orthodoxies for new and carried no threat of revolt against fundamental positions or tenets.

It was Philo, in the first century, who brought out prominently the allegorical method in biblical exegesis. He had drawn it from its source in remote Egyptian crypticism. An eminent modern biblical scholar, Robert H. Pfeiffer, in his work, *The History of New Testament Times*, speaks of "the allegorical interpretation of the Scriptures, used with such amazing virtuosity by Philo."[1] The early Christian fathers made a valiant attempt to apply the principles of the method to textual exegesis, and in the case of Clement and Origen it was by no means a futile endeavor. "Origen's allegories," as the historians refer to the exegetics of this most learned of the early church fathers, still stand as brilliant, illuminating revelations of the Holy Word. But the church successfully warded off whatever disturbing force the effort carried, and the historical code of interpretation has prevailed down to the present. The life of the Christian system was so powerfully activated by sheer faith that anything like a cold intellectual scholarship, which would subject the scriptures to dialectical criticism, was never able to gain a real hearing. Any such agitation was simply stifled by pietism. As a professor in Columbia University said in 1926, the Christian ecclesiastical power put a clamp upon the thinking mind of Europe for fifteen hundred years.

Now, however, that clamp is pried loose. For perhaps two centuries we have heard the hue and cry of scores of scholars as they have laid violent hands upon those venerable scriptures, to take them apart, study the mechanism of their structure, and discover their innermost motive and meaning. This work by now has progressed to the point where it puts in jeopardy the basic historicity of the entire scriptural corpus. Scholarly exegetes of the Gospels and the life of Jesus are bluntly declaring that the incidents of Gospel narrative can no longer be regarded as actual event, but must be taken as one or another form of literary artistry, legend, poetry, fiction, allegory, or Mystery play. The declaration of one writer as to the miracle of the feeding of five thousand with five loaves and two small fishes—that "whatever else this episode may be, it is assuredly not history"—is applicable to scores of incidents narrated in the Gospels. Under the blows of this sort of textual criticism, delivered with the remorseless power of fact and logic, the edifice of historical interpretation is fast crumbling.

In proportion as the historical view weakens, the allegorical approach must be reexplored. Truth emanates from the supernal world of divine ideation, and, as Plato said, comes forth in ideal forms. Man's feeble power to discern abstractions limits him to the effort to represent ideal forms by the imagery of concrete structures perceptible to his senses. Hence he must exotericize all esoteric truths. Having done so, he then faces the fatal risk of mistaking the objective representation for the ideal reality. When spiritual vision is blurred, the human mind sinks into idolatry. In the Gospels it is reported that in his questioning of Jesus, Pilate asked "What is Truth?" The canonical Gospels do not record Jesus' answer, but it appears in an apocryphal Gospel: "Truth is from heaven."

Truth does indeed emanate from the cosmic ideation and is brought down from that high source by the soul, for only the soul can grasp and carry it. Souls descend from on high, bearing the light of divine consciousness. But, says the profound Greek philosopher Plato, this light is dimmed and nearly extinguished by being plunged into the darkness of the body. As Browning has put it, "Wall upon wall, the gross flesh hems it in." St. Paul long ago stated the case: "For God, who hath caused the light to shine out of the darkness, hath shined in our hearts . . . but we have this treasure in earthen vessels." Well has the poet said that the glory of God is "imprisoned splendor" in man's being, "cribbed, cabined, and confined" in the dungeon of the body. The weak vision of man has distorted the archetypal forms of divine truth, which he sees but dimly in the darkness of his earthly prison.

It has never been clearly perceived that the universal, immemorial symbol of light in religion represents *mind*. Mind is that light eternal that God caused to shine out of the darkness of unconscious being to generate consciousness. It was the projection of invisible reality into visibility, as the forms of the divine mind arose out of the darkness. A line from John Greenleaf Whittier's charming winter idyl, *Snow-Bound*, felicitously expresses the concept. Describing the effect of pale moonlight falling upon the countryside all blanketed under snow, he speaks of the "unwarming light,"

> That only seemed, where'er it fell
> To make the darkness visible.

To make the primeval darkness visible, from its fathomless depths was generated the light of mind. And the images, the archetypal forms that arose in that mind, became the realities of all existent things. The whole process of creation can be envisaged as the generation of God's divine ideas and their being crystallized into the concrete visible objects of our world. Thus creation is the materialization of the noumenal world, the abstract made concrete. Even modern physical science discloses that all material things are crystallized sunlight. Every tree leaf is produced by photosynthesis—and *phos* (phot) is the Greek word for "light."

Over the pattern of cosmogenesis we may discern the numberless archetypes embodied in ancient religious literature. If, to become manifest, God's truth assumed visible substantiality, likewise the lofty concepts of the celestial mind, if they were to be discerned in the lesser light of man's recognitions, had to be similarly made concrete. Divine ideation took material form; therefore, intelligent men had to follow this creative process when they undertook the task of expressing truth for the apprehension of human minds. Every truth had to be externalized in some form sensually or imaginatively perceptible; and, beginning with basic words (including even the letters of the alphabet and numbers, which are themselves miniature allegories), such various devices of representation as myth, allegory, drama, figure, symbol, parable, apologue, and astrological typology were resorted to in order to portray the archetypal forms of "the wisdom hidden in a mystery." Inevitably the bibles were collections of allegories, myths, dramas, and "such-like tropes," as Plato observes.

Doubtless the original formulators of the divine myths never dreamed there would come a time so degenerate in reflective capacity that the products of their allegorical genius would be mistaken for the body of reality itself; that the diaphanous character of their imagery would fail to be apparent; that spiritual vision could not penetrate the symbols. They could not have guessed that the allegories and dramas would be taken for objective factuality and the *dramatis personae* for living humans, or that their ideal world of living imagery would become frozen into ostensible history.

This development represents the wine and bread of an exalted conscious potential turned to stone. It offers us the archetypal forms of truth fixated in impossible "historical" events. Ancient Egypt's cryptic but luminous paradigms of spiritual truth were turned by Christian stolidity of mind into Hebrew miracles at the historic level. No one has seen this more lucidly than the English scholar and Egyptologist, Gerald Massey, as two passages reveal:

The human mind has long suffered an eclipse and been darkened and dwarfed in the shadow of ideas the real meaning of which has been lost to the moderns. Myths and allegories whose significance was once unfolded to initiates in the Mysteries have been adopted in ignorance and reissued as real truths directly and divinely vouchsafed to mankind for the first and only time! The early religions had their myths interpreted. We have ours misinterpreted. And a great deal of what has been imposed on us as God's own true and sole revelation to man is a mass of inverted myths. . . . Much of our folklore and most of our popular beliefs are fossilized symbolism.[2]

The lost language of celestial allegory can now be restored, chiefly through the resurrection of ancient Egypt; the scriptures can be read as they were originally written, according to the secret wisdom, and we now know *how* the history was first written as mythology.[3]

The world of scholarship which once repudiated Massey's contentions is now proving him right. When, however, he said that we have misinterpreted our Bible myths, it would have been nearer the truth to say that we have taken them without any interpretation at all. If we have progressed far enough beyond fundamentalism in its grossest forms to understand that the scriptural allegories of the Jonah-whale story have some recondite meaning, we still think that the ancients believed the myth unconditionally.

Massey has had corroboration from other astute investigators in the field of mythicism. Godfrey Higgins, in his monumental work, *Anacalypsis*, says that "what are called early histories are not histories of man, but are contrivances *under the appearance of history* to perpetuate doctrines . . . in a manner understood only by those who had a key to the enigma."[4]

The noted scholar Gerald Massey says, "I have amply demonstrated the fact that the myths were no mere products of ancient ignorance, but are the deposited results of a primitive knowledge; that they were founded upon natural phenomena and remain the register of the earliest scientific observation."[5]

Surely a Christian should give heed when Origen, the most learned of the fathers of the church, speaks as follows: "The priests have a secret philosophy concerning their religion contained in their national scriptures, while the common people only hear fables which they do not understand. If these fables were heard from a private man without the gloss of a priest they would appear exceedingly absurd."

The sad truth is that in those early centuries of the Christian upsurge even the "gloss" of the priests on the hoary fables and allegories lost its true luminosity, as the cryptic keys themselves were lost and never recovered. This tragedy comes home to us in the realization that the modern mind is so unacclimated to the rarer atmosphere of true mystical apperception that it is unprepared to grasp the recondite significance of the Jonah allegory even if the true "gloss" of the ancient priest were to be clearly expounded.

With the near-total extinguishing of the genius of the ancient interpretation—that fatal fading out of what was not only the luminosity but a still deeper numinosity of mystico-spiritual vision—the Dark Ages were born. The loss of the subtlety of mind that was able to devise and interpret the divine allegories committed the succeeding ages to a mental darkness so profound that it amounted to a veritable derationalization and a hypnotic paralysis of Western mentality. And no remedy can be found, no awakening from the delusion, until the whole body of our heritage of ancient literature and dramatic genius is reexamined and reinterpreted through the lens of allegory.

The epic of the soul on earth, its battle of evolution on the horizon line between the heaven of spirit and the earth of sense, can again irradiate the lives of thinking men only if the paralyzing obstruction of the historical incubus is lifted. The symbols, graphs, images, and devices for the expression of spiritual truth that were converted into alleged history must be turned back into their original purport. The figures personating the divine central Sun of Righteousness that is to rise in the collective consciousness of the race with healing in its wings, along with its retinue of attributes and qualities that were transposed into men and women, must be reentified as conceptual forms. There is no incident or detail of narrative in the scriptures that cannot be made to glow with a far more inspiring luminosity of meaning when taken allegorically rather than objectively. The content of the sacred literature, expressing the noumena of Nous, the God-mind, and the materialization of the divine ideas in the living world, must be reoriented to the plane of its original conceptuality. The analogical genius of man must be sharpened once again to the acuity of reading back from the concrete image to the abstract conception of which it is a hieroglyph. The entire body of scripture must now be transfigured in our consciousness with the light it was designed first to conceal, then to reveal. The task now confronting modern intelligence is to throw off the blinders of a shallow realism that have obscured mystical vision and to awaken the long-stifled faculties of insight into noumenal verities. It will inaugurate finally a reenlightenment and transfiguration of human society.

In ancient times, the principles of a lofty soul-science were the substance, the nub, and the core of the Mysteries. Knowledge and instruction were not withheld from any who manifested potential capability and worthiness, as well as the desire and the will to attain the high goals. Thus began the tradition of secrecy. Only the reflective, discerning mind can see through and beyond the outer appearance and catch the spiritual counterpart in the noumenal world that remains hidden to the less thoughtful. This phenomenon is well described by the philosopher Santayana. In his *The Life of Reason* he writes, "Plato and Aristotle failed in spite of the immense and lasting influence of their work, for in both cases the after effects were spurious, and the spirit was smothered in the dull substance it strove to vivify. The Christian movement laid hold of the great body of imagery designed to depict spiritual truth and recondite wisdom, and transliterated it into 'history.'"[6]

Christianity never could have emerged out of Judaism if it had not deviated from previous and more general religious acceptances to receive a separate character and identity. Its novelty lay in the fact that it had departed from former anchorage in the esoteric wisdom, which in certain of its forms and elements still activated and characterized the Hebrew religion. True, Hebraism itself had not maintained vital connection with the high, mystical esotericism manifested in Kabalism. It, too, had moved some distance in the direction of a literal reading of the sacred scripts, the Torah, the Law, and the prophets. The psychological pressures impelling Judaism to interpret the scriptural allusions to a spiritual Israel in the terms of an ethnic Israel, with a divine commission to implement God's purpose in history, were almost irresistible, and they prevailed in direct proportion to the waning and final obscuration of the purely spiritual or otherworldly reference of the Israelite tradition. Jewish orthodoxy had swung away from the primal revelation of divine truth to a distortion that was a concession to mass ignorance very much as the Christian leadership did in its turn.

The two great religions, Judaism and Christianity, represent two somewhat divergent defections from the ancient occult heritage emanating from the shades of remote antiquity, but transmitted out of historical darkness into historical day by the ancient Egyptians. There may not be scholarly unanimity on the question of the primeval divine illumination from which came our revered holy scriptures, but there is a weight of academic opinion that the wisdom emanated from Egypt, or at least that Egypt transmitted it to such nations as Greece and Palestine from some remoter source. Academic authority is not lacking in support of Egypt's claim, and we find such an eminent scholar as

Dr. Robert H. Pfeiffer of the Harvard Divinity School, in his exhaustive work, *The History of New Testament Times*, writing that "Sirach's teaching illustrates the growth of wisdom from its mundane origins in Egypt to its identification with normative Judaism."[7] It is almost a universal tradition that the flowering of philosophical genius that gave the world the Platonic wisdom in Greece was fostered by contact with the Egyptian culture.

Chapter Two

EGYPT'S WAYWARD OFFSPRING

A better religious perspective might be gained if it were understood how both Judaism and Christianity developed as the product of two movements stemming from Egypt's heritage. It is not adequately realized that the central axis of religious ideology is the Messianic concept. This was an allegorization of the gradual coming to expression in human consciousness of the mind-soul-spirit of Christliness. But when it was travestied into the coming of a divine cosmic man-Christ in the flesh of one human body, it became the nucleus for a complex theological superstructure. At this point, it is above all desirable to look at the two lines of divergence, which were taken, first by the Jews and later by the Christians, from the pristine concept of the Messiah as the spiritual evolution of man.

Departing from the principles drawn from Egypt's basic lore, and cultivated for some time among the Hebrews by the Kabalists, Jewish theology veered away from the conception of Messianism as the advent of Christliness in all humanity. It interpreted the doctrine instead as a special manifestation of the destined rulership of the world by and through God's dealings with one particular group of people expressly chosen for such agency, this group being the Jews themselves, who had arrogated to themselves this function by dint of having identified themselves with the "Israelites" of the Old Testament. As outlined in the Mosaic books, the divine drama was to be consummated by the appearance of the long-prophesied and long-expected offshoot of the rod of Jesse and the "star out of David" foretold by Amos, Micah, and Isaiah. In the language of the Messianic allegory, this exalted personage, when he appeared, was to lead Israel in the fulfillment of God's marvelous design for the spiritualization of the nations through the Jewish people. The concept in this form necessarily carried the implication of the coming of divine influence into the world, but it stressed primarily the appearance in human form of that shoot from the rod of Jesse, that "branch from the tree of Eden" that was to redeem humanity from the Adamic curse. So it is true that the Jewish conception humanized and personalized the Messiah, as did the later Christian.

The Christian diverged from the Jewish conception in deleting entirely its reference to the Jews as the chosen instrument of God's purpose. In the Christian form of the concept, the Messiah was personalized at the human level and his whole function was focused in his person. He was at the same time to come as the full and final embodiment of God's own nature, which the Father thus projected into the world for the salvation of the people. He was to be the sole bearer of the Messianic power and glory.

Presenting many facets in its entire scope of meaning, this analysis outlines sharply the basic distinction between the two schematic views. Had the Christian included the exaltation of Judaism along with the birth of the Galilean Son of Man, there would have been little to distinguish it from the Judean ideal. Christianity also preached the coming of the Messiah as fulfillment of the Old Testament prophecy. Possibly at the start there was no definite design to exclude the Jewish world from participation in the drama of world salvation. But it was inevitable that the Jews would refuse to accept the extension of the tradition to universal mankind and the delimitation of Messianic function to a single personality, thus ignoring the role of the Israelites. These differences created the breach between the two positions that was destined to inundate Western history with rivers of blood. The Christian move stripped Judaism of its historic role of special divine agency. It asked Judaism to abrogate its historical birthright as God's chosen people. This was an insufferable humiliation, a dismantling of Israel's national and racial epos. To have accepted the Christian concept would have destroyed the structure of Judaism itself.

Any scholar who examines the evidence can readily determine that the name *Israel*, in its first connotation and usage, never carried any reference to any nation, tribe, or race. It was a term, one among many, used to designate the heaven-born sons of God, the pure offspring of God's creative mind and spirit. Had the formulators of the Jewish religion ever looked at corresponding terms in Hindu religion—*Manasaputras* and *Agnishwatta Pitris*—they would have been warned away from the error of limiting the reference to their own little Palestinian tribe. In the sense in which Minerva is said to have sprung full grown from the forehead of Jove, men can be conceived as generated from the cosmic power of mind. The term applied to no earthly beings, but when these spiritual monads of divine consciousness descended to earth to fulfil their mission, they thus became citizens of our mundane world. The evolution of their seed divinity could not be consummated save through union with the force locked up in the atom of matter, which they could utilize in the prosecution of their work in cooperation with the demiurgic oversoul of the universe. Thus arose the need for their incorporation in physical bodies. Their real birth out of spiritual potentiality into conscious power could come only through the intercourse of their spiritual fatherhood with the material motherhood, called by the Greeks *physis,* or "nature."

The heroes of ancient myth were all born of the union of a spiritual, heavenly, or divine father and an earthly mother. The force of this typology carried over even to the legendary birth of such exalted mortals as Pythagoras or Plato. The latter was acclaimed as the son of Apollo. Hence the name attached to the monads, in the reconstruction of the archaic heritage by those sages who from remote Egyptian sources formulated the religion for the Palestinian tribes, was *Israelites,* or "children of Israel." Some eminent scholars have lent their dictum to the derivation of this name from the Hebrew verb *Azor,* to "help," and *El,* "God," declaring it to mean, "God is my help." But no scholar is in a position to pronounce an apodictic judgment on the philology of this word. This etymology seems strained, and there is no warrant in the lettering for the introduction of the "my" in the rendition. It appears far more probable that the word is a compound of three units, *Is - Ra - El. Is* could well be an abbreviation or shortened form of Isis, the Egyptian goddess of motherhood. Even the Hebrew word for "woman" is *isha* (issa). The *Ra* comes direct from the great Egyptian father of spirit, Ra; and *El* is the Hebrew singular word for God. It would then read "Mother-Father-God," precisely what its generic character would make appropriate. The Hebrew heritage *was* drawn from Egypt, and in that land the name of the divine father principle not associated with Ra was Osiris; significantly enough, the original name of this deity was Asar (Azar). The Hebrews carried this very name forward in the title of their High Priest, who stood for the spiritual fatherhood, *El(e)azar,* and again, *Azariah.* (It was the Greeks who made Azar into Osiris.) The spiritual progeny of this God were called the children of Azar, and with the addition of the Hebrew *El,* God, as "Azar-el-ites." This derivation may be speculative, but it is worthy of consideration.

Gesenius' *Hebrew Grammar* was a text previously in popular use in the academic world. Gesenius states that the Jews appropriated unto themselves both the terms *Hebrews* and *Israelites* in token of their claimed descent from an illustrious ancestry. Virgil wrote the *Aeneid* to glorify the Caesar dynasty in Rome and to immortalize the glory of Rome itself by tracing the line of descent back to the goddess Venus. Most national epics were inspired by a similar intent to represent history as embodying the fulfillment of divine purpose.

But it remained for the Jews to interpret literally and to apply to themselves historically not only the three principal esoteric designations of the twelve celestial orders—Israelites, Hebrews, Jews—but to go to the extreme of identifying their own small ethnic group with these Israelite children of God. They took a name, in fact three names, originally designed to apply universally to collective humanity, endowed with the spark of the divine fatherhood. No tribe, group, nation, or race of mortals could justly appropriate any of these names to itself exclusively.

Such an attempt at self-glorification brought upon them the inevitable opprobrium of the rest of mankind. Having committed themselves to the notion that they were in fact those Israelites of Genesis and Exodus, having poured their intense national spirit into the mold of this conception, they paid the grievous penalty of having their national and racial consciousness imprisoned in the narrow sphere of a character and a destiny fixed by the explicit delimitations of the scriptural role. The Israelites were God's "chosen people," the special objects of his concern, his care, his favor. Just as they had stumbled over the meaning of the word *Israel*, likewise they blundered in their reading of the word *chosen*. The idea that God, the all-righteous ruler, would look out over the hosts of earth and select one small tribe of Palestinian herdsmen from among all mankind for special concern and favor should have appeared unconscionable from the start. The inner implications of the word should have told them that this "choosing" of God was not made among ethnic groups on earth. It was his selection and deputation of twelve legions of angelry in heaven! Their divine assignment was to migrate to earth and there fulfill a commission appropriate to them in God's plan of creation as it touched his progeny at a given contingency in the process. They were chosen to come to earth to *be* humanity.

More than one ancient people had attempted to intertwine the divine allegory with their own history and geography. This impulse arose from the reflection that history in the small epitomizes history in the large, and that the career of a nation (as also the career of an individual) may closely follow the outline of general evolution. If lofty intelligence governed the undertaking, the result would be an epic of Homeric order, but if ignorance and self-righteousness prevailed, and the allegorical intent was replaced by credulous belief, the result would be a disastrous falsification of history. This blunder did occur, and as a result most biblical "history" is misinterpreted allegory and myth. The name *Israel* applied to no ethnic group. Its reference was wholly to the divine spiritual origin of humanity, said to be twelve legions of "angels" sent to earth bearing the seed germ of potential divinity, which, when planted, grown, and fructified by evolution, would make mankind the legitimate heirs of God's patrimony.

In a purely spiritual sense, all humanity is potentially Israel. Charles Guignebert, the outstanding modern exegete, in his work, *Jesus*, quotes Philo of Alexandria as saying that any man who forsakes the worship of idols for the true God is a member of the *true* Israel, which is not to be confused with "Israel of the flesh." St. Paul declares that merely being born in a Jewish family does not make one an Israelite. The criterion is spiritual unfoldment; an Israelite is one who is bringing his spiritual potential to birth, and he may be of any race.

Christian apologetics has found it dialectically necessary to accredit the distinctive claims of a divine status for Jewry, assumed to be the "Israel" of the Bible, in order to vindicate its claims for the divinity of its own Messiah, Jesus of Nazareth, born to fulfill the Old Testament prophecy. In the Christian theological view, there would have been no gulf between the two religions had the Jews recognized Jesus as the Messiah, born of their own divinely commissioned race. But by denying him they forfeited the glory of having produced him for humanity. We find a typical expression of Christian support of the Jewish "Israelite" status in a work entitled *Introducing the Old Testament*, by a Catholic writer, Frederick L. Moriarty. Expounding the biblical-rabbinic view, he states that Israel is not a "natural" nation; it is not like other nations; it rates a "supernatural" status, having been called into being by God to serve his special cosmic purpose. God made a special covenant with Israel, first through Abraham as the progenitor of the race, then with the entire community of Israel at Mount Sinai. Only by God's gratuitous and gracious election of this race to a special place in his divine favor does Israel play its part in the scheme of world destiny; apart from this covenanted relation to God, Israel would be as nothing.[1] The Catholic writer does not repudiate this Jewish evaluation of Jewish election and destiny, because it strengthens Christian claims as to the divinity of Jesus.

We have, then, these two streams, each diverging from the original connotation of *Israel*. The Christians cherished a misconception of the word *Messiah*, which in later years drove them to the contradiction of believing that the love of the humanized Christ child could sanctify the slaughter of nonbelievers. The Jews cherished the misconception of the words *Israel* and *chosen*, which drove them to self-isolation and sequestration from other peoples. Never in human history could it be said that so great a tragedy eventuated from so seemingly trivial a cause as the misreading of a term in sacred literature. Yet the phenomenon is understandable if one considers that when a nation or culture takes a single book as the determining source and monitor of its entire psychic life, every chapter, every letter becomes crucial, and its misinterpretation can hold countless minds in bondage.

It is a significant fact of history that when Alexander the Great swept the Near-East world with the besom of his Macedonian phalanx, it was Jewish Palestine that alone stubbornly resisted absorption into the Hellenic culture that followed in the wake of his conquest. The fact that Philip of Macedon engaged the philosopher, Aristotle, as tutor of the young Alexander is evidence that he dreamed of spreading Greek philosophical culture over the known world. Had the conqueror lived to age seventy and given his life to cultivation of the Greek influence in the area he had overrun, the course of ensuing history might have perpetuated "the glory that was Greece" for the blessing of mankind. Greek philosophy did spread its benign influence over much of the terrain of Alexander's conquest, but it fought a losing battle on the soil of Palestine, because the Jewish consciousness was sealed against any system that rested on pure rationalism. When every aspect of a nation's life is imbued with the conviction that it is inspired by God for the accomplishment of his divine will, all philosophy must be shaped to fit this conception.

Instead of melting into the broad universality of the Hellenic wisdom, therefore, the Hebrew theology remained unmodified and retained those elements that ultimately conduced to the eruption of Christianity. Had Judea been more receptive to the Greek influence, Judaism would have been so modified that the misconceptions as to the nature and significance of the Messianic advent could never have taken form to derationalize the Hebrew consciousness. Hellenism looked for the glorification of the human spirit in a general and collective apotheosis of humanity, and it would have effectually debarred any concept of a personalized avatar or Sun God from displacing the spiritual and evolutionary interpretation.

Finally, the world would not have suffered the loss of any true religious motivation had Judaism not personalized the Messianic entity as a son of David, and had Christianity not existed at all. For its only excuse for divergence from Judaism was likewise its still more literal personalization of the Messiah. Would the world have suffered a religious loss had history taken this course? Many will answer yes, yet the record of Western history would have been spared its long chronicle of war and religious persecution had Judaism not restricted to itself the conception of Israelite, and had Christianity not personalized the Messianic light of deliverance, meant to shine upon the hearts of all men.

THE BREACH BETWEEN JEW AND GREEK

S cholarship is almost universally agreed that the Christian movement created by the disciples of Jesus would have disappeared in a generation if St. Paul had not grafted on to it the essential substance of the Hellenic philosophy. Christianity was in effect saved from extinction in embryo when it incorporated in its scriptures those documents known as the Epistles of St. Paul, which enabled it to rationalize its Messianic tenets. Later, under the massive pressure of an ignorant population that flocked into its fold by the third century, the Greek influence was suppressed. But still later, finding that it would have to meet the problem of exegesis at the level of a more learned society, the church was happy enough to accommodate its doctrines to the fundamentals of the much-despised Hellenic systematization, and by the twelfth century it had taken refuge entirely in the shelter of Aristotelianism. St. Paul was eulogized as the divinely appointed instrument for the conversion of the pagan world to Christianity; it was also he who, to make the Gospels acceptable to the Greek cast of thought, recast the figure of the Christian's personal Christ in the character of the Greek Christos, for the concept of the Messiah personalized in a man of flesh was totally alien to the Hellenic ideology.

The first group of simple country folk, the *am ha'arets* of Israel, who comprised the personnel of the nascent Christian upsurge, could be content with their entified Christ man, Jesus. But such an interpretation of the Messianic tradition was impossible for a Greek. For him the Christos was a spiritual consciousness, not a man. This is clearly the reason why Paul preached "Christ-in-you, the hope of glory" for mankind, and never mentioned Jesus as a man of flesh and the founder of the movement he is declared to have carried beyond the borders of Palestine to the "Gentiles." It can even be affirmed that Paul was more truly a "Christian" than those with Jesus in Judea, for the agitation set in motion by the twelve "fishermen" had nothing to do with the name *Christian*. "The brethren were first called Christian at Antioch." The name is wholly of Greek origin and connotation. Before its later adoption by followers of Jesus it never bore any reference to a man-Messiah. It is an anomaly, a contradiction of terms, to call any man the Christ, *the Christos*. To have said, in the hearing of a Greek, that "Christ" went to Cana and turned water into wine would have caused him mental pain, thus to identify and personalize the very spirit of divine Being as a man of flesh. It would have been to him blasphemous and degrading to his concept of transcendental deity. Even Judaism would not tolerate the conception of the Messiah as a man who could be killed ignominiously by the Roman power. An intelligent Greek would not have used the term *Christos* without the definite article *the*, just as the Egyptians usually spoke of "the Osiris." The Hebrews, too, dignified the deific name with the article prefixed, which accounts for the *el* beginning or ending so many names, as Bethel, Israel, Eleazar. A fact of etymology that seems to have eluded scholarly recognition is that this little article *the* is itself basically the designation of deity, equivalent to *God* itself. *El*, Hebrew for "God," is the Spanish masculine singular word for *the*, as in *el sombrero*, "the hat." The English *the* is the whole stem of the Greek word for "God," *theos*.

Far from the truth is the commonplace idea that St. Paul, after his spiritual awakening through his Damascus road vision of shining light, threw himself in with the Galilean band about Jesus, espoused their cause, and then went out and preached their doctrine and founded a dozen "churches" of the movement. What the Apostle promulgated was the basic principia of ancient wisdom that belonged wholly to the Mysteries and to Hellenic philosophy of the Orphic strain. He himself characterized it as the "wisdom hidden in a mystery." It was indeed so incongruous with the Galilean's preachment of the imminent coming of the Kingdom of Heaven that the party attached to Jesus menaced Paul's life when, with Barnabas, he first visited Jerusalem. If the pupil of Gamaliel can be said to have preached Jesus Christ and his crucifixion, death, resurrection, and ascension, it is an unwarranted assumption that he was talking of Jesus of Nazareth. The germ of divinity implanted in the human constitution *was* crucified, went to its "death," was buried and rose again, even on the third day, and returned to the Father, according to all esoteric legendry. The Greeks did not need to hypostatize a *man* to yield them the understanding or to afflate the consciousness of the miracle-working power of the deific fire of soul in all mortals. Their definition of *ho Christos* was a psychological potency active in the human constitution that was itself the agent of their regeneration. The knowledge of its presence and psychic dynamism within the sphere of their own control was the cogent spur to self-realization.

It is a degradation of the human spirit to believe that one is subject to the impact of forces over which he has no control, to which in dire distress one is driven to implore help or mercy. It was the weakening of the tradition of esotericism (which raised man's endeavor and aspiration to peak level by its predication of man's own divine capability) that caused Christianity to externalize the Christos in a living human. Turning from the God-seed within to a man-God without, Christianity drove the humanity it touched to the status of beggary. The ultimate criterion of a religious value is incontestably the degree to which the human being comes into a conscious recognition of the nature and value of his own activity. Is he a creature under the control of forces external to himself, or is he, and to what degree, master of his own life?

Religion has always clung to the possibility of man's attainment of an unimaginable glory. But there can be no glory for a creature that cannot direct its own career and destiny. The transforming glory can only come with the development of forces, energies, faculties, and powers from within the being of self-conscious creatures themselves. There is warrant for the categorical pronouncement that all growth is an outward movement of forces emanating from an inner core of nonphysical energy. The activity of life energies invariably is in the movement from latency in germ or seed outward and upward to physical manifestation. The line of march is from seed to fruit. The seed once planted, there is set the tug of polarity between the vital fire latent in the seed and the opposite fire in the environment. The power without and the power within are thrown into tensional relationship with each other. The impact of exterior influences stirs the seed into activity, confronts it with the necessity of self-exertion, and so brings it to the realization of its own nature.

As this realization deepens and clarifies, the procedure passes from implicit passivity to greater self-generated exertion. For every individual embodiment of life must ultimately be self-conscious, self-contained, and self-governed. Without this condition, no deification of life is possible. If the glory is not a product of growth in the consciousness within, it is no glory, for it represents no conquest. The transfiguration scene vividly dramatizes the glorification of man. It shows our Christhood, the divine figure in the myths and Mysteries, radiating a veritable flaming fire of spiritual light. "For his face did shine as the sun and his garments became white as light."

The instructive essence of all this is that a religion which shifts the center of man's conscious effort from development of the powers within, and focuses aspiration upon some saving power external to the self, will dissipate psychic energy in futile endeavor, while it lets the dormant divinity lie unawakened.

The clash of Jew with Greek was in itself one of the most fateful crises in the cultural history of our race. It arrayed the two forces in opposition in a battle fought right down to the present. It was a tragic denouement, all the more so because the great break need not have occurred at all. One mind was brilliant enough to see how unnecessary it was, and he strove valiantly to prevent the breach or to heal it. This was Philo Judaeus, whose greatness and potential service to religious harmony and fraternity have not been adequately recognized. With philosophical insight he discerned the recondite principles of the archaic wisdom hidden under "glyph and symbol" in the Mosaic Pentateuch and in the Hellenistic abstractions of myth, allegory, and drama alike. Beneath the symbols and representations, he traced the graphs of one and the same occult philosophy and effected a working synthesis. But his work encountered the same stolid incapacity to recognize truth that has ever been its defeat. It has to be said that his elucidations were not sufficiently authoritative and convincing to establish the esoteric theses, and although Clement, Origen, and other early church fathers carried his methodology into their interpretative efforts, his work lapsed into desuetude.

Just as scholarship has reported different religions as worshipping different gods, when all the while they were worshipping essentially the same divinity under a wide variety of names, so the religious formulators of different cultural systems exploited the content of one set of allegories and arrived at a systematic codex of their faith conditioned by the particular semantic structures they had used in the process. Thus one religious system appeared to differ from another. Had Judaism and Christianity

been discerning enough to probe deeply into the hidden significance of their literary symbolism, they would have found themselves standing on the same ground of meaning, developing the
same truth under various tropes and figures. This immense variety of forms that meaning takes can be appreciated only if one
surveys the myths of ancient peoples. Fully understood, the mythologies would be found to embody the same basic and still-living
truths. In this light it seems evident that the Palestinian religious development caught up one thread of allegory and worked
it into a fabric of creed and worship, while Greece fell heir to
another line of typology and built upon its intimations of
meaning. Had there been competent study of comparative religion in that early day, the identities hidden under dissimilar
forms would have been caught, and the Hermetic wisdom would
have come down in the life of Near East nations fairly intact.

Failing to find Hellenism compatible with its own religion,
Hebraism conditioned itself to breed a daughter who was to
turn against her parent almost from the start. This ungrateful
daughter of Judaism was Christianity, and her alienation from
her parent source was the penalty Judaism had to pay for its failure to embrace the essence of Hellenism. For the presence of
elements of Greek philosophy in Judean religion would have
prevented the personalization of the Christos; hence Christianity
would not have taken its present form. The self-questioning
that presently engages Christianity may in part spring from
doubt that the infinite magnitude of God could be compressed
in the body of one single human being, no matter how spiritually noble. Taken abstractly, however, the doctrinal statement
that God in the Logos aspect of his being became flesh and
dwelt among us contains a profound truth. If one takes the
noumenal instead of the physical connotation of the word *flesh*,
signifying the corpus of humanity itself, then the idea of the
incorporation of the divine Being in man regains its universality and its spiritual message for all men.

A further principle of the arcane science, if retained, would have served to balance understanding of this recondite statement. This is the doctrine that the visible universe is the _body_ of God, itself one vast organism whose order and coherence are the result of his ensouling consciousness.

Pantheism ?
Panentheism ?

In outline, then, we can perceive the currents flowing in Judaic religion that generated its offspring, Christianity. In Hellenistic philosophy the concept of the divine manifestation, epitomized so widely in the doctrine of the coming of the Messiah, was steadfastly held to the abstract level, connoting the presence in humanity as a whole of the spirit and consciousness of the divine Principle. But in the Judaic religion the concept had advanced a half-step away from philosophical abstraction toward human entification, the Messiah being conceived as the spirit of Jehovah animating the "Israelites" and destined to be embodied in a man-born son of David who should sit on the throne of Jerusalem and be God's vice-regent, for the execution of the divine will over the nations. Finally, in Christianity the concept of Messiah came to be identified with the form of one babe, divinely endowed but born in a lowly stable among animals, representing the polar opposition of spirit and matter, the tension out of which the Christ-consciousness is born.

In summary, Hellenism preserved the Messianic concept in its purely noumenal and abstract form; Hebraism kept it half-spiritual, half-personalized; Christianity completely personalized it. As already indicated, the primitive Christian movement swung away from its roots in both Hellenism and Judaism to take the path toward the full human entification of deity in one personality. Scholars are nearly unanimous in asserting that if it had held narrowly to that path it would have died after a brief upsurge, just as scores of other group movements in religion have flickered and died out. In a comparatively short time, however, the Christian movement was impelled to reach back to the original Greek mystico-spiritual concept of Christhood, joining that purely nonphysical doctrine with its sarcolatrized, i.e. "fleshed," entification of the Messiah. This dichotomy of the Christ character has left Christian doctrine divided between the concepts of Christ as spirit and Christ as Jesus of Nazareth, both of which have, over the years, served the purposes of exegesis.

A New Orientation, Not a New Revelation

Christianity has persistently claimed that it is the one true religion among all other faiths. Yet the sad fact is that more untruths have been promulgated in its name than by any other major religion in the civilized world. Over the centuries, the Christian church has enforced the acceptance of many dogmas that have since been discarded. Today Christianity is undergoing a self-reappraisal which is painful, even agonizing, to many of its believers. So deeply does an old and hallowed institution like the Christian church become interwoven in the culture that it becomes sacrosanct and inviolable; its traditions, to its inheritors, are beyond criticism. Only the slow progress of reluctant recognition of the validity of criticism will at last bring recognition of past errors and a willingness to change. Only when the pressure of cultural change becomes relentless do these believers evince any such willingness. The purpose of this volume is to assist in this process of reevaluation by pointing to the torch of truth which has been almost totally extinguished, but which gave Christianity its birth and its genius.

The study of comparative religion and mythology, to which many scholars have contributed, discloses overwhelming evidence of the parallelism, unity, and kindred origin and structure of all ancient systems of national, racial, and tribal religious rite and belief. This evidence attests the homogeneity of Christianity with, and its obvious derivation from, a common source of religious expression in history. The study of the religions and the myths on a comparative basis reveals that not a single teaching of the Christian faith was new or unique. Without exception, every element of this "revealed" religion was extant before the first Christian century, in the traditions, practices, and literature of many other lands and peoples. (When, for instance, l'Abbé Huc was the first Christian to enter the region of Turkestan, what was his consternation on finding the Tartary natives celebrating the Eucharist with bread and wine? Or the amazement of Pizarro and Cortez when they found Aztec and Mayan rites and beliefs similar to those of the Roman Catholic system?)

One might even say that when Christian congregations celebrate Holy Communion, and thus "partake of the Lord's body till he come," they are perpetuating, in a refined sense, the aboriginal tribal custom of cutting up and eating the body of the local god, in order thus to incorporate his *mana* in their own nature. The distaste we feel for ancient barbaric practices, when primitive child-mindedness misjudged the profound intimations of a once high ritual, is paralleled by our dismay when we realize that the Christian practice of the Eucharist is also inspired by a misconception. In both cases the custom derived from the literalization and materialization of a mystical drama. The inner psychological dynamic of the allegory was lost, and only the outer enactment of the rite was sustained. It became an empty shell, due to the failure of the mind to pierce through the outer form of an ideal figuration and discern the noumenal truth that dramatic genius had incorporated in it.

Herein lies the lost clue to the eclipse that has darkened the religious consciousness antecedent to Christianity in many lands and throughout Christianity itself. The religion that preached charity seized many a convenient opportunity to denounce paganism. Yet if humane standards and sentiment be made the criterion, the history of Christianity is far from blameless. Christianity never offered up human sacrifices, and it advanced beyond the Judaic use of animal sacrifices on temple altars. But it did not scruple to torture and burn millions of people for their honest and courageous dissent from declared doctrine. Its victims can well be called sacrifices on the altars of Christianity, and it has often forfeited its right to spiritual leadership by permitting this killing in the name of the Prince of Peace, a cruel contradiction of its basic principles.

However, since the motive of this essay is not to castigate Christianity, but to reaffirm its real message, nothing is to be gained by dwelling on the past. The attitude of the church is already changing toward recognition of its own record. The past must be remembered and acknowledged, however, not to make the present generation feel guilty, but that we may thoroughly repudiate the causes of what we condemn. But if Christianity, in spite of so much good, has in the past inflicted so dire a dementia upon the West, is not this ample justification for a reexamination of its history, to discover the mistakes and chart a better course?

Religions are basically mankind's efforts to relate the content of human consciousness in both feeling and thought to the life of the world. They are man's endeavor to ascertain the meaning, the context, and the laws of life and to relate himself most harmoniously with what he can learn of these. The impact of his experience causes him to exert himself and to equilibrate his position in the midst of the forces, both physical and psychic, that he must seek to control. Defining *soul* for the moment as the synthesis of all psychic experience, religion may then be said to be the ultimate outcome of the effort of souls to harmonize themselves most felicitously with their world. What the senses experience, what the emotions feel, what the intellect cogitates in response to living, must precipitate in consciousness a sediment of integrated psychic elements. Whether the individual knows it objectively or not, this deposit is his religion.

Religion therefore embodies, in addition to its revealed truths, a loosely knit content of aesthetic, emotional, and intellectual elements. The ancient sages, drawing upon the living mythos of their world and other ages, which Plotinus called the World Soul, formulated an organic integration of the principles governing the play of the living energies. This synthesis of knowledge was treasured as the priceless heritage of mankind from the gods. From time to time there arose societies, associations, and brotherhoods that aimed to preserve, to cultivate, and to practice the principles and techniques of this arcane science. Christianity developed out of the efforts of one group to exploit certain elements of the archaic wisdom, elements that were common to many sectarian movements of that time. By placing special emphasis on certain of these (and, it must be said, by misinterpreting their significance) it produced a unique crystallization of religious force that strangely survived when so many others perished.

Such in fact was the new orientation of basic ingredients in this development that the groups concerned were persuaded that their production was an entirely new revelation, indeed the one true revelation, never known before. And such were the psychological repercussions from the impact of the dynamic elements in the compound that there was generated a ferment such as had never been seen before. The rise of Christianity was marked by a release of pietistic fervor that swept reason aside and produced an afflation of religious zeal unique in world history. In his famous work on *The Decline and Fall of the Roman Empire*, Gibbon states that the devotees of the new faith in many instances virtually badgered the Roman magistrates to sentence them to martyrdom, repeating an offence if the first one was pardoned. Precisely what the constituents were of the teaching that engendered perhaps the most passionate religious feelings in all history is, at this late date, difficult to determine. Yet it is clear that what comprised a blending of many incongruous elements already existent in Hebraism and other contemporary systems was able to seize on the imagination and the hearts of its followers in an overpowering way. Contemporary scholarship recognizes that Christianity borrowed many of its rites and doctrines from earlier cultures; nevertheless, Christian apologetics still largely contend that in every case a new and more spiritual rendering was substituted for the crude pagan interpretations.

This view, however, has been negated by the findings of numerous scholars, all men of unimpeachable integrity, many within the ecclesiastical system. It has required moral courage to publish these determinations of honest scholarship. But the action of the Roman Catholic hierarchy in legitimizing the allegorical interpretation of the scriptures marks the dawn of their vindication. It will be a considerable time before the import of this epochal move will be seen. It sharply reverses the policy of the Christian hegemony in an effort to correct a blunder perpetrated in its early history. During this period of anti-intellectualism when the darkness began to creep over the Western world, all things having to do with learning, erudition, and philosophy were subject to suspicion. The scriptures were held to be the literal, solitary truth. The reaction against all scholarship grew so violent that it sent up in flames the invaluable library of the Serapeum in Alexandria, destroyed the priceless *Hexapla* of the church's most learned pundit Origen, and posthumously anathematized him. It forced Jerome to recant and apologize for his unguarded expression of love of classical literature. It menaced Augustine with the same charge and caused Tertullian to shout, "What have Homer and Virgil to do with the crucified Jesus?" It murdered the brilliant Hypatia as she took refuge within the "inviolate" sanctuary of the altar. It compelled the emperor

Justinian to close the Platonic Academies and thus extinguish the light that, if suffered to continue shining, would have saved Europe from its devastating and fatal plunge into the medieval Dark Ages.

When Rome declares that the divine voice out of the heavens at the baptism of Jesus was perhaps an "exteriorization" of an inner state of the divine mind, and not an objective historical event at all, the world should note it as a momentous event, unprecedented for many centuries. Once before, Christianity had to reverse its position. Having earlier eliminated the philosophy of Plato and Aristotle from its doctrine, it was glad to call their works in to support its inadequate intellectual foundations and to give back to Christian doctrine its philosophical roots in Greek rationalism.

As in the case of many an individual and many a nation, Christianity's path to future power and beneficence for humanity has had to run for a time through the valley of humiliation and contrition before it ascends again to the uplands and heights of a new vision. This new ascension is only possible if mankind's demand for the inner truth of Christian teaching and history is answered. "The hungry sheep look up," as Milton said, and will flock to the hand that offers to feed them. But who is their rightful shepherd, and with what provender will he feed them? They flocked into the fold in those early times, and it was not long before the Christian leadership awoke to the realization of power that was thrust into their hands. But as always, power corrupted, and churches have never been free of this danger.

As religion arises out of this tension in the duality of man's nature between the animal-human and the Divine, so it is inevitable that in the welding of the religious influence into institutionalized forms there will be a clash between the Divine and human motives. Human interest, wayward and recalcitrant, as it is bound to be, must in the end bow in meekness and docility, if not in awe, before the mystery of the Divine. And the Divine must take what measures it can to maintain its supremacy. These two elements are inevitably interwoven in man's religious life.

C h a p t e r   F i v e

RELIGION AND THE ILLUMINATION OF MIND

Religion is that sphere of thought and feeling in which the human being shows himself both at his heroic best and his tragic worst. It is the field in which man stands firmly for his ideal values, or surrenders himself to delusion, thus corrupting his innermost nature. When adversity, danger, or tyranny challenge, he shows himself capable of the loftiest nobility, the most godlike self-sacrifice, and the most loyal spiritual consecration. But in long periods of commonplace existence, man may succumb to lethargy and let his spirit sink low. In such an inert state, he submits to orthodoxy. He has neither the incentive, the intelligence, nor the courage to subject doctrinal impositions to robust criticism and so determine his code of belief for himself. He relies on the competence and good faith of the priesthood. He feels a certain safety in keeping in line with communal sentiment. He thus ordains for himself and his children a mental or psychological subservience to established consensus in his religious life, and this amounts to a virtual abandonment of that which makes man unique—the faculty of reasoning and the hunger of the soul for understanding.

Mind is the primal, as it is the ultimate, creative force in the cosmos. Either in conscious operation or stored in man's unconscious mind is the governor of all organic life. To the ancients, mind was "the serpent charmer," the reptile symbolizing the fiery power (in Egypt, the *uraeus*, a "serpent of fire") locked up in the atoms of the body and its animal instincts. Intellect and reason must eventually "charm" these writhing serpents into harmlessness. In reverse symbolism, however, the serpent may charm the soul, the mind itself, under the symbol of the bird. Thus the reason and the sense can each dominate the other, so there is a dual hypnosis. In the end, if the purpose of evolution is to be served, life will come fully under the governance of conscious mind. Science today supports the view that the drive of life is toward greater awareness. In men, each individual becomes in time what the nature and the contents of his mind make him. His thoughts will stamp upon him their true or false design. "As a man thinketh in his heart, so is he."

Plato outlined this view of man some four-and-a-half centuries before the Christian era. Greek reflection had extracted it out of the more venerable Egyptian structure a millennium or two earlier. For this is what the hierophants of the Nile had meant by their gods. Those divinities were the archetypal Forms of the Noumenon of the creation, the living energies of matter and of mind. A Form was the shape, structure, and organic unity of a brooding cosmic ideation. When it hardened into matter it passed from aeri-form to fluid, became concretized, and finally became the object of perception to sentient creatures.

The young germ of mind implanted in the creature—unfolding in ovo from first cell, reaching in millions of years the self-consciousness of the human order and groping toward the expression of that same power in itself which it had inherited from its father Nous—began to think, act, and create after the model and pattern of the cosmic archetypal Forms. The natural creation, being the projection and precipitation in matter of the divine ideation, held before its generated sons, in every tree, stone, cloud, brook, and lightning flash, those multitudinous concreted shapes of the celestial beauty and verity. Living among them daily, facing them at every turn, the minds of the children of God could not fail in time, in spite of ages of blinding nescience, to reflect in consciousness the Forms of the primal cosmic Logic. The son-mind must come in time to match the father-mind. For the creature-mind is a fragment, but at the same time a potential integer, of the Creator-Mind. So St. Paul said that now we see in part, obscurely, dimly, but in the consummation of the cycle we shall see all things as integral and whole. And Kant's synthetic unity of apperception will end in synthetic unity of understanding and vision.

The conceptual form and coherence that dominate any individual consciousness constitute for that individual his religion. It is also his philosophy, his psychology, and his theoretical and practical ethics. It is his philosophy as far as it is intellectually formulated. It is his psychology to the extent that it gives him feeling and motivates conduct. It grounds his ethics insofar as he endeavors to adapt his conduct to the idealities it recommends to him. It is his religion in-so-far as the synthesis of all these elements engages his loyalty, his devotion, and his deepest consecrations. The total involvement of a man's consciousness in the business of relating his life to his world would be the large and inclusive definition of his religion.

But it is the power of thought that becomes so crucial an element. The ideas, notions, fancies, intimations, and yearnings that make up the endless stream of mental activity constitute for the individual the reality of what he is. He is thus mesmerized by them in the state in which they hold him. This is the strange truth of the assertion that all thought is mesmeric. And the only way by which the spell can be broken is through a change in the form and nature of the thought. Where can we look for help? Our scriptures have given us the answer:

"Ye shall know the truth and the truth shall make you free." To be put to sleep by falsehood is tragedy. To be obsessed with the beauty, truth, and goodness of life is to live in beatitude. One is hell, the other heaven. Well does the book of Proverbs exhort us, "With all thy getting, get wisdom, get understanding," assuring us that these are precious beyond all imaginable evaluation.

The philosophers have said with unanimity that there is no blessedness in life equal to that achieved by the mind that will lift itself to a synthetic view of all reflective ideas in an integrated structure of significance. The Greeks insisted that the life of reason was the divinest attainment of the human being. The word *meaning* is perhaps the key of all philosophy. A person who truly grasps meaning feels himself to be at one with the dynamic of the universe, in tune with the infinite. His mind pulsates with the universal life, it sweetly senses its harmony with the blessedness of being. Under divine spur, the soul of man, like a seed pushing upward toward the light of the sun, seeks for this bliss of self-illumination. It is Ajax crying for the light. True philosophy is more than intellectual ratiocination; it is beyond that, the complete irradiation of consciousness with the perception of truth and beauty and the beneficence of all things in harmony. Such union of thought and feeling brings, as Spinoza exulted in saying, the intellectual love of God and produces the "God-intoxicated philosopher."

Each religion makes its own special appeal. Our particular task is to scrutinize the system known as Christianity to determine to what extent it has been a salutary, and to what extent a deleterious, influence. The task is difficult, because Christian origins are shrouded in a cloud of obscurity. There is not only a lack of basic historical data, but early Christian literature was not at all motivated to strict historical accuracy. Modern study discloses that ancient religious writing aimed always at a sort of mystical efficacy, which might better be gained by means of allegory, myth, drama, or other mode of representation than by simple historical recital. A fanatical zeal for the propagation of the faith seemed to the scribes sufficient warrant for the production of a great quantity of literature of such doubtful authenticity that to it has been attached the designation of *pseudepigrapha*, "false writing." Books have been found that are thought to be in part or wholly spurious, including a Gospel of Pseudo-Mark, Gospels of Peter, James, Ignatius, Gospel of the Infancy (of Jesus), Gospel of Mary, Gospel of the Nativity, Gospel of Pilate, Letters of Paul and Thecla, Nicodemus, Seneca, and others. One evident motive inspiring these books was that of enhancing the faith by accounts of such wonder events and miraculous tales as were designed to show the immediate agency of Providence in worldly events.

Many historians stress the fact that the Near East was full of the coming of the Messiah at the time when Christianity arose. Apocalyptic prophecies abounded. The stage was set, the psychological atmosphere tense with expectancy. However, we shall never know precisely what influences, trends, forces, and pressures came to a balance at that unique point in history, uniting to give the new movement its specific form, character, and content. But one recognition now taking shape, after centuries, is that virtually every commonly accepted notion about the series of events that supposedly brought Christianity into being is no longer tenable. The tradition that has ruled Christendom is that, while all other religions were products of human origin, Christianity was ordained by God, who once and only once sent his only-begotten Son to institute this true and final code of faith, belief, and conduct for all mankind. Perhaps it cannot yet be said that this is now widely questioned; nevertheless, many thoughtful people are now attempting a reinterpretation of the long-cherished legend.

Tradition held that if the Christian movement was not instituted by God himself, it was the work of men completely under divine supervision and inspired by the divine mind and will. Yet the evidence points to the conclusion that Christianity came into being when and because both the Judaic and the Hellenic world had sunk from the exalted peaks attained some four centuries earlier to a state of philosophical vacuity. If it is not true that Christianity was born out of that darkness, it can truly be said that it was born *when* that darkness was densest. Christianity has never ceased to claim that it was the supreme revelation of true light to the world, decreed by God to end the reign of benighted paganism. Yet if it was that transcendent light, history itself poses a natural question, "Why was the night of pagan ignorance prolonged into the Dark Ages that held Europe in twilight for a millenium and a half, during which Christianity was the ruler of Europe's mind?" The logic of events and the development of history even suggest that the Christian religion must itself have generated much of the darkness that covered the lands it dominated. Christianity must accept the challenge that, having the light of divine truth, it failed to let that light shine forth upon Europe for fifteen centuries.

Christianity is now definitely known to have been an upheaval of religious pietism among the ignorant populace of the Judean province, and for a considerable time it was shared by none of the intelligentsia. It is difficult to believe that there was enough intelligence and theological acumen in the unlettered, unschooled group of fishermen around Jesus to have launched the highest system of divine truth ever given out to humanity. Christian writers have extolled these twelve peasants as the most fitting agents for the propagation of divine truth precisely *because* they were simple and not intellectual. Humbleness of station does not presuppose ignorance, and erudition is no guarantee of wisdom and spirituality. Nevertheless, that a small group of Galilean fishermen (and they were fisherfolk only by virtue of Piscean allegory) and their humble associates should alone in all the world have possessed the keenness of spiritual vision to recognize the Logos of God when he "came eating and drinking" with the lowly is again hard to accept. We should remember that the central Sun-God character in ancient dramatic representations was always attended by twelve disciples, and that they were designated by a name connotative of each sign of the zodiac in turn in the precession of the equinoxes. They were shepherds in the sign of the Ram and herdsmen in the sign of Taurus. Thus was repeated the basic symbolism underlying all ancient religious scriptures.

The fact that things of this sort had been lost sight of attests the decline of that genius for dramatization of abstract forms of truth that had enabled the Greek mind both to discern and then portray in vivid outlines those archetypal designs of cosmic thought. This was that failure of vision, that "failure of nerve," which Sir Gilbert Murray decried as the cultural tragedy of the ages, the paralysis that afflicted the Greek mind following its efflorescence in the Periclean epoch. In that bright day, the Hellenic spirit had faced life with a zest for its beauty and a sense of its infinite value and wholesome *joie-de-vivre*, because the Greeks had a deeper insight into the *meaning* of life than has been achieved at any other time in world history. When that insight dimmed, the prospect became confused, the perception of beauty and goodness vanished, and men's souls sank into doubt, hopelessness, and gloom. At the very nadir of this depression, Christianity flowered. With earth's values all discredited, men's minds perforce turned to heaven for hope of beatitude. Interest in attaining the "good life" in this world ebbed away. The only salvation that might be expected was to be found in the promise of the coming of the Messiah written in the scriptures. Help must come from heaven, since the joy of earth had fled. Must we not admit the candid verdict of history itself that Christianity was the product of the Hellenic mind when its brightness was dimmed?

This judgment is affirmed by the fact that while Greek thought centered upon the positive interests of health, beauty, and sensual wholesomeness, the Christian conscience became almost at once submerged under the dark and morbid conviction of sin. Under the spur of Greek philosophy, a mortal might cherish the idea that he could, by the exercise of intelligence, self-discipline, and wisdom, make steady progress toward the unfoldment of his divine potential. Christianity, however, afflicted consciousness with the sense of man's total depravity and the hopelessness of any effort of his own to redeem his fallen condition. This was the portentous change in outlook that swept over the peoples inheriting the Greek culture.

The modern mind is hardly prepared to credit the statement that the bitterest of human strife has come from sheer stupidity, the inability to appreciate poetic and mystical significance, and failure to discern the difference between allegory and history. Yet a mountain of evidence rises up to support this statement. It has to be said that our age seems to have lost the perceptive genius that a fresher, earlier age possessed and that enabled the human mind to relate itself to life and nature in a closer intimacy of feeling and understanding than now appears possible. In the childhood of the race, when people lived intimately with nature, they intuitively sensed her forms and functions with a clarity that fades away when the sensibilities of childhood are replaced by less imaginative, if more rational, modes of consciousness. In youth the natural world impresses the psyche with a direct and naive sense of the reality and the meaning of life. The world is seen as the very picture and form of real being. The mind's effort to grasp and communicate the truth of things inevitably resorts to this natural world for all the types, figures, and images by which it essays to formulate ideas and concepts. Truth telling becomes thus the art of poetry, the ideal representation of meaning through imaginative constructions suggested by nature. How could a concept be represented except by a symbol? But the symbol had to be itself a part of reality and truth if it were not to falsify the representation. To the ancient mind, the natural world was the lexicon of truth.

In childhood, this sense of the affinity of mind and nature is instinctive, spontaneous, and not consciously rational. At a later stage, when reason deploys into activity, the poetic rapport of mind with nature may fade, but if the mind is given to philosophical reflection there develops a faculty for the perception of its affinity with nature. This is through analogy, the discernment of similitude, parallelism, and correspondence, suggesting a fundamental identity between the forms and phenomena of nature and the apprehensions of abstract thought. Children, like humanity in its youth, intuitively sense the truths of life as reflected in the face of nature; sage philosophers rationalize the affinity between the concrete world and the archetypal ideation that had in the beginning generated it. The books such wise men wrote in the past were designed to convey the truth of the ideal world to the human mind through forms of symbolism, for such was the most graphic device of communication. So the language of the great scriptures was that of allegory, drama, poetry, legend, myth, and appropriate symbol.

Loss of the knowledge that the scriptures were collections of ancient documents of this character precipitated the culture that was founded on religious literature into the darkness that cost humanity so dearly. Moreover, the catastrophe was avoidable, because the evidence that the writings were cast in the mold of allegory and expressed in symbolic language was everywhere abundant at Christianity's inception. That its promulgators appeared to be unaware of this traditional mode of expression, and made the unconscionable mistake of reading the allegories as factual history, is testimony that they were ignorant and uncultivated people.

When Martin Luther came to the task of translating the Bible into fifteenth-century German, he had to devise virtually a whole new vocabulary to express the concepts of the ancient

Egyptian sages, which had already been recast in the phraseology of the Hebrews and then again modified by their translation into Greek. So when the illuminati of an earlier time, with minds aglow with apprehension of spiritual verities, came to express in writing the principle of understanding of the loftiest spiritual science, we must stand in awe at their ingenuity in devising an alphabet, a lexicon, and a language of such involved and abstruse technicality that it required a special training in its subtleties to render a mind alert to its significance. It was a code of semantic forms, drawn mostly from nature, but made more complex by employing artful devices of myth, allegory, and drama. Plutarch speaks of Plato's methodology of portraying the profoundest mysteries by resort to tropes, figures, fables, and similar modes of depiction. The truth the sages of old dealt with was indeed "the wisdom hidden in a mystery" and further concealed in an enigma.

Most students of ancient literature have known that the archaic writings were of this sort, but by some quirk have remained impervious to the implications of the fact. Failure to read the scripts in this special way has left the books of the arcane science still sealed in their original mystery. But we now at last have our finger on the key to the tragedy that consummated the long centuries of philosophic decline in the Hellenic world, with the conversion of the great occult Mystery drama and the scriptural Gospels into the biography of Jesus of Nazareth.

One cannot be dogmatic about all aspects of this development, but there are substantial signs and intimations that the codices of understanding and the manuals of wisdom were turned into wraiths of alleged history. Two monumental works of the Egyptologist, Gerald Massey, *The Natural Genesis* and *Ancient Egypt: The Light of the World*, have been largely ignored. With brilliant scholarship and insight he pierced Egypt's enigmatic scriptology and documented the provenance of both Old and New Testament literature from remote Egyptian sources. He forced us to ask how the four Gospels of the Christian canon could be the biography of any Messianic personality living in the first Christian century, when he traced their texts back to Egyptian documents that must have been venerable even in 3500 BC. He has noted some one hundred and eighty points of similarity, parallelism, and identity between the archaic figure—never mistaken for a living person—of the Egyptian Christ-type Horus and the Jesus personage in the Gospels. As one scans this table of identities,[1] there is no escaping the conviction that "Jesus" is just this Horus-model of our divinity presented under a new name—a name, however, that is found to have been attached to the Messianic character even before Jesus lived.

We are faced with the inescapable realization that if Jesus actually lived in the flesh in the first century AD, and if he had been able to read the documents of old Egypt, he would have been amazed to find his own biography already substantially written some four to five thousand years before he was born. Tertullian, Justin Martyr, and other writers have noted that the leaders of the Christian movement confessed that many of their doctrines, rites, creeds, and symbols were identical with Egyptian antetypes. The late outstanding American Egyptologist, James H. Breasted, found evidence of such similarities between the Old Testament book, Proverbs, and addresses to the Pharoah of Egypt dating as far back as 3500 BC. All this confirms Massey's conclusions.

There are strong indications that Christianity today faces a time of crucial testing. But as broader studies of comparative religion are supported by fresh discovery of ancient documents and are sharpened by higher criticism, the position of Christianity in the *whole* religious world spectrum will emerge more truly and, we believe, with greater stature.

Chapter Six

SOME CONSEQUENCES
OF ESOTERICISM

The catastrophe that befell the pagan world following the close of the glorious period of Athenian philosophy still casts its shadow over the human mind and spirit. It is evident that at times a combination of fortuitous circumstances lifts a people to surpassing heights of vision. And after every such peak of cultural achievement there seems to come a regression to mediocrity or worse. During these regressions there is little ability to appreciate the subtle refinements of art and the heights of philosophy achieved in that earlier period of grandeur. Perhaps it was because of their realization of the inevitability of such pendulum swings that the sages of old clothed their insights in allegory, poetry, drama, and symbol, that these coins of mystical value might be preserved even in a period of cultural darkness, under the guise of myth and fable. Thus we have inherited a priceless legacy of truth and wisdom from the past, miraculously preserved in spite of ignorance and neglect. The world has possessed this treasure only to ignore it, and so to lose its benefits, time and time again.

There is a fine Latin word, *numinous*, which is closely allied to "luminous." *Numen* means not a god in person, but the light

of the mind of a god as present to, and sensed by, a human. It
is the "presence of God," that which the Hebrews called the
Shekinah, and which the Romans represented by their household gods, their Lares and Penates. It was what the palladium,
the image of Pallas Athene, meant to Athens, and what Minerva
meant to Rome. Athens had ignited the torch of enlightenment
from the altar fires of ancient Egypt. Moses, too, was learned
"in all the wisdom of the Egyptians" and made it a fundamental in the majesty of the Pentateuch, the prophets of Israel, and
the wisdom of Solomon. Persia, Babylon, and Assyria shared
the ancient light and, if only in allegory, sent its three Magi to
welcome the King of Kings at his advent. But, melancholy as it
now appears, the high tide ebbed, insight dimmed, the *numen*
faded out, and philosophy lost its metaphysical fire and became
cold and empty. Yet Sir Gilbert Murray could only tell us of a
"failure of nerve."

Macedon Phillip's dream of hellenizing the world, surely
one of the noblest undertakings to advance human culture, did
not entirely fail. His son's founding of Alexandria lighted a lamp
that burned brilliantly for several centuries and whose rays gave
early Christianity its brightest light. Here Philo Judaeus developed the insight that enabled him to synthesize the heritage of
Greek and Hebrew systems. Philo was born about the time of
Jesus. One might say that the births of Jesus and Philo represented the beginning of the clash of the two forces they
launched into history. The Jewish philosopher's work went far
to unite Hellenic philosophy with the Mosaic Pentateuch and
the sacred Torah of Judaism, thereby opening the door to the
entry of Greek enlightenment to the Eastern world. The recon-
ciliation of Hellenic intellectualism with Hebraic theocracy and
devout moralism in Philo's synthesis might have perpetuated
something approximating Platonic-Aristotelian wisdom into
the Christian era. In fact, in the second century AD the
Neoplatonists launched their magnificent effort to restate the

principles of the great Orphic-Hermetic tradition. Out of those systems both Judaism and Hellenism had taken their rise, and in them would have found the common elements that could have brought them into unity. But unfortunately this effort was short lived and destined to have little effect upon the course of European history.

A ferment was brewing among the peasantry of Galilee in Judea in the first century—a ferment that grew to proportions and power sufficient to block the marriage of Judaism and Hellenism. The anti-intellectualism natural to such unlettered and simple folk led to the tragic destruction of the Serapeum, the priceless library of antiquity at Alexandria, by a frenzied mob led by the notorious Cyril, Bishop of the East. When the flames of that fire died out, it symbolized the extinction of the light of the world for that time and the beginning of the Dark Ages, which lasted for fifteen hundred years. The great Italian Renaissance of the fourteenth century lifted a corner of the shroud of ignorance in Europe; the Protestant Reformation of the sixteenth century let in a bit more light. But the first real promise of our emergence from medieval ecclesiastical tyranny came with the discovery of the Rosetta Stone in 1799 and the discovery in the twentieth century of the Dead Sea Scrolls.

It has been the sad fate of humanity, consistently demonstrated down the line of history, that the dream of a purely ideal state for mankind inevitably turns into the aspiration and then the determination of some one nation or people to realize the achievement itself. When a group has attained recognized supremacy, as in the ancient world Hellas had done, it entertains thoughts of a divine commission to dominate the earth. The Hebrews had similarly felt the sense of their mission. Each great religion has speculated on its special agency in the world's apotheosization. Greece experienced the perilous afflation at the time of the Platonic exaltation and pressed toward its actualization through the might of its arms and ships, only to have the dream shattered by the destruction of Alcibiades' fleet in the siege of Syracuse. Hellenic philosophy went into decline with the fall of the hope of Athens for world hegemony, for man's inner life is inseparably bound in with and conditioned by his outer fortune. The Greek philosophy courageously postulated the possibility of man's realization of his innate divinity on earth, but instead of creating a utopia wherein eternal values would guide human life, Greece reaped the harvest of human inadequacy in the devastation of a fratricidal war.

The sudden blasting of Greece's national hopes in military defeat, in conjunction doubtless with other causes not so clearly delineated, conditioned the Greeks to a favorable reception of another philosophy, the Zoroastrian system of the dualism of good and evil, heavily tinctured at the time with a still further Eastern philosophy, that of Hinduism. The Greek soul, its wings singed and its aspiring rationalism destroyed by a panic similar to that which destroyed Phaeton driving Apollo's chariot too close to the sun, sank back wounded and confused. It was thus ready to be caught up by the following wave, and Christianity, by virtue of influences inherent in the context of the age, chanced to be in position to be carried forward on its crest. This may be a poetical way of saying it, but the rhythmic upsurges and recessions of the spirit are indeed a historical fact. The Christian surge was the result of a convergence of many currents into a channel that proved viable enough to permit a steady flow, while other streams were diverted or arrested. Germane to this point is the cultural and intellectual background against which a new and rising statement of truth, beauty, and goodness must be studied. This observation can be fittingly applied to the Christian movement. Christianity arose out of a momentary cultural vacuum, in a time of obscuration of the inherited tradition of religious truth.

Christian historians have always tended to ignore or pass over the previous existence of such bodies as the Essenes and the

Gnostics, not to mention the Mandaites, the Elkasites, the Therapeutae, the Ebionites, Ophites, Mithraites, Sabaeans, Manichaeans,
Orphics, Hermeticists, Mystery cultists, Hellenists, and others.
Yet the Mediterranean area in that epoch was deeply saturated
with the spirit of religious esotericism. In pagan society, Mystery brotherhoods developed strict codes of behavior based on
esoteric philosophy and refined rituals designed to effect a
moral and spiritual catharsis. Notably, among others, Cicero
has testified to the spiritual dynamic released by the ceremonies
of these "initia," as being in truth the real beginnings of the
activation of innate human divinity. These schools were secret
because, to these ancients, truth must be guarded from desecra-
tion by the ignorant. With the right to possess goes the obligation to use aright, and in this view only those able to assume the
obligations of knowledge could rightly claim title to its possession. The power of knowledge is a two-edged sword, like fire.
It can construct, enlighten, vivify, and save mankind; it can
also destroy. Therefore, the ancients instituted drastic and rigid
requirements for admission to the Mystery Schools.

This attitude persisted in early Christianity. Jesus himself
distinguished between the deeper wisdom imparted to the inner
circle of his disciples and the simple parables given to the multitude. The early church itself for some time was so steeped in
the spirit of esotericism that it instituted a graded system of
instruction, even to the point of conducting Lesser Mysteries
and Greater Mysteries. Direct and significant testimony that
doctrine was interpreted at two distinct levels is found in a
statement of Synesius, bishop of Alexandria, in the fourth century: "In my capacity as bishop of the church, I shall continue
to disseminate the fables of our religion; but in my private
capacity I shall remain a philosopher to the end."

The compulsion to conceal truths that might be misinterpreted or misunderstood by the ignorant is revealed in a
declaration of the church father Gregor Nazianzen in a letter to

Jerome: "A little jargon is all that is necessary to impose on the people. The less they comprehend, the more they admire. Our forefathers and doctors have often said, not what they thought, but what circumstances and necessity dictated." Here we have testimony to two facets of historical truth: the tendency of the ancient religions to practice their rites in secrecy, and the moral permissiveness which justified the "paternal deception" of the people. Perhaps there are legitimate grounds for deceiving the ignorant for their own good. History must pronounce judgment in such cases. But conscientious historians must confess that the early Christians carried secrecy to excess, even to the point of dishonesty.

It is possible to understand, however, that the esotericism of the pagan religions had come to be resented by the populace. The secrecy of the Mysteries came to be associated predominantly with the intellectual and social aristocracy of the ancient world; to the unlettered it appeared as a symbol of their inferior status and their exclusion from the higher ranks of society. Out of a situation of this kind is born a spirit of iconoclasm. The spectacle of a superior class of society engaging in elaborate rituals that are baffling because never understood becomes, in time, a source of irritation and antagonism to those who are excluded. Thus the secret tradition of the Mysteries, while preserving the inviolate sanctity of esoteric wisdom, evoked a smoldering hostility among the populace and so prepared the ground for the new faith, which from the very first stood out in strong reaction to paganism. The possession of secret knowledge tends always to detach its holder from the remainder of society and diminish his influence upon the community. Such knowledge carries its own dangers, and one of them is that the possessor is lured to labor at his own salvation and let humanity as a whole flounder in its ignorance. Against this temptation the esotericist must constantly be on guard. Pagan mythicism, pantheism, polytheism, and animism each had its day. While they should be given credit for having at least provided the conditions that fostered so magnificent a product as the Greek philosophy, both Platonic and Neoplatonic, this was the pinnacle of their achievement. And the brilliant sunlight of intellectual eminence in that pagan world did not penetrate the dark valleys where the masses dwelt. Christianity can be justifiably proud that it valiantly struggled to bring light and salvation to the downtrodden.

The history of the Christian movement underscores the problem of how cultural growth and knowledge are to penetrate mass ignorance and moral blindness. Truth and purity of life have little appeal to those whose way of life is vulgar and brutish. This has always been the reason and the excuse for secrecy. Pagan genius adopted a device that provided safeguards against the misuse of knowledge while giving access to the higher concepts of truth even to the ignorant. Life and nature deliver eternal images of truth to all men. If inertia blocks intellectual comprehension, the human mind will not be entirely impervious to the silent instruction of the omnipresent images and archetypes. Through fables, parables, myths, allegories, and symbols, truth will seep into consciousness. In due time, developing capacity will bring rational understanding and enlightenment.

It could well be true that Christianity embodied some disastrous consequences of a breach in the esoteric code. It demonstrated what could happen to the loftiest concepts once the popular mind, with its materialistic predilections, gets hold of them. The English writer, G. R. S. Mead, has described the phenomenon clearly in *Fragments of a Faith Forgotten*:

> The new method was to *force out into the open* for all men a portion of the sacred Mysteries and secret teachings of the few. The adherents of the new religion itself professed to throw open everything; and many believed that it had revealed all that was revealable. This was

because they were as yet children. So bright was the light to them that they perforce believed it came directly from the God of all Gods—or rather from God Above, for they would have no more of gods; the gods were straightway transmuted into devils. The "many" had begun to play with psychic and spiritual forces *let loose from the Mysteries*; and the "many" went mad for a time and *have not yet regained their sanity*.[1]

This statement supports our proposition that Christianity was a product of the ancient arcane systems. Strangest of all, it is Christianity itself, which arose in large part from a revulsion against pagan esotericism, that has stamped the seal of verity and authority upon this same esoteric principle. In the first place, by breaking the tradition of inviolability and exposing hidden teachings to the multitude, it threw the minds of common people into a state of confusion that lasted for two millennia. And in the second place, having from its own seat of power observed, over the centuries, the disastrous consequences of letting ignorance degenerate into religious fanaticism, the church has, in the end, itself wrapped up its inner codes of doctrine and interpretation in secrecy, forbidding to the laity the liberty of dogmatizing on its own account. In short, it has had to resort to that same esotericism that it originally repudiated.

Christian antipathy to paganism is ungrateful, since it derives every element of its theology, ritual, and symbolism, along with its sacred scriptures, from that source; it reconstructed its entire dogma over the model of pagan—that is, of Platonic and Aristotelian—philosophy; it has perpetuated the celebration of most of the pagan religious festivals; and, finally, it has adopted, as its own policy, the pagan emphasis on esotericism. One distinctive new element it has added, however: authoritarianism over the lives of its followers, which has lasted almost down to the present time. It is only now that we are at last witnessing a questioning of absolutism within the Catholic Church. In the United States today, many priests and bishops are urging the revival of individualism, appealing for the growth of personal responsibility and spiritual assertiveness and resistance to the growing automation of social and intellectual life.

Such an awakening of robust individualism is needed to resist the pressure from groups that seek to impose organization programs and policies on their members. Uniformity of thought and supine loyalty to organization, be it the big industrial corporation, the labor union, or the political party, leads to the hardening of prejudice and the reduction of individual responsibility. It is a measure of the great changes taking place under contemporary social pressures that the religious organization which for some seventeen hundred years demanded blind allegiance from its followers is now loosening the rigor of many of its strictures. The long history of the Roman Catholic Church exemplified its dogma that salvation could only be won through such allegiance; and every move toward individual freedom was for centuries met with excommunication, and even with death. Thereby the church tacitly postulated the dogma that allegiance to the church is the highest form of liberty of the human spirit. So precious is the soul's right to this freedom that for centuries the church considered it a holy act to save a soul from eternal perdition, if it rejected this pathway, by destroying its body.

THE MIRROR
OF TRUTH

The psychology of religion has not yet adequately ana-
lyzed the forces that play upon the human psyche when
it succumbs to the influence of pietism. It is not that the religious man surrenders the authority of his senses, his feelings,
and his mind, but rather that, over and above these ordinary
faculties, he feels the potency of divine forces that overshadow
him as they do all else and can sanctify a life that is otherwise
quite ordinary. In one form or another, from the earliest times,
the man turned religious has become the object of a tacit belief
that he is thus overshadowed or possessed by a measure of the
divine power.

For some eighteen centuries, the Christian mind has been
trained in the conviction that the first promoters of the faith were
people of extraordinary and unique spirituality, in fact the first
holy worshippers of a true God. The Christian tradition has
endowed the first scenes in the Christian drama with such an
aura of sanctity that it has been impossible to study them objectively. Miracle, magic, and marvel have colored the entire picture.

The decay of rationalism into superstition and devaluation
of learning, especially of classic literature, were characteristics

of the Christian movement for many centuries. They caused untold harm. For the revulsion against intellectualism led to the uncritical acceptance among Christians of a mundane and material interpretation of the scriptures. The profound spiritual message of Jesus was degraded into the crudest of literalizations. The revolt against paganism early took a turn that was fated, not only to plunge Christianity into gross superstition, but also to inspire within it a tendency toward intolerance. Acceptance of the ancient myths did not lead to sectarianism, because a myth, an allegory, or a drama leaves the spirit free to digest its truth in terms of its own genius and experience. A myth can instruct, enlighten, and inspire without binding. But when that same myth becomes a story that is believed to be actuality, freedom to evaluate its edifying power is gone. As an allegory of the soul's stressful imprisonment in the body, the story of the crucifixion can generate a variety of reactions that lead to spiritual insight. Regarded as a physical experience of one man, however, it becomes an alleged historical fact that one accepts or does not accept, according to what one regards as binding evidence. Scholars have never fully recognized, in religious history, that most of the virulence of sectarianism was bred by the transposition of scriptural allegory into history. As one writer expresses it, "The same myth in cruel hands becomes a goad to fanaticism." Over a myth, people can compare their feelings and reflections, their sense of its meaning, without rancor; over an alleged event, however, one agrees or disagrees; and this leads to parties, movements, causes, and all sorts of discord. In one case the outcome was tolerance, if not fraternity; in the other case it led to war and persecution.

If one were to proclaim that most of the troubles of Europe were caused by a mere misreading of some old documents and an insensibility to the intimations of their poetic and dramatic fancy, one would be dismissed as a fool. Yet this seems to be what history itself implies. The course of many events in the

West has been affected by the position of the accent on a Greek word, the substitution of a plural for a singular noun, or the question as to whether Plato was merely punning or hiding the most recondite wisdom in the etymology of words in *The Cratylus*. Origen, the most learned of the Christian fathers, complained that he was not permitted to express the meaning of the resurrection in tropes and symbols, while the pagan commentators were able to indulge their fancy freely. The modern world is only now beginning to recognize a fact that is bound to have profound effects upon Christianity: the fact that the ancient and revered scriptures of antiquity are not history, but rather spiritual truth dramatized and illustrated by some history.

The ancient world never wrote its religious books in the frame or the spirit of what moderns call "history." Not until Herodotus does there appear to have been any appreciable amount of history written at all, and much even of his work has seemed implausible as history. The literary objective of the ancient sages appears to have been simply to perpetuate the principles and archetypes of truth in such forms of imagery as would preserve their meaning and their potential. They aimed to illustrate, to dramatize, to pictorialize truth. Myth, allegory, and drama were their main resources, but number significance and, to an astonishing degree, astrological pictography and symbolism were also employed. Gerald Massey has taken us far toward the recognition that the dramas of the spiritual life of humanity had been inscribed on the night sky before they were copied on earth.

The zodiac was the first graph of cosmogenesis and anthropogenesis. The sages of old discerned that in the fact of three plus four equaling seven, and three times four equaling twelve, they possessed the key to a constructive cosmology. The number seven occurs ubiquitously in ancient scriptures and mythologies, because, as Pythagoras taught, the physical universe is built upon this number. It has been said also that man's evolution on this earth will unfold twelve facets of his potential divinity. The primacy of the number twelve in the ancient cosmogony led to the division of the year into twelve periods, the months into thirty days, and the week into seven days.

This zodiac was of central significance in ancient religious conceptions, as testified by its presence on the ceilings of ancient temples and in such structures as the Somerset zodiac in southern England, wrought into the features of the landscape and covering one hundred square miles.

Christian scholarship has never considered the basic numbers that appear with such frequency throughout the Bible as of more than incidental importance. For example, the number forty recurs again and again in all sacred scriptures, and there are at least four periods in the calendar of religious festivals of the year that extend over forty days, the Christian Lent being one of them. Yet no work on Christian theology known to the present author has noted that the number forty occupies this place of prominence in symbolism because it signals the period of the incarnation of the spirit in matter: e.g., rain fell for forty days in the story of the flood; Jesus was tempted by Satan in the wilderness for forty days; Lent was ordained for forty days; the Israelites wandered for forty years in the desert of Sinai; Halloween and All Souls' Day fall forty days after the autumn equinox. To the theologian, this is just a bit of odd coincidence, as it has to be if the scriptures are to be taken as actual history. Yet the recurrence of this number forty in such diverse contexts strongly suggests an allegorical rather than a factual meaning. The fact that the dates of Christmas and Easter are clearly determined by the winter solstice and vernal equinox—the more so because Easter is not even a fixed date, but shifts each year—should long ago have shaken faith in the purely historical view.

For many years, the adherence of Christians to the fundamentalist thesis blocked the evolutionary view of man's ascent. Another radical deficiency in scholarship that has been equally

damaging has been the intransigence of Christian interpretation to the implications of the data encountered in the study
of comparative religion, as well as in the study of its companion
science of comparative mythology. Against overwhelming evidence of the fundamental relationship between various religions
and their sacred books, which obviously point to some common origin, and the equally massive evidence of a primordial
identity of structure and significance in all systems, Christian
theology has stood obdurate. Since scholars failed to trace allegorical imagery back to its roots in the world of noumenal
archetypes, the meaning and reference of the texts was located
in the wrong world. Reading the scripture in a way that distorted its significance, Christian sectarians have, for centuries,
engulfed themselves and the Christian world in a delusion that
persists to this day.

The open-minded investigator of comparative religion finds
it difficult to excuse the obtuseness of Christian writers to the
universals that emerge so clearly within the scriptures and link
Christianity in the closest bonds with its pagan heritage. In the
first and second centuries, Christian leaders like Justin Martyr
were very ready to contend that the fundamentals of the new
religion did not contravene pagan systematics. But the third
century brought a drastic reversal of policy, and all things pagan
were declared anathema. If Christianity wishes to hold its place
in the growing community of religions, it must drop its claim
to a unique and exclusive status and admit its fellowship with
other faiths in a common origin. Growing familiarity in the
West with the scriptures of the five or six major world religions
clearly reveals that their doctrines and rituals represent cultural
modifications that dramatize the same basic conceptions of the
relation of man to God and the universe. Every facet of Christian
creed, rite, and symbol reflects an ancient belief and ceremony
that may be found in the literature of Palestine, Persia, or
Egypt. It is difficult indeed to reconcile this fact with the pre-

sumption that Christianity is the sole possessor of divine truth. To take only one example, the church asserts that Jesus instituted the blessed sacrament of the Eucharist. Yet for ages before him, tribes of the forest and the sea isles had been partaking of the body and blood of their gods, in the assurance that they endowed them with eternal life.

As long as the Bible was held to be directly inspired by God, delivered to his chosen people, it was, of course, venerated and implicitly believed. It was The Book, a unique once-and-for-all statement of eternal truth. Today, however, Christian scholarship is beginning to realize that the Bible is only a collection of scattered documents. Much positive knowledge of the origin and history of these documents has recently come to light. Instead of being a unique vehicle of the divine Logos to mankind, it is evident that another whole volume of similar material could be collated from ancient sources. Far from damaging the Bible's authority, however, the new knowledge of its history may help it to deliver its true message.

It is only some eighty years ago that the academic and theological world gained enough courage to begin a serious examination of the scriptures. The study was begun outside the circle of orthodox scholarship, by those less bound by tradition and ecclesiastical authority. But their revelations were so startling that orthodox scholarship was put on the defensive, and defense required critical study. So the quest has gone on. If the Bible still retains its prestige and authority today as God's holy Word, it is now seen to have suffered much in human transmission. But the degree to which it has suffered from unintelligent misinterpretation is still not fully perceived.

Chapter Eight

THE GHOST OF
ANCIENT EGYPT

C hristianity has long held that the documents assembled
by the Council of Nicea in 325 AD and ratified by a latter council as the canon of Christian scriptures (having been
selected out of a multitude of "gospels" extant at that time) were
original literary products of the latter half of that first century. In
the second century, Irenaeus, first Bishop of Gaul, declared that
four gospels were chosen because there were four cardinal directions and four winds. The dating of the composition of these four
books becomes at once a matter of crucial importance if they are
indeed the biographies of Jesus of Nazareth who lived in the first
years of that first Christian century. As such, they would naturally have had to be written during his lifetime or shortly thereafter. Scholarly speculation has been fairly unanimous in placing
their authorship at various times between the years fifty and
ninety of our era. Much internal evidence indicates their provenance at that epoch. Yet there are signs which point to the existence of the Gospels prior to the first century. The discovery of
the Dead Sea Scrolls may yield corroboration of this fact. Beset
as the subject is with difficulty, its critical importance and the
availability of new data make further consideration imperative.

It may be said that Christianity is the product of the four New Testament Gospels of Matthew, Mark, Luke, and John. These appear to be four variants of the same theme. The acumen and efforts of thousands of scholarly investigators since the early centuries have been spent upon the problem of their authorship. Still, many capital questions remain unresolved, and conclusions are still speculative and indecisive. Much opinion holds that Mark's Gospel was the first to be composed. It is acknowledged that little is positively known about these documents. But from the unquestioned fact of the evident similarity that exists among them, it has been speculated that either three were copied from a fourth, or all four were copied from what has conjecturally been termed "a common document" antecedent to them all. Criticism has never candidly faced the problem of the similarity of the four Gospels. That four men, each writing his own history of the great figure of Jesus, should turn out nearly identical chronicles seems most unlikely.

We have, then, the theory that all four authors of the Gospels based their accounts on a common source. Everything thereafter hinges upon the date and authorship of this document, or series of documents. Even if we avoid the possible pre-Christian provenance by maintaining that it was produced after 33 AD, how can it be certified that this document was not itself a transcript of one still earlier that likely preceded the first century AD? The libraries of the Essenes, and no doubt of the Gnostics, Manichaeans, and other groups, were large and well stocked. There is certainly a strong possibility that an earlier document, on which the four evangelists based their accounts, might not only have antedated the lifetime of Jesus, but might even have been a book or books that originated prior to the Christian era.

Among European Egyptologists, there is one whose research and discovery have contravened the Christian claims relative to the first-century origin of the New Testament scriptures. Gerald Massey, rated in British literature as a minor poet, is far more accomplished in the field of Egyptian studies. Nothing but a full reading of his six major works and lesser volumes would be adequate to the significance of his material, the sum of which is that not only the canonized scriptures of Christianity and Judaism, but much apocryphal and pseudo-epigraphic literature afloat in those early centuries, is demonstrably of Egyptian origin.

The question of what may have been a still more remote source from which Egypt in its turn drew this material is one that lies hidden in the darkness of antiquity. It is asserted, for example, that the Egyptians knew of the interior structure of the atom. Their mechanical resources for the building of the pyramids are still a matter of mystery. Their knowledge of the astronomical periodicities was amazingly accurate. Many hints are found in the literature of Greece that her wisdom derived from remote Egyptian sources. Plato recounts the legend of Atlantis told by an aged Egyptian priest to Solon.

Fixed in the opinion that nothing could have been embalmed in literature save facts (although we realize today that even the most scrupulous accounts of events are always colored by the observer or narrator, if only by the selection of what is reported), the scholarly mind has gone off on many a wild goose chase after the ghosts of history entified out of allegorical and dramatic type-figures. The ancients, to whom facts were far less powerful than they are today, did not write a mere chronology of events; they wrote tales depicting the *meaning of all* history. The venerable scriptures will never be read aright until the spiritual essence of the events, and not the events themselves, are understood to be the heart of the narrative. The events that never occurred, and the actors and characters who never lived, still carry the significance that is always and finally the true event of life. To the ancients, it was soul and not body that held the essential being of existence; the one uppermost objective in religious literature in antiquity was to devise ways to represent the pilgrimage of the soul. And because the system of hieroglyphics was developed to conceal as well as to reveal, empirical study has been unable to sift the gold of meaning out of the gravel of mythical events.

It seems clear to this writer that Gerald Massey has come closer than others to plumbing the depths of Egypt's well, yet his work has largely been ignored, primarily because his revelations did not agree with orthodox historical findings. For example, only five hundred copies of his book *Ancient Egypt: The Light of the World* were published, and, of these, few were read with serious attention. After years of research, during which he mastered the hieroglyphic writing, Massey arrived at the conviction, on evidence that could no longer be discounted, that the scriptures of Judaism and Christianity were basically Egyptian formulations; reedited, redressed, and reoriented to a new cultural milieu. He affirmed to the West that he had traced every doctrine, rite, and symbol of Christianity back to its Egyptian sources. He listed some one hundred and eighty particular similarities, parallels, and identities between the figure of Horus and that of Jesus of the Gospels. Much of the evidence of this resemblance had come out in the first centuries of our era, but was subsequently suppressed. The time is long overdue for its publication.

In the face of such evidence, we are forced to consider the possibility that the New Testament contains remnants of Egypt's legacy of arcane teaching. It is an impossibility that the detailed career, character, and very words of a person who lived in remote times in Egypt should be repeated in the life of another personage, living many hundreds of years later in Palestine. That Jesus recapitulated the life of Horus is unthinkable if both were actual historical figures. Also, that both should occupy the same place and fill the same role in the sacred scriptures of two widely different lands and peoples is improbable to the highest degree. If Egyptian religious literature exhibited a figure of divinity clearly characterized to typify the nascent divinity burgeoning in humanity, and the Hebrew-Christian literature closely matches this figure in innumerable ways, it seems only logical to wonder if both representations are not kindred portrayals of one and the same figure. It is very difficult to defend the thesis, attempted by some, that the birth story of the Son of God as a baby in Bethlehem was copied centuries before in the image of Horus as a divine child. It may well be a blow to Christians to learn that many events in the life of Jesus had already been lived out, in a manner of speaking, by a long-previous figure in Egypt. It may be even more startling to realize that this earlier figure whose career Jesus duplicated in astonishing detail was never a living man. For no scholar of repute has ever suggested that Horus was a mortal being. He was the luminous, intensely spiritual figure designed to embody the nature of man's incipient divinity. If, then, the life of Horus, with all its wealth of details, survives today as allegory, what are we to think of the historical account of Jesus' life, so startlingly similar? Is it not likely that this, too, must be construed as a divine allegory of the spiritual life?

The revelation that came to Massey, as he sifted through the Egyptian sources, was that the Jesus of the Gospels could not have been any *man* who lived in the first third of the first century AD. No man's life can be written before he has lived it. Yet Massey had found an account of Jesus' life written down possibly five thousand years before he had "lived." Those hundreds of parallels and identities were hard evidence that the Gospels were not histories written in that second half of the first Christian century. They were, instead, spiritual allegories and ceremonial dramas that had escaped from the Mysteries, collected around a central religious figure in order to put the spiritual message into dramatic focus.

The method of exegesis we shall try to employ here is simply the substitution of the allegorical mode of interpretation instead of the factual. It will not detract from the inner spiritual message of Christianity any more than does the abandonment of the creation stories of the Old Testament as fact and their replacement as symbol. If the Occident loses the psychological uplift of its humanized divine archetype, it will gain in its place the archetype of an everliving, everdynamic ideal reality. And just as an anthropomorphic deity has lost its hold on the modern mind, so will the canonized personage of history yield to the more universal and durable ideal archetype of Spiritual Man, the full realization of the human potential that is of divine origin—the Christ within the heart. The universality of this religious concept is certified by the presence in many world cultures of those very figures whose message and works of wonder the life of Jesus so amazingly recapitulated.

Chapter Nine

THE DIVINE ARCHETYPE

A central tenet of Christianity is that God made the first and only manifestation of his own divine nature in Jesus of Nazareth. As has been demonstrated before, if Jesus' career and individuality provided for the world this solitary epiphany of the God-nature, it was a revelation that presented to man not a single feature that was not already extant and publicized in the "lives" of Horus, Tammuz, Adonis, Atis, Marduk, Balder, and other messiahs and avatars of the world's religions. Christians may reject as barbarous some of the modes of representation of the nature of these gods, but this is largely because the inner significance of the myths is lost in translation, misconstrued, or distorted. The pagan mind was conditioned to see and to know that the divinity dramatized by these figures of the many sun gods and the mythological heroes (*hero* is from the Greek *eros,* meaning "divine love") was that remote goal toward which the stream of evolution was bearing the children of earth, but which could by no stretch of imagination be attained at present by humanity. It was conceivable that some men could have scaled the higher uplands of the pilgrimage, since most religions predicated the existence of saints, sages, seers, and other advanced souls. And there were legends of great ones who had completed the cycle of humanity and had reached the threshold of Godhood, but who returned to earth to aid in the upliftment of the generations of men.

The image of man perfected, or as the Egyptians said, "Osirified," was still the ideal; early man was never left without the guidance of the divine archetype. This shining ideal, it was said, was given to early humanity by the gods, so that there would never be wanting the potent psychological stimulus to constant striving, the ever-present spur to aspiration.

It is here that the basic difference between Christianity and the earlier pagan systems is to be seen. Paganism presented the image of the ideal in ideal form; Christianity, too, presented the image of the ideal, but with the difference that the image was that of a living man. The figures offered by paganism were mythic, fictional, lifeless, and therefore they generated no psychological efficacy; they lacked healing, saving power. From them emanated no divine initiative or potency to touch and transfigure mankind. Furthermore, they were often grotesque and even horrid types. According to Christianity, it was only in the living man-become-God, Jesus of Nazareth, that God had embodied the perfection and majesty of his nature, and this incarnation of the Deity in his Son alone made effective the power of his life for the redemption of fallen man; the idols of the heathen are dead; Jesus, the Christ, alone brings the gift of divine life to the world. Therefore, it was proclaimed that only in the Christian Jesus could the world contact the living and miraculously saving power of God.

Yet Judaism had for centuries before that day proclaimed with equal fervor that only through the unction of the power of God's covenant with the children of Israel, and the promises of God to Moses on Sinai, could the sanctification of the race be achieved.

The Christian construction of the salvation "scheme," as it has been called, has a certain appeal—as is testified by the rapid spread of Christianity throughout the Western world. Yet over the centuries the transforming power of the Son of man has lost its efficacy, as C. G. Jung has pointed out. Christianity believed fervently that in Jesus, the living archetype, divine unction had been released to the world for the first time, so that whosoever would lift his mind and heart to contemplation of this ideal would be blessed with soul-regenerating force. Had not Elijah demonstrated on Mount Carmel the superiority of the living power of God and the utter defeat of the Baalim?

Jung, however, clearly identified the flaw in this belief. In offering to the world the living waters gushing from this single fount, Christianity demanded that its people drink of this life-giving spring—and of this only. Here was the one and only source of blessedness. In his state of utter dependence, there was danger that the Christian aspirant would lose faith in his own inner spiritual resources and his ability to achieve regeneration. In giving us the Christos in Jesus the man, the church declared him to be the "only begotten" of the Father, the unique mani-festation of divinity, the mediator between heaven and earth, the One alone exalted to sit with the Father. For the worshipper to believe that he, the mortal, the child of sin, could ever be equal to Jesus was blasphemy and sacrilege, demeaning to the solitary grandeur of God the Son. All that was left for the sin-ning mortal was to abase himself before this ever unreachable Excelsior, first pleading guilt, then seeking mercy. The source of salvation was therefore to be sought without, beyond the self. Before the image of Jesus, the stainless and pure, the splendor of whose countenance blinded Paul on the road, there was nothing the humble suppliant could do but bow his head in worship. Loving and tender though Jesus might be, the gulf between him and mankind was too deep to cross.

Here, then, is the difference between the Christian Jesus and the pagan sun gods. The pagans presented the image of div-inity in ideal structures; the possibility that men might realize this ideal, this divinity, was implicit in the nature of the image. But in Jesus the divine ideal was already realized, a fait accompli, a unique, unrepeatable event. The special role of the Savior precluded its duplication again on earth. Mankind could never hope to reach a similar height. Jesus made salvation available for all in whom faith was strong. Yet because Jesus was the only intercessor and mediator with the Father, there was no hope for the Christian believer unless he were to surrender himself wholly, and thus surrender the only divinity to which, as the pagan system constantly reminded him, he does have instant and constant access—the Christ within himself. But what avail was it for Christianity to give the man Christ to the world, yet hold him eternally beyond human reach? Paganism, in contrast, gave men the ideal image of the Christos, the power eternally present and potent for blessedness within the devotee's own life, and therefore accessible to him at every moment.

Thus the Christian claim to have replaced the "dead" sterility of the pagan deities with a living ideal can be regarded in a different light. Faith in the pagan image was effective because it was grounded to earth, like the lightning rod, whereas the divinely inspired dynamic of Jesus was powerless to transform man, because his uniqueness was its own statement; human beings benefited by his mission and ministry rather than by the application of his example to their own lives. Christianity had somehow subverted the ancient conception that there is, within the heart of every son of man, a divine seed, dormant perhaps, yet giving him the potential of, at first, a partial, then a full, Sonship with God. There might be many gods in the heavens and numberless avatars of awakened divinity to appear on earth. But according to the ancient teaching, there could never be the miracle of salvation for any man until that latent spiritual power within himself was stirred to active expression of its divine capabilities. Do not the scriptures themselves assure us that all unction of salvation wells up from within? Out of the heart are the issues of life. The "life hid with Christ" must be brought out from its concealment in undeveloped selfhood—which is undeveloped Christhood—to open manifestation in the organism wherein God has ensconced it.

The "imitation of Christ" is an ideal that has impelled millions of people over a long historical period to the sincere effort to emulate the spiritual perfection embodied in the figure of Jesus. Yet such imitation is no substitute for the individual's struggle to find his own spiritual source. As Jung has said:

> The Imitatio Christi will forever have this disadvantage; we worship a man as a divine model embodying the perfect meaning of life, and then out of sheer imitation we forget to make real the profound meaning present in ourselves.
>
> If I accept the fact that a god is absolute and beyond all human experience, he leaves me cold. I do not affect him, nor does he affect me. But if I know, on the other hand, that God is a mighty power within my own soul, at once I concern myself with him.[1]

Imitation has something specious about it, something secondhand; at best it can only serve as temporary surrogate for reality, and at worst it can delude us into taking it for that which it imitates. The object of religion is direct knowledge of God; for this there is no substitute.

As long as men expend their energy upon the worship of a Deity external to, and remote from, his creation, hoping that living unction will flow forth from that Source in response to their entreaty, the divine unction that sleeps within the human heart will not be aroused. The Christian misdirection of devotional energies has resulted from the idea that the transforming power emanates from the image itself. Yet that image has no more power to illumine or to save than has a picture or a statue.

Its beneficence lies only in its function as inspiration. The potential of power resides in the individual, and the model only points the direction of his striving. No deity was ever sent to earth to save humans from the necessity and labor of saving themselves, nor has God left any of his children bereft of the power of self-salvation.

The power of God for salvation is not only within man, but around him on all sides in the world of nature. This power from without also helps redeem man, along with the power within, for beneficent influences emanate from nature and bless man both physically and psychically. Deity is immanent in everything—every atom, flower, creature, and star derives its being from Being itself, which remains ever transcendent and unchanged by its creation.

Even today, Christianity still maintains that Jesus is the only efficacious generator of salvation, because in him God has demonstrated the divine life for man. But this is to assert that a divine model has no power to elevate man until it has been demonstrated in the flesh. More than that, the Christian theology postulates that the beneficence of such a model had to await the advent of this one living demonstration to be efficacious in human life at all. In other words, the way of salvation was never open to man until the year 33 AD. Yet historical evidence testifies that the ancient world did not lack demonstration of the efficacy of the divine power to change human life in the lives of many personages to whom divine or near-divine status was attributed. How could Christianity assert that it alone had given the world a true Son of God when the East had exalted its Buddha, Krishna, Zoroaster, Hermes, Orpheus, Bodhisattvas, Nirmanakayas, and avatars in considerable number? The Christian will protest that these were not the very God, but only highly spiritualized humans, whereas Jesus uniquely personified in himself the wholeness of the Godhead. But the East will rejoin that this statement cannot be accepted in the light of its ancient and well-articulated metaphysics. If there is but one God, then there cannot be a second; that Oneness permeates all. If spirituality is inherent in man because of his divine origin, its revelation must be gradual and diverse: It is hidden in many lives but revealed in the great. Indeed, the Eastern faiths name hundreds of such divine incarnations.

The pagan religions rejected Christianity not because they denied the divinity of Jesus but because they could not accept the claim that he was a unique manifestation of divinity.

Other world religions, such as Islam, have accepted him in their pantheon of saints and prophets. Judaism had cherished the tradition that the radiance of God's benignancy had shone out through the personalities of Noah, Abraham, Moses, Joshua, and David. Were not the mind, the purpose, and the shekinah of God manifested even through the messages of the inspired prophets? It could not be expected that the ancient world would repudiate its commitment to these apotheosized figures whose sacred histories dramatized and focused its religious heritage.

The arcane wisdom envisaged salvation as a process taking place within the complex of psychic and spiritual "bodies" that together constituted the inner mechanism of consciousness in man. The evolution and spiritual attainment of man could come only through experience and the development of a culture that would integrate the conscious forces activating and being activated by these several interior states of consciousness in a relation of harmony and unity. This integration could be consummated only under the direction of a central intelligence presiding over the activity of these "bodies" in their community of function. Such an understanding of the nature of man at once precluded the notion that the process of inner growth and enlightenment could be either affected or dominated by any forces exerted upon the individual consciousness from outside. External circumstances would, of course, call upon the powers within, and instruction, inspiration, and training could come from external sources. Still, the operation, control, and use of the psychic forces at play within man were, in the final analysis, wholly within the purview and under the control and direction of the inner self. Self-transformation could result only from the redemptive power of individual self-awareness. This understanding is supported by Jung's argument that the process of redemption must be engineered within the interior complex of man's organic functions and under the conscious direction of the individual Self. This Self is the indestructible unit of the deific energy that is the God-in-man himself; man is not deified until this divine spark grows in wisdom and knowledge and becomes the master and ruler of his own household. It is to this end that God sends forth his children into the world, for this mastery cannot be won in heaven.

There is here a clear analogy between the soul in the human body and the buried seed in the soil of earth. By virtue of the primary endowment of living energy inherent in the seed, there are at hand from the start all the essentials necessary for the growth that is to come. The indispensable requisite is that the seed be put in that relation to the physical environment that will nurture and sustain its growth. Incarnation in fleshly bodies establishes this relation for the soul. All conditions are provided for normal growth; nothing more is needed. In the case of the plant, no one would ever think of postulating the introduction of some extra super-dynamism from a cosmic seed-life external to the seed itself as a necessary adjunct for successful growth. The dynamic of growth is already implicit in the organism. The same is true of man.

The crux of this problem of psychic efficacy is, as Jung states, a matter of the point at which the forms of worship and consecration are focused. The adoration of an external image directs these forces outward. That is, the ego of the individual conceives that it must reach out and seek the blessing, the intercession of a power beyond the self that may be enticed to exercise influence in favor of the suppliant. His fundamental motivation in such worship is grounded in the belief that he himself is impotent to win his own salvation. Even though a man may pray that Jesus help him to self-regeneration, the focus of the appeal is still on the efficacy of Jesus' saving power. The suppliant relinquishes his initiative and surrenders himself. So long as man accepts a surrogate for his own spiritual self, he is not the decisive and responsible initiator of his own salvation. Any attempt to stand alone—even if it results in failure—is better than reliance on another. For it is only when the soul learns—with pain and difficulty—that his personal salvation depends wholly and solely upon the divine potential latent within his own being that he will gain the incentive to struggle through to his own redemption.

The weakness of the Christian position is that Christianity asks the individual soul to fight his battle for God's grace without giving one ounce of power into man's own hands. It sends him into the struggle unarmed, urging him to plead total helplessness and to throw himself on divine mercy. It asks him to "negotiate from weakness," not from strength. When the ideal of pagan philosophy was dominant, and with it an understanding of the complex inner constituents of man's being, the spirit of the individual was braced to wage his battle with courage, knowing that he could have direct access to the source of spiritual power even if that power were not as yet evident in him. The knowledge that the divine potentiality was available was itself the guarantee of ultimate victory. Paganism armed the individual with certitude of his invincibility; Christianity swept away this inner certainty and left man clinging precariously to the single lifeline it extended to him.

The Christian church has never ceased to denounce pagan religion for its alleged idolatry. Idolatry, however, is degrading only to the extent that the worshipper attributes the living reality of divine power to the idol or image itself and fails to see that the image is merely a representation. If the devotee gazes upon the idol in full knowledge that it is a device designed to stir in him a more vivid sense of the high realities it symbolizes, there is in fact no idolatry at all. The image serves as an outward reminder of an inward and invisible truth and beauty. The Christian has, in his houses of worship, many images of saints as well as those of Jesus and the Virgin Mary. If he adores these representations in the belief that the divine essence of saving power is actually embodied therein, he, too, is guilty of idolatry. One could even say it would be idolatrous to worship Jesus the man in his character as the cosmic God in human person.

The ancient sages regarded as idolatry the worship of any power outside the range of man's own capability and potential. Since the power that sleeps in him is the power of God, both first and last, his concern and his contact with God were immediately a matter of the governance of his own life. The manifestation of Godpower revealed in external nature, to be sure, could be revered with wonder, gratitude, and praise, as its benign influences charmed and beautified the soul. But it was peripheral to the power within and never usurped the central role in pagan worship.

In the end, it seems necessary to say that no other religion in the world has so completely turned its people's worship from inner subjective to outer objective levels as has Christianity. By centering the means of man's salvation in a hypostatized historical person, it has been forced to deprive man of his own divinity.

Chapter Ten

WHEN MESSIAH COMETH

I n the vast complex of scriptural interpretations produced in the third and fourth centuries, one central and powerful motif was the expectation of the coming of the Messiah—an expectation that constantly aroused and agitated the Christian congregation. The origin of this concept is lost in the mists of antiquity, being found in the oldest of religious systems. Among the initiates of the Mystery Schools and even among the less informed, the Messianic tradition was a concept that could be rationally related to actuality. The idea of the Messiah could be clothed in forms other than that of human flesh: for example, it might be thought of as the advent into life of a *spirit* of love and fraternity that would redeem humanity as a whole from its crude state of animality. When "the spirit of truth" shall have come into all human hearts, the scriptures said, man will consummate his salvation. When the Christos reigns in the hearts of all men, that will constitute the advent of the Messiah. Thus the lofty concept of Messiah signified to wise men the transfiguration of mankind by the "emergent evolution" of the divine spirit from the depths of human nature itself. The introduction of a human figure as agent, bearer, or daemon who performs the miracle of inner

grace was adventitious. Not what divine spirit in one man could
do, but what the birth of divine spirit in all men could do for all
men—this was the essence of the great Messianic tradition.

The pagan mind did not look to the heavens for the coming of the Messiah, but into the hearts of all men. It was a subjective, not an objective, realization, although the subjectivity
would be made objective, since all objectivity proceeds from
subjectivity. The esoteric form of the Messianic concept was,
however, too abstract and philosophical for general appreciation. For this reason, the illuminati of the period withheld the
teaching from the populace. Even the Christians at first had
their Greater and Lesser Mysteries; St. Paul recommended meat
for strong men, but milk for babes. There is evidence that in
its early days Christianity sympathized with the notion of esotericism always embodied in pagan culture, for neophytes were
held in the class of catechumens a considerable time before
being admitted to full communion.

At what level of understanding the Messianic concept prevailed among the generality of the Roman Empire is not hard
to determine. After its first impulse, Christianity made its appeal
mainly to the general populace. The writers of the time testify
amply to this fact, indicating that people of more sophistication
looked upon Christian converts as deluded fanatics. Edward
Carpenter, in his *Pagan and Christian Creeds,* states that antipathy to learning among early Christians was so great that intelligence was a positive bar to membership in the movement. As
the humble have, throughout history, been uniformly the economic underdogs in the social organization, they are at all times
certain to look for the possibility of human betterment in any
religious tide that sweeps in with force. Many books have traced
the rise of Christianity out of the soil of Judaic theocracy, in
which the future political fortunes of the Israelite nation were
grounded on the prophecies of the restoration of David's line
and the inauguration of a new era of universal peace and abun-

dance for all. Such concerns soon tend to taint the high religious appeal of such a movement with the economic motive. When the reforms advocated by Martin Luther became powerfully convincing, he found the German peasants flocking to his banner with such vengefulness against their feudal oppressors that he was forced to suppress them ruthlessly. In the case of primitive Christianity, the two elements—religious and political-economic—combined most forcefully to engender in the populace a vigorous resistance to power and status, and consequently to culture and learning, since the latter was usually evidence of social superiority. Some scholars have asserted that it was when Jesus told the multitudes, swarming around him to witness his miracles, that his kingdom was not of this world but to be enjoyed in spiritual consciousness only, that they quickly abandoned him and shouted for his crucifixion. They wanted conversion to bear immediate fruit—to throw down established authority and to usher in an era of abundance and prosperity for the poor and the humble.

In the context of this situation, the dominance of the personal-historical form of the Messianic concept was fated to cast Christianity in the mold it took for the centuries ahead. Semi-esoteric, semi-Gnostic as it was at the outset (else it could not have enlisted the allegiance of such perceptive men as Augustine, Jerome, the Gregories, Basil, and others of the fathers), and embracing as it did the mystico-rational school of Clement and Origen in Alexandria that expounded the allegorical method of apprehending spiritual truth in the scriptures, the Christian church soon became dominated by the lowest common denominator as represented by the illiterate masses that flocked into the movement. The esoteric elements in its teaching were abandoned, and superstitious zealots gained control of its policies and dogmas.

So the expectation of the coming of the Messiah was a deeply felt impulse in the religion of the age. The pagan world believed in the periodical appearance of avatars. According to the sibyls and in conformity with the pagan conception of the hierarchical governance of the world, such divine emissaries were expected at stated intervals, the cycles being determined by astronomical periodicities, mainly of the sun and moon and such great stars as Sirius and Spica. One of the chief of these cycles was called the Cycle of Neros, of six hundred or six hundred and eight years. However variously the cycle's significance may have been interpreted, it was inevitable that some would look for its fulfillment in the form and person of a Messiah. Once this aspect of the historical situation in the Near East during the first centuries of the Christian era is fully appreciated, we have, under our eyes, the most potent cause of the origin of the Christian movement.

The hope of the imminent coming of a Messiah was certainly widespread at that time. More than in most periods of history, in that age and in that region there was an extraordinary proliferation of religio-philosophical cults. If the Homeric-Olympian age of the mythic gods was decaying, it was being succeeded by an age of concern with spiritual movements that were profoundly engrossed with esotericism and occultism and a mixture of mystical and magical elements. In general, the inspiration behind these movements was the possibility of contacting and activating the power of divinity latent in the nature of man. In the hands of the more learned and more cultivated, the movements developed highly rational systems of philosophy, as in the case of the Gnostics and the Stoics. In more ignorant hands they tended to become involved with less rational and more meretricious forms of occultism. There is little question that the "churches" organized by St. Paul were associations of this character, promulgating variations of the Mystery teachings. It is significant in this connection that the name *Christian* that was taken up by the "brethren" was a term applied first to the movement at Antioch in Syria and was purely Hellenic in usage and meaning.

The age was rife indeed with every shade and flavor of esotericism. One has only to mention the many monastic settlements of the Essenes, the Therapeutae, and Gymnosophists, which represented one strand. Then there were the Gnostics, with schools headed by Marcion, Basilides, Valentinus, Bardesanes, and Marcus. Lower in the intellectual scale were the Ebionites, who were Jewish Christians, the Ophites, with the serpent *(ophis)* as symbol, and many minor groups. One must not forget also that the great world figure of Apollonius of Tyana— seer, sage, and prophet—was at the height of his career and influence, which extended from Rome to India. So notable was his work and impact upon the time in that first century that the Roman emperor, Septimius Severus, had a statue of Apollonius erected in his court at Rome, along with that of Jesus. It is far from being merely an outrageous conjecture that he might be the true historical protoype of St. Paul himself. Both men have the basic syllable *pol* (from Apollo) in their names; both were educated in Hellenic philosophy at the same time at Tarsus, a center of Greek culture; both traveled widely and founded esoteric associations at many of the same places and at about the same time; and both had a secretary and traveling companion—Demas in the case of St. Paul, Damis in that of Apollonius. And there are other points of similarity and coincidence.

It is clear that the cult of the Mysteries was giving place to new associations aiming to advance one or another aspect of the arcane spiritual wisdom. Worship of the old deities still prevailed in the cults of Isis, Serapis, the Great Mother, Cybele, Atis, Adonis, Jupiter, Apollo, and Dionysius. Mithraism was being carried everywhere by the Roman armies. Manichaeanism had even gathered in Augustine; Montanism had caught Tertullian; Orphism had its temples throughout the Empire; Egypt's venerable philosophy had a strong vogue in the presence of Hermetic societies. To crown all this philosophical effort was soon to tower the peak of Neoplatonism.

It is probably true that the Messianic concept was in one way or another integral to all these expressions. The more perceptive groups viewed it as the spiritual regeneration of mankind. Others, less metaphysically minded, translated the concept into the person of a Savior to appear in human form. The fate of half the world for the ensuing two thousand years hinged on the issue as to which of these two interpretations would prevail and win general acceptance. The victory went to the man-God conception over that of the God-in-man.

Christianity has the distinction of being the first of the world's great religions to make the Sonship of the Supreme Deity a man born on this infinitesimal speck of stardust that is our earth. Other systems had their images, their idols, and their representations of the Supreme, but except in those cases where ignorance of worshippers led to the confusion of the image with its invisible spiritual substance, nowhere was the idol held to be more than a form designed to draw men's minds and hearts toward a deeper reality. Christianity alone reduced the ineffable majesty and magnitude of the concept of the one God to the proportions of a man of flesh. Ancient philosophy had refused even to name the deific Being, since to name it brought it under limitation; it was spoken of only as the One. Ignoring the obvious manifestation of the divine Being in his physical universe, the new religion proclaimed that God had made his ultimate manifestation in the form, life, and history of one man among earth's millions. Now that modern science has succeeded in probing farther into the starry reaches of the heavens, it is becoming increasingly clear that we are not alone in space—that there are other solar systems like ours and doubtless life-bearing planets. With all this immensity before us, this history of evolving worlds embracing tens of billions of years, the importance of our own earth and its humanity shrinks. It begins to seem astonishing that the Supreme Creator of these island universes, each with its millions of stars, could have designated one man alone, no matter how great his spiritual stature, to be the sole instrument of his creative power, the sole embodiment of his ineffable Being. Yet Christianity, for some sixteen centuries, has proclaimed that all the universe revolved around our tiny globe and in fact existed solely to promote the glory of our race.

The Greeks had put forth in their notable philosophy the rational nature of the cosmos, which they conceived to be the expression of the Mind that had generated the universe over the pattern of its primal ideas. To this concept they gave the name of the *Logos*. As a word uttered in human speech carries the form of an idea, so God's voice, which rang through boundless space when it caused the morning stars to dance and sing together, carried the form of God's ideation and stamped it upon the material creation. The Logos was thus the Word enunciated by the creative Voice as it energized the substance of the universe and shaped it according to the noumenal patterns. The Logos was the Cosmocreator, the generator of the innumerable hosts of the suns, galaxies, and island universes.

We are today realizing that much of what has heretofore been thought of as miraculous comes within the province of natural law and so can be understood. We are coming to realize how universal the laws of evolution are, both in the large world of stars and star systems and in the smaller world of living things. We are also beginning to understand the circumscription as well as the potentiality of human life in such a context. Therefore, we know that the prediction that one human could embody the highest divinity and constitute "a special case," outside the evolutionary stream of natural progression, violates all that we know of the laws governing human life. The human species covers a span of evolving life that stretches from its animal heritage into the still-veiled future, where, it may be, man will fully acknowledge his divine nature. But even then he will be man, not God. The Supreme Deity could not be human and at the same time infinitely transcend the human. The sphere of life denominated human extends over a certain range of the vibrant dynamic of creation, and what lies beyond that cannot be called human. How can one tiny fragment of the infinite range of being embrace, contain, or include the infinite whole, which is indeed and always will be greater than the sum of its parts? The Christian theology is predicated on the belief that the ocean of deity could be condensed and offered to mankind in one incarnation. In the order of nature—whose very lawfulness attests its nonmaterial or divine origin—no stage, grade, or order of life can transcend itself. It can manifest only the attributes it has slowly won and passed on to its progeny. By learning the lessons of experience, and so developing its conscious response to environmental pressures, it presumably produces at its cycle's end the seed of a higher order. Having developed its potential at one level, life moves on to the next higher level of expression. What the human being really is has not yet been fully specified, but we can judge what a human may be, even at such a peak of perfection as is yet seldom realized. A superior man may be compassionate, heroic, wise, tender, perhaps creative or even a genius, but he assuredly falls far short of divinity, even in his highest moments. There is an inexorable forward movement in the evolution of consciousness: the weak become stronger (or die out); the creature skillfully learns the uses of its inheritance and exploits that heritage ever more fully. Nothing in nature retrogrades, for even a seeming dead end in evolution may provide the impetus for a new transcendence.

Considering the possibilities further, if one speaks of divinity as resident in all nature in the pantheistic and deistic sense, then the affirmation of the incarnation as applied to Jesus has relevance. But this position is rejected by Christianity, for if it renders Jesus divine, so does it all men equally. Another ancient tradition predicted the unfoldment for all men of the divine life latent within them. Christianity asserted, however, that Jesus came to earth in the full glory of his divinity. As Jung sees it, the founders of Christianity believed that no presentation of the drama portraying the allegorical "death" of the soul in its incarnation in matter and its subsequent "resurrection" at each cycle's end could exert psychological catharsis potent enough for the human spirit unless and until the very Creator of the cosmos himself came down, put on mortal flesh, and ritually dramatized the spiritual reality by going through the pageant in his physical body.

All living things have within themselves a power of growth, but Christianity seeks to exempt the human species from this universal law. Believing in original sin, it has held that man, left to his own resources, will struggle upward for a time, then miserably perish of his own corruption. All that can save him is a divine force that comes from on high. Christianity asserts that this force came in the person of Jesus, born to save man, for man's most consecrated effort at righteousness was otherwise doomed to failure. This beneficence, therefore, really denigrates man, for it denies the human ability to transcend its sins and realize its spiritual nature. Yet even the most pious of religious zealots, John Calvin, attests that religion can only take hold of men's minds because of the innate religiosity in man arising like a fountain from his innermost nature:

> I confess indeed that artful men have introduced many inventions into religion to fill the vulgar with reverence and strike them with terror, in order to obtain greater control over their minds. But this they never could have accomplished if the minds of men had not previously been possessed of a firm persuasion of the existence of God, from whom the propensity to religion proceeds. And that they who cunningly impose on the illiterate under the pretext of religion were themselves wholly destitute of any knowledge of God.

As regards the purely psychological efficacy of the demonstration made by Jesus on the cross of Golgotha, antiquity had long known the famous fifty-third chapter of Isaiah, in which the "suffering servant" was contemplated as the image-model of the "pangs of the Messiah" and the "oblation for sin." Unable to name any historical figure with whom to identify Isaiah's portrait of this man of sorrows and meek victim of our sins, theological opinion has been forced to ascribe a purely allegorical character to the Old Testament description. There are many indications that the Gospel story of Jesus in the New Testament is just a later (or more lately published) statement of the same dramatization, but Christian theology so far has rejected the suggestion that the later version is likely to be no more factual than the earlier one. The central figure of the drama found in The Dead Sea Scrolls, the so-named "Teacher of Righteousness," "King of Righteousness," "man of truth" (persecuted by his adversary, the "wicked priest," or "man of the lie") exhibits some of the same marks of the Messianic role of suffering. In spite of this similarity, scholars have ranged over the field of ancient history in a desperate effort to find a historical character who might fit this description. The fifty-third chapter of Isaiah, however, was only one fragment of the allegorical picturization of the Messianic prototypal figure, which, in a variety of depictions, had portrayed the spiritual Messiah's "life" ages before the Gospels gave it forth as ostensible first-century biography.

Recognition of the allegorical quality of the Gospel narratives is heightened through acquaintance with the indispensable *Golden Bough,* by Sir James Fraser, and Thomas Bulfinch's *The Age of Fable,* both of which deal with the parallels between the accounts of the hero-gods and the legendary folklore and basic religious traditions. Many characters were revived after three days of "death," languished in prison, wandered in darkness, or toiled in slavery for six days or years, being released on the seventh; many Old Testament kings or judges ruled forty years, or were forty years old when their reigns began; many heroes crossed a sea, lake, or river either dry shod or with the aid of a great fish, to find happiness on the farther shore; many infant deities were suckled and saved by shepherds, herdsmen, or by animals and lived to found kingdoms; many were born in a cave, slew a lion or dragon, and descended into a dark under-world to release a captive maiden watched by a three-headed monster; many heroes were accompanied by twelve followers; many god-figures had their bodies cut into twelve or fourteen pieces and asked their followers to remember them. Added together, these accounts become too many for us to single out one as uniquely authentic and historical. The perspective thus gained, however, was lost during the early Christian centuries when scholarship, during the Dark Ages, was at its lowest ebb.

It is beyond the scope of this book to array a body of specific data that would demonstrate the truth of the observations just made. But perhaps in one paragraph it can be shown that even such a central constituent of Christianity's basic literature as the Sermon on the Mount was composed of material long embodied in the literature of Judaism. The Talmud, Mishna, or Midrish haggada of the Jews long antecedent to the first century contained passages often matching in exact words such elements of the "Sermon" as the following:

- To look upon a woman in lust is to commit adultery.
- One will be dealt with according to the measure of one's dealings with others.
- One must first pluck the beam from one's own eye before seeing the mote in the neighbor's eye.
- If one's eye or hand offends one, it must be cut out for spiritual salvation.
- One must swear not at all.
- Almsgiving and long prayers should be done unostentatiously.
- One must not lay up treasures on earth, but in heaven, where no one can steal them.

- Anxiety for the morrow must not crush the glory of today, which is to be freely enjoyed as the lilies of the field enjoy it.
- One should not indulge in repetitions and vain babblings.
- Love of neighbor must be as strong as love of self.
- Love must go out to one's enemies; vengefulness must be displaced by meekness and charity.
- Good works far outweigh the strictest obedience to ceremonial observances.

An objective comparison of the ethical code taught in the school of the famed Rabbi Hillel in Jesus' own time reveals that its spiritual morality is equal in purity and idealism to the ethics of the great "Sermon" itself.

In his discerning work, *Why Jesus Died,* Pierre Van Paassen recounts the consternation with which he and his fellow students heard the learned Abbé, Alfred Loisy, who was among the most distinguished of modern exegetes, solemnly announce at the end of a lecture in the College de France that he had been forced to the sad conclusion that the Sermon on the Mount had never been preached by Jesus in any sense of an original construction formulated by him, but was instead a collection of Hellenistic maxims and aphorisms. The impact of this statement was such, Van Paassen writes, that one student burst into tears and others left the room in silence.[1]

The statement made by the Abbé Loisy has been confirmed by the modern Jewish scholar, Joseph Klausner. Klausner states that the Sermon on the Mount expressed the basic principles of Jesus' ethical teachings, but he doubts that they represent an original formulation. He makes the point that throughout the Gospels there is hardly a single item of ethical instruction that cannot be found in near-identical phrasing, either in the Old Testament, in the apocryphal books, or in Jewish literature—

the Talmud, Midrash, or other Haggadoth of the period of Jesus' alleged lifetime.[2]

Van Paassen has also made the sweeping statement that there is no ground for the belief that Jesus ever lived at all. He bases this assertion on the fact that, in the records that have come down to us from Jesus' time, there is no reference to him or his works. The Dutch scholar goes so far as to affirm that the New Testament documents are not contemporary with the life of Jesus and cannot be accepted as history, being rather a form of poetic legend. In support of this statement he mentions that, although historians of the time know a great deal about Herod's evil actions, they make no mention of the so-called Massacre of the Innocents, for the good reason that Herod had been in his grave at least four years before the supposed birth of Jesus, or in 4 BC.

Understood in its proper relevance, which admittedly is only fully to be discerned in the light of the universal principles to be found in all great religions, the Messianic tradition is a basic element of man's religious philosophy, and, like all such elements, it can be the source of the greatest spiritual inspiration. Conversely, when misunderstood and misused, it can lead to gross superstition and denigration of a lofty concept. Such, unfortunately, was the fate of a magnificent idea—the divine origin of the inner spirit of man—in the hands of the early Christian church.

Chapter Eleven

JESUS—MAN OR MYTH?

I t is significant that Jesus was one among many throughout
the course of Hebrew history who claimed Messiahship,
most of whom were also summarily executed by the Roman
power. Such claims were put forth, for example, by Mani,
around whom grew the cult of Manichaeism; this group num-
bered Augustine among its ranks. Tertullian was a member of the
cult that advanced the claims of Montanus. Simon Magus, mentioned in the Acts, also figured in the role. A cult grew up around
the person of Arion. Sigmund Mowinckel, in his book *He That
Cometh,* expounds the concept of the Messianic hope as it found
expression in the religious life of the Jewish people. He states that
it assumed two distinct forms. Among the learned of the schools,
it was an expectation of the manifestation of the veritable presence of God himself among his people—not in the person of the
prophesied scion of David, but in an exaltation of the nation and
an overshadowing by a divine influence that was transcendental,
universal, and individualistic. This form of the tradition was
never popular with the people at large, who looked for the coming of the national Savior in the person of the King, who from
his throne in Jerusalem should rule the nations of the world.

This is an understandable hope in times of social unrest. All kinds of speculation thus centered about any outstanding figure, whether he appeared in the political life of the nation or came forward as a religious teacher. Mowinckel speaks, for instance, of a series of such characters mentioned by Josephus. He also lists Zerubbabel, spoken of by Haggai and Zechariah; Simon, mentioned in Maccabees xiv ff.; Pheroras, brother of Herod; Hezekiah, recognized by Hillel; Herod's son, Judas the Galilean, and his brother Menahem; Theudas, a prophet who led a host of followers to the banks of the Jordan, where he had assured them that the Lord would dry up a passage for him across the river; an Egyptian Jew who led his followers to the Mount of Olives to see the walls of Jerusalem fall as he had declared. All these men were executed by the Procurator Felix. Another unnamed Jew had led his group of devotees out into the wilderness, only to be cut down by Roman soldiers. And even the great and illustrious Rabbi Akiba sanctioned the proclamation of the Messiahship of the last military hero of Jewish resistance to Rome, that "Son of the Star," Simonbar Kochba. A number of leaders similarly appeared among the Samaritans.

Jesus was thus preceded by many other claimants to the Messianic mantle. The question must therefore be asked, How can we be assured that all the others were conscious impostors, or sincere but deluded claimants who paid the penalty for their aspirations to Messiahhood with their lives?

The conscientious student of Christianity sooner or later becomes aware of a consideration that grows more significant as he reflects on it. This is the contrast between the Jesus potential and the Jesus accomplishment. The fact is that Jesus' life ended without the institution of any agency to implement his message and that the abrupt termination of his teaching in his thirty-third year brought him only defeat and anguish. The problem the theologians faced was how to resolve this defeat into victory, this failure into the most climactic success in all history.

That spirit can conquer only through the crucifixion of the flesh is the dialectical foundation of Christianity. Its central thesis is that, paradoxically, the glory and triumph of Jesus' life could be sealed only by his yielding to suffering and death. The question that comes to mind, however, is this: If the career of Jesus had been crowned with success during the years of his mission and ended in the conversion of a multitude of followers instead of a mere handful, would the faith still have taken the stand that this was not as it should have been, that he should have agonized in defeat in order to save mankind? The reason why the Jews refused to accept Jesus is precisely this defeat. As Mowinckel expounds it, the Jews could not commit themselves to the cause of a Messiah who suffered ignominy and death. Their Messiah was to be the Davidic King, who should sit on a throne in Jerusalem wearing a crown of gold and whose rule would extend to Rome. The exquisite irony here lies in the fact that the faith that glorified the man of sorrows now sees its leader enthroned in his seat of majesty in that same Rome, while the faith that lived in the hope of seeing its King on that throne has endured the anguish of merciless persecution and defeat for two thousand years.

Jesus *was* crowned; yet neither Christians nor Jews have proclaimed the truth that the only crown of victory mortal man will ever wear must be shaped by the pure rays of the light of his own spiritual consciousness, once that consciousness has been awakened in him. This is the significance of the nimbus, the halo, and the aureole that ancient symbolic art drew around the heads of its deities. It has been called the hundred-petaled lotus by the Hindus, the Augoeides by the Greeks, the Sahu by the Egyptians, the Shekinah by the Jews, and the Holy Spirit by the Christians. Thus the human imagination has universally dreamed of the immortal crown of glory to be won by man.

How is it that Jesus came and went, leaving the world in ignorance of the meaning of his death? No Christian has ever advanced a rational explanation of how Jesus' bodily crucifixion on Golgotha became the power of salvation for human souls. The doctrine that the seed of Christ-consciousness must experience imprisonment in the flesh and endure the pangs of mortal life on the cross of matter is a mystical truth.

The sacrifice inherent in the act of pouring out the essence of his spiritual life, symbolized as his blood, for the eventual transfiguration of his lower nature is the dynamic of man's evolutionary aspiration. Had the knowledge that this Christ power was the divine potential within every mortal man been retained, the causal nexus between the "death" of the Christ soul and the redemption of the human man of flesh would also have been kept in clear perspective. For this God-seed, which lies so long dormant within the body, suffering a constant trial under the wild instincts of the flesh—a veritable crucifixion—nevertheless works as a leaven in the ferment of the psychic forces that long dominate man's consciousness. In spite of, or rather through, suffering, it is destined to transmute these psychic energies into agents of its own higher ends. Greek esoteric philosophy had framed the concept of the descent of souls into incarnation in the allegory of their descent into the realm of death, believing that the soul's imprisonment in the body is like a death that lasts until the resurrection out of latency into dynamic self-consciousness and awareness of kingly power. True enough, the Christ soul from the heavens of higher consciousness does pour out its lifeblood for the divinization of the baser part of man, infusing body with spirit and thus metamorphosing the creeping fleshly creature into a winged being. This is the sum and substance of all that the shedding of a God's blood for the salvation of man could ever mean.

The Christian version of this allegory withdrew from man his confidence in the power available to him and left him a nonentity, a helpless chip adrift on the ocean of life, crying to be led to some safe harbor. The historization of the Christos-principle severed the dynamic, living connection between man human and man divine, which, in fact, is the true mediation between man and his salvation. A medieval saint warned the church of this danger. Angelus Silesius put it thus:

> Though Christ a thousand times in Bethlehem be born
> But not within thyself, thy soul will be forlorn;
> The cross on Golgotha thou lookest to in vain
> Unless within thyself it be set up again.[1]

The Christian dogma has thus thrust man into a position of hopeless denigration, for on the one hand it asserts that he is morally responsible for his sins and answerable thereto, but on the other hand it holds that man's redemption is not within his power to achieve, since it is due to a spiritual agency above and beyond him. Christianity first blackens man as a sinner, then admonishes him that nothing he can do will avert his punishment save appeal to a higher agency. Earnestly as he may strive to merit some credit or consideration, obey as he will every demand of the law, his fate nevertheless hangs upon the will of heavenly power, even though it is said to have been focused in Palestine for humanity's benefit. Goodness alone will avail him nothing if he be not saved by Christian grace; yet a life of crime and violence may be redeemed by last-minute repentance and acknowledgment of allegiance and obedience to Christian codes. This is the inequity established for man in the moral sphere.

Life is today universally rated as being under the governance of natural law, and one of the principles of law is that of causation; cause produces consequent proportional effect. The forces at play being known, one and only one series of effects is possible, but everywhere and always the operation remains within the area of the forces involved. This abstraction finds immediate relevance to the theological predicament set up by Christianity. Christian doctrine does not apply the principle of law to the moral-spiritual problem in man. It segregates man's moral action from the realm of moral consequences. This has the effect of making moral and spiritual law inoperable in the sphere of man's daily life. So long as men assume that action motivated by good intent will bring good results, they will have a proper incentive to right conduct. But if they are deprived of the right to look for such reward, they will become hopeless of the success of moral action. The drive to do one's best is sapped at its source, which is man's will to the good.

The doctrine that human life is, in the final analysis, to be weighed, judged, and recompensed by an Intelligence, a Power, which is totally beyond human control or even human understanding, can only vitiate human dignity. Herein can be found no evolutionary goal toward which man can purposefully strive; he can only try to propitiate these external forces. Evolution itself will not save him. If he yearns for salvation, he can only hope and pray. What is more, Christianity asserts, the source and power of such salvation only became available for man in the year 33 AD, and those born prior to that date were fated to live and die oblivious to spiritual truth, for no true light pierced the heathen darkness until the advent of Jesus. This has been the stated position of most Christian writers in the past, in spite of the fact that the very founder of Christian doctrinism, the sainted Augustine of the fourth century, stated in unequivocal terms that the religion that in his day came to be called Christianity had been in the world since remotest time and therefore was the cherished treasure and legacy of the pagan world.

Greek philosophy was essentially anthropocentric; it approached the study of the problem of the universe, and of man's position therein, from the standpoint of man himself. What is more, the Greeks proceeded on the assumption that the elementary factors of the human problem were comprised in the constitution of man himself. They held that the factors in play in the human drama were all in view, or amenable to study, experience, and logic. They saw in man four levels or grades of consciousness: sensation, emotion, thought, and spiritual will, symbolized by the elements earth, water, air, and fire. As the interplay of these four elements in nature generated physical bodies, so the interplay of their counterparts in consciousness generated the sum of human psychic existence. Absorption of the conscious interests in the two lower forms or energies—sensation and emotion—held men captive to "sin," to "the law which is in my members," as St. Paul phrased it, imprisoned man in "Egyptian bondage." When man learned to enthrone reason and the sweet influence of divine love as the rulers of his life, he liberated his soul from bondage to the flesh or the material world and then enjoyed the "freedom of the Sons of God." The arcane science of the soul was, therefore, the study and cultivation of the balance of these different forces in the constitution of man. If the grosser elements overruled the finer, the mortal was held back in his progress toward the deific state. If he strengthened the authority of reason and the spirit, his advancement proceeded apace. The arena of the battle was his daily conscious experience, and the four modes of consciousness were the forces in contention. The fate of the individual was determined by the success of the struggle within his own heart, as the divine potential burst into fuller expression out of the depths of man's own constitution. Success was essentially a human achievement, failure a human responsibility.

The Christian concept of the Messiah, as previously stated, placed man's source of salvation beyond himself, in heaven, and taught man not to rely upon himself, but to look to others for guidance and strength. One of the results may have been the Dark Ages of superstition, ignorance, and fanaticism.

The expectation of the Messiah's advent involved another belief, the "fulfillment of prophecy." The expectation was universally strong because it had been universally prophesied. In the venerated scriptures, Amos, Hosea, Micah, and Isaiah had all foretold this event that would verily bring heaven down upon earth and transfigure dreary human history with celestial radiance. Even the pagan sibyls united their oracular voices, prophecying that a virgin would conceive by Apollo, by the power of the Sun God, by the Holy Spirit, and give birth to the Avatar, the Aeon, the Christos. All Jews were looking forward to the day when the Son of David, the *natzer* or branch of the Rod of Jesse, would ascend the throne of Israel in Jerusalem, rule the nations, and transform society. This dream was the midriff of the Hebrew theocracy.

A misunderstanding of the meaning of the words *prophet* and *prophecy* has perpetuated a misconception. These words derive from the Greek *pro,* meaning "forth," "forward," or "ahead," and the verb stem *phanai,* meaning "to speak." A prophet is one who speaks forth; he is a proclaimer, an expositor, a teacher, a preacher. The subtitle of the book of Ecclesiastes is "or the Preacher." The main character in ancient Egyptian spiritual dramas was "the Speaker." Books of Gospel-like nature found in Egypt, containing discourses attributed to Jesus, had the title *Logia,* or "Sayings," of the Lord. Jesus preached or *prophesied* the Sermon on the Mount.

It is therefore significant that scholars are now declaring that the prime usage of the word *prophet* in the purview of scripture writers carried no *necessary* connotation of prophecy in the sense of prediction of future objective historical events. *Prophecy* would readily enough include a broad perspective of developments, predicting calamity for Israel for its waywardness from Jahweh, or blessing for obedience to his commands. But the prophets were not concerned with the prediction of specific events. A number of savants in biblical exegesis have gone on record as stating that the several pronouncements in the "prophetic books" of the Old Testament, declaring that a virgin shall bear the Messiah, can *not* be considered any longer as a reference to the birth of Jesus by Mary. Yet Christianity all along has claimed divine authorization because the events engendering it occurred that Old Testament prophecies might be fulfilled. It has been asserted that some of these "events" have every appearance of having been introduced into the narrative to make sure that the record, if not the reality, did not fail to fulfill ancient prophecy.

Thus the true significance of prophecy as pure preaching of spiritual truth under the guise of symbolic drama, allegory, or parables was debased into the prediction of future events. The central "event" of all such teaching was the birth and growth in human society of the spirit of Christhood; this universal concept, personalized, became the incarnation of spirit in a human body. In this light, we are forced to the conclusion that the Christian religion was born out of a misreading of the cryptic ancient scriptures, by sincere but unschooled minds.

Today, all Christian sects agree on the historicity of Jesus and his authorship of Christianity. Let it be reflected, however, that when Christianity arose there was no such unanimity. The new sect was alone in its predication of the Messianic fulfillment in the babe of the Bethlehem stable. So far was it from universal acceptance that it was looked upon at the time by all cultured ranks of society as the fantasy of poor, deluded fanatics. It was pronounced a dangerous superstition by such thinkers as Pliny, Suetonius, and Celsus, among others.

Chapter Twelve

PETER'S JESUS AND PAUL'S CHRIST

C hristianity thus transformed the Christ principle into Christ the man. In so doing, it captured the imagination of those to whom the abstract concept of Christliness would have little appeal. The birth, baptism, temptation, sermonizing, miracle working, transfiguration, trial, crucifixion, resurrection, and ascension of a *man,* whose effort and agony were bent on eradicating the sins of mankind, could stir the most torpid minds. The spectacular growth of the Christian religion (which was essentially little different from a score of religious cults of its day) was due in large part to its startling proclamation that the universal dream had been fulfilled, the Messiah *had come* in the person of the babe of Davidic descent.

To those people whose prospects of earthly happiness were stifled under the tyranny of the Roman power, Christianity's heralding of the advent of the Messiah sounded much like the ringing of a liberty bell, promising their release from servility. They were to be redeemed by God himself, come to earth to fulfill the glorious promises of scripture. The poetry of the birth story itself was filled with mystery and magic. At the divine birth, angels had announced the glad tidings to shepherds watching their flocks by night in the fields. (Thus the humblest person felt himself the direct recipient of divine grace.) The virgin maid had been mystified as the angel Gabriel announced to her that she should conceive and bear the child of heaven, fathered by the Holy Spirit. Three Magi came from the East to greet the celestial visitant with threefold gifts; heaven and nature united their songs in jubilation over the Lord's birth.

The beauty and wonder of this story never fails to touch the heart. The tragedy is that its acceptance in literal form robs the mind of the true mystical experience that can be imparted by the universal truth contained within the nativity story. The imagery of the scriptures was designed to elevate consciousness above the mundane into the pure realm of the spirit.

It has generally been forgotten that the advent of the Messiah was inseparably connected with the concept of the apocalypse. The consummative event was to take place when the scroll of the heavens was rolled up and the earth dissolved. In the view that prevailed in the Jewish world at the time of the upsurge of Christianity, the Son of God was to come "at the end of days." The delineation of the event was heightened in the imagination of the age by the universal distress of the masses and, among the Christians, by oppression under an exaggerated consciousness of sin. The distress of nations would bring repentance as the first step and the necessary condition of the consummation. Then preliminary heralding would come in the appearance of the prophet Elijah, the legendary forerunner of the Messiah. This role is played in the Gospel story by John the Baptist, who was said to be the prophet reincarnated, and who must appear to announce the near coming of the Lord and call the nations to repentance.

It was believed that with the avatar's appearance and the assumption of his seat on the throne in Jerusalem would come the restoration of the kingdom of Israel. The Messiah would judge all the nations in addition to the twelve tribes of Israel.

Transgressors would be consumed in fire. There would be anguish of nations, famine, earthquakes, and convulsions of nature. Son would turn against father, daughter against mother; cities would be destroyed, laws forgotten. False prophets would abound, deluding the people. A few of the good would be preserved and purified out of the welter of iniquity.

Instead of bringing the consummation of all things in the eschatalogical sense, much Messianic expectation contemplates only the end of the present cycle of darkness and evil and the beginning of the reign of peace and the golden age of the world. Happiness and prosperity, both material and spiritual, will universally prevail. At the sound of the heralding trumpet, there will be a gathering together of the exiles—all the Jews scattered over the four quarters of the earth. The Gentiles who survive the day of judgment will all turn to Judaism and call upon the name of the one and only God, and all will be united in one society to bow to the will of the Most High with singleness of heart. The glorious kingdom of the saints will be established in the land of Israel. The temple will be rebuilt, and though the nations will continue in their separate existence in the brotherhood of the world, they will all stream into the mountains of God and serve him along with his own chosen people. The earth will increase its fruitfulness; even the beasts will be at peace with men. All grief, pride, oppression, slavery, and inequality will pass away, as all recognize their common brotherhood as sons of the Father in heaven. Then will come the resurrection of the dead; the righteous dead will come to life, and even the ungodly will turn to virtue following their purgation in the fires of hell. The righteous will sit in the company of Abraham, Isaac, Jacob, and Moses, and all will be sheltered in the shadow of the Messiah. Then will dawn the halcyon age in which the need to eat and drink will be overcome. Even the begetting of children will pass away, all being spiritual; sharp dealing, jealousy, and strife will end. But the righteous will sit with crowns on their heads in the bright light of the presence of Shekinah.

This, avers Joseph Klausner in *Jesus of Nazareth,* was the ideal that Jesus heard proclaimed in his day; and this, he adds, is what Jesus had in mind when he predicted that the kingdom of heaven was nigh and that those hearing his voice should not pass away before they would see this kingdom realized. Is it not a sobering thought that even his divine genius was misled and that his prediction was followed by two thousand years of strife, violence, war, and human exploitation?

Christian theologians insist that their religion demands only one thing: belief in the existence, divinity, and saving power of Jesus of Nazareth. The Christian manifesto is that, whereas in the Old Testament the Messianic advent is still the hope of the future, in the New Testament, this hope has been fulfilled, and the event has released upon earth a beneficent reality for all men. This saving power did not arise from any evolution of spiritual capacity in mankind, any growth of conscious capability to apprehend truth or any natural unfoldment of inner quality. It came simply and entirely from the events of the life of Jesus of Nazareth. In effect, this doctrine asserts that spiritual truth would be powerless to redeem human nature unless first demonstrated by Jesus. In other words, truth as an abstract principle is impotent on the human level unless and until it has been hypostatized by Jesus' life and death. Hence, nearly every address to deity in the Prayer Book of the church ends with the phrase, "through our Lord Jesus Christ." That Jesus was God, and alone of all men divine, is the cornerstone of the Christian religion.

The early fathers of the church did not realize how precarious was this commitment to one set of alleged historical events, for the events themselves might be questioned or even disproved. Their authenticity was maintained down the centuries by the sheer force of dogmatic assertion. But now investigation, criticism, and definite historical data have cast considerable doubt on the facts of Jesus' life. If the entire foundation of the religion rests upon historical fact, its fate may hang precariously in the balance, depending on whether increasing knowledge will confirm or disprove certain historical events. And indeed the claims for its historicity are losing ground before the steady advance of contemporary research and discovery.

But surely Christianity has much more to offer in the teachings of its founder than in his life. It should therefore be said at once that what is lost as history will come back with immeasurable gain as spiritual allegory. As the Petrine contention for the historical Jesus of the early church weakens, the Pauline contention for the *Christos* that is, or is to be, resurrected in all hearts, grows in truth and power. More and more significant will become the outstanding fact that Paul cared so little for the historical Jesus that he did not think it worthwhile to mention him in connection with a single event of his career. Paul's conception of the Greek *Christos* was that of a principle of divine consciousness in the souls of men, and not merely that of one man from Galilee.

Modern man and ancient man held widely different views as to what deserved to be perpetuated in written accounts. Today we have unlimited resources for communication, and so we freely publish the trivial along with the meaningful. Antiquity had no such resources, and therefore it conserved what it had by recording only that which was considered most vital and precious. What people did was held to be secondary, derivative, and subordinate to what they thought and felt. The center of interest was not the eventful content of history, but the structure, the frame, and the *meaning:* its elan, its spirit, its logos. There are any number of indications of this attitude. The mind of antiquity continually strove to discern and reconstruct in human terms the rationale of the Overmind of the world. The nature of the ancient scriptures openly reflects this purpose, and it is more than confirmed by the fictional and symbolic method of representing truth in multiple images. History needs no such instruments to narrate its factualities.

This methodology is revealed, not only in the contents of the works, but also in the subtle and cryptic devices introduced into the structure of the composition. Study indicates that the authors intended to convey or embalm meaning as much by form as by wordsense. As nature reveals its meaning in its morphology, so it seems to have been the intent of the ancient writers of the sacred books to present truth in forms whose very organic structure would be revealing to the discerning mind. Investigation has traced some highly ingenious and subtle ciphers and cryptograms in our Bible itself. The word *chiasmus,* for example, will be found in the dictionary; it appears in the title of an epochal book, *Chiasmus in the New Testament,* by Nils Wilhelm Lund, of the faculty of a Chicago theological seminary. In it, he reveals the presence of a structure in the arrangement of verses in the Bible, based on the great key number of the universe—seven.[1] Arcane science of the ancient day said that the creative force emanating from the heart of being, and proceeding from spiritual to dense material levels, descended through planes A, B, C, to D and went no further; but on its return it took the course back to its primal ethereality through the same planes, D, C, B, and A, in reverse order. Lund traced the presence of many chiasmic structures in the Bible, such as the fact that the last three verses in a series of seven virtually repeat, in reverse order, the first three.

Here is evidence that the authors of the Bible tried to copy in a literary structure what they conceived to be the form of procedure in cosmic creation. Pythagoras was not alone in holding that God built the universe on number: the Gnostics, Kabalists, and Hermeticists also expounded this theory. In both Greek and Hebrew, every letter of the alphabet had a numerical value, so that the words and sentences not only carried a message through their words, but also framed a pattern of meaning over mathematical design and proportion. The scriptures there-

fore stand not only as books enshrining the most profound ethical meanings; they also structuralize the frame of the patterns
or *archai* of the Logos. A careful counting of the numerical
value of the Bible texts reports that every verse totals a multiple
of the number seven. The first verse of Genesis, in the Hebrew,
is composed of seven words and shows nine combinations of
the words and phrases that equal multiples of seven. Facts of
this kind enforce the recognition that the purpose of scriptural
composition was something far more profound and more potent
than mere narrative.

Along with this, there are numbers and symbols interwov-
en in the texture of the composition that also indicate a purpose
and modality other than historical factuality.

At the marriage feast in Cana, for example, the servants set
out six pots of water to be turned into wine, signifying the six
days of creation of the natural world that generate a birth of
"spirit" in the crowning seventh. Jesus tarried here or there for
seven days (as indeed, so did the Buddha and many another
great religious character). Kings reigned forty years. Twelve stones
were set up by Joshua in the dry bed of the Jordan River at his
crossing; twelve baskets of fragments of bread and fish were
gathered up after the multitude had been miraculously fed on
five small loaves and two small fishes. Circumcision was performed on the eighth day. The very name of Hecate, Greek
goddess of the moon, means six. The Israelite world was nearly
split in twain over the question whether the Passover fell on the
fourteenth or fifteenth of Nisan, the fourteenth being implied
by lunar, the fifteenth by solar symbolism. The seventh day of
the tenth month had special sanctity. More events than Jesus'
resurrection—notably, Jonah's voyage in his piscatorial ark—
were consummated "after three days." Atergatis and Semiramis
and other goddesses were named "the Goddess Fifteen."

Many intimations point to the general fact that the documents authored and cherished in ancient times were cryptic

constructions devised with incredible artistry to prefigure and dramatize both the form and the meaning of cosmic ideation, natural law, and living spiritual truth. Beyond question, this secret language was among the most important arcana of the Mysteries. To the ancients, literary composition had one preeminent purpose: to reveal the heroic struggle of the soulfire of man to overcome its material bonds, to free itself and transform mortality into immortality. The evidence for this is ubiquitous in mythology, in iconography, in epic and lyric poetry, in the universal science of heraldry, in astrological pictography devised and attached to the constellations and major stars in the heavens, in the zodiac, and in such elaborately constructed symbolic systems as the Tarot cards.

The very life of the people from remote time down through the medieval period was saturated, one might say, with an endless diffusion of arcana in the form of folklore, tradition, proverb, fairy tale, legend, castle ballad, and hero epic—even to Mother Goose jingles. Inspiration sprang from an overriding concern with the rich inner life of man, in relation to which the haphazard and often meaningless and cruel sequence of outward events was of but transient significance. We should note, in this connection, the relation between the two central words in arcane literature, *Logos* and *Mythos*. Logos is the power of the universal Mind; Mythos, related etymologically to mouth and therefore signifying utterance, is the effort of man's mind to express what it has comprehended of the supreme Mind. Myth is man's admittedly partial and incomplete statement of the truth of the Logos. Even though fragmentary, myth embodies truth at the highest level on which the human mind can envisage and pictorialize it. The scriptures of the Eastern world will not be read in their proper context until their imagery is penetrated to reveal the forms and figures of truth that have been so cunningly wrought into their texture. Many secrets of ancient men of wisdom still lie hidden, a rich resource which awaits discovery and decipherment.

Alfred Loisy has framed one of the problems that confront biblical scholarship. If the Gospels can no longer be accepted as history, what may they be other than history? It seems clear to us that they must be allegory, drama, and myth, which thus convey to man a grand panorama of spiritual truth. The discourses in the Gospels may well have been speeches to be recited by the principal actors in the Mystery plays, especially the utterances of the central figure, the Christos-Messiah. The movements, actions, and miraculous labors of Jesus could well have been the dramatist's efforts to portray histrionically the occult experiences of the soul in its evolution. Such features as the birth, the awakening of intellectual power at age twelve, the temptation or stress of conflict between the body and the soul, the development of the soul's divine potency to heal the ills and weaknesses of the flesh, the overcoming and casting out of the demonic forces of the natural man by the Christly influence, the symbolic raising of the "dead" inert spiritual power to a new birth of life, the anguish at the height of the clash between the two poles of life (the whole experience of the soul under the long domination of the animal instinct being itself the essence of crucifixion on the cross of matter), then the final victory in the soul's radiant transfiguration of the mortal man by the spirit's light, and the ultimate resurrection of the soul out of its "death" under the suffocating heaviness of the life of sense—what are all these but a dramatic rendition of the phases of the soul's life under the duress of its incarceration in mortal body? As asserted before, these elements of the narrative that constitute the ostensible life history of the man Jesus coincide at every point with critical situations in the drama of the Mysteries and other rituals in religions long antecedent to the first century. It would be extraordinary if long after earlier religions had elaborately portrayed a series of stages in man's spiritual experience, one man should have recapitulated every scene of the drama in his own life, even to the point of using the identical words put into the mouth of the Sun God of ancient Egypt.

There is an aspect of the Messianic conception that deserves special attention in this connection. Certain forms of the presentation had linked the advent to the moral condition of the people of Israel. Since the world was to be regenerated at the great day of the coming, the inference had been that the event was contingent upon the moral regeneration of God's chosen people. Israel's sins, her waywardness, disobedience, and apostasy from Jehovah were holding back the dawn of the Day of the Lord. In fact, one faction held that the Messiah had already come, but that he remained unrecognized, a beggar wandering among men who, because their spiritual sense was deadened by immorality, could not identify him as God. This legend, of course, is the precursor of many expansions of the poetic theme of human failure to discern the godly under the guise of the commonplace, as in Lowell's *The Vision of Sir Launfal* and the stories of the Grail cycle. It can readily enough be presupposed that the birth of any higher spiritual quality in human nature is retarded by a low level of general morality, just as continued ignorance inhibits whatever advance greater knowledge would bring. But this point is not the one expressed by the Messianists. Their thesis was simply that, in the terms of the great tradition, Israel might be expected in a few years to transfigure its mores so radically as to constitute a climactic point in human history. From one point of view, this thesis can be seen as a rational belief that the field must be tilled and ready before the seed can be planted. But from another, it signifies that heaven must wait upon man, which would be absurd.

Another belief inherent in the tradition was that the divine Child should be born on the day of the destruction of the temple. If one uses Paul's vivid figure of the *body* as the temple of the living God, this implies that when the weaknesses of the flesh (epitomized in the concept of original sin) have been over-

come, transmuted, or "destroyed," the Christ spirit, ever present but until then submerged, will flower into full life. The spiritual man, the Christ, will be born when the natural man dies.

Then again, the legend asserted that the Messiah was to
come up out of the sea. What does this mean? From the physi-
ological point of view, it is true that every human babe is born
out of sea water—the amniotic fluid. In another sense, all living
matter is symbolized by water, from which and by which all life
proceeds. Life on our earth began in and came out upon land
from the sea. Greek myth recounts that Venus (Love) was born
out of the sea foam that was stirred up around the knees of Zeus
as he waded through the waters. As life started in water, then
emerged into the air, so man is said to be born first of water, the
psyche, and then of the spirit. Since the element water has long
been held to represent the animal or psychic nature, the Christ,
representing the spiritual soul, would be seen as arising out of
that watery element, the sea, into the free air of the spiritual life.

Integral in the Messiah legend was the notion that the child
had to be spirited away immediately after his birth to escape
destruction—often by a dragon. In the Egyptian tradition, the
name for the symbolic serpent typifying the lower nature of
man, along with Apap and the Hydra or water dragon, was the
Herut reptile. A Syrian form was likewise *Herutt.* Mythology is
full of stories of the God-child who must be hidden from the
danger of destruction by a serpent, which the Egyptian myths
represented as lurking in the bight of Amenta (this physical
world) to devour young souls. So, also, Hercules had to stran-
gle two great serpents in his cradle. Can there be a connection
between the danger to the divine Child from the snake "Herut"
and that from the tyrant "Herod"?

Another story is connected with a figure named Taxo or
Taxon in the *Apocalypse of Moses.* It is said that Taxo and his
seven sons hid themselves in a *cave* in order to pray for the
people, but also to be able to live in accordance with the

people's strict interpretation of the law. The cave is a companion symbol to the stable as the birthplace of the Savior in the legends. If ever theology could recognize that this "strict law" is not Jewish legalistic religion, but that which is characterized by *geburah,* the unbending immutability of natural law, it might perceive therein a hint that the divine soul, when it comes to dwell in mortal body, would conform its life to the law governing its house of flesh, while it "prayed" for the elevation of its host.

The above forms only a small part of the existing evidence that the expectation of the immanence of the Messiah was widely prevalent in that first century.

THE TRIFORM MESSIAH

T he Messianic concept has been a fundamental and indeed universal element in religious psychology. Each of
the world's great religions can be shown to have taken its particular historical form of doctrine and rite—its constitution, as
it were—from the particular way in which it formulated and accepted the Messianic concept. In its most refined form, the theory of the coming of the Messiah was inseparably interwoven
with that of the divinization of man, whether evolutionary or
apocalyptical. The insight of the religionists in each case determined the form in which the concept came to expression. The
Avatar might be expected to appear in one of many guises, usually described in poetic or dramatic terms that might be taken
literally or symbolically. Literalists would take it for actuality,
while those with more discernment would look for a higher
interpretation in the mystic-spiritual realm. In the three religious
systems with which the theme of this work is most vitally concerned—Hellenic philosophy, Judaism, and Christianity—the
Messianic concept took distinctive forms which merit study.

To the Greeks, the Messianic ideal may be described as the
most philosophical, the least influenced by religious psychology.

It was regarded as the climactic stage of the long, slow evolution of the divine potential that was the source and ground of man's natural life. The new birth was to come as the denouement of the growth of soul in body and inferentially as the outcome of many incarnations of soul in different bodies. The latter qualification seemed necessary if the soul was to have an experience adequate to carry evolution over a long stretch of slow development—for one life (which might be curtailed to a few years or months) seemed far too brief for such an achievement as the soul's transition from animal to god. This philosophy argued, too, that if after one short life a continuation of spiritual growth was postulated as the mode of further evolution, then the necessity for restriction to but one life could not be dialectically vindicated. Reasoning would justify the conclusion that, if souls are to go on progressing toward supernal divinity and beatitude in a discarnate world, in an eternity beyond time—as religion generally has predicated—there is no utility in restricting incarnation to a single life. On the doctrinal grounds laid down in theological beliefs, the presumption that the one life on earth is to be followed by an eternity of spiritual progress in ethereal realms and higher states of consciousness makes the cause ridiculously inadequate for the effects. Momentous indeed would be the issues of this one all-too-fleeting mundane life experience if it alone determined the future of the soul that stretched forward into eternity. The injustice and irrationality of such a situation has always challenged men's minds. Before that challenge, Christian theology, having in the sixth century cast away the ancient theory of reincarnation, has remained mute. Yet until we are able to relate the pains as well as the peaks of individual experience to the whole of life, how can we gauge their significance?

It was to be a weakness of early Christianity that it abstracted its system out of the context of contemporary and contiguous religious life and then sought to rationalize its doctrine in isolation. Having repudiated the notion of human rebirth, it likewise rejected the concept of the growth of the individual soul toward eventual divinity through the lessons learned in earthly experience. The Christian teaching that the soul saved by Jesus, upon release from earthly woes, would rise at once to the bliss of heavenly courts, might rouse its followers to happy acceptance. But it could not convince the Greek mind, because it was not a rational belief, and in the Hellenistic view, rationality was intrinsic to the spiritual world. Therefore, to the Hellenist, speaking in the New Testament through the voice of St. Paul, the concept of the Messiah could mean nothing other than the coming, in the conscious life of humanity, individually and collectively, of the spirit of Christ.

As we have said before, Hellenism inherited many of its religious teachings from Egypt, from which also flowed the heritage of Judaeo-Christianity. From that ancient source came the idea of the advent, the "coming" to man of his divinity. There the power of righteousness and beauty, of grace and blessedness, that was to sanctify and transfigure man was called the "Comer," Osiris. His two sisters, Isis and Nephthys, who personify the material worlds, both visible and invisible, plead with him to hasten his coming.

> Come to thine abode! Come to thine abode!
> God An, come to thine abode.
> Do not stay from me, O beautiful youth;
> Come to thine abode with haste, with haste.
> Mine eyes seek thee;
> I seek thee to behold thee.
> Will it be long ere I see thee?
> Beholding thee is happiness.[1]

This was the precursor of the hymn, "O Come, O Come, Emanuel." Isis and Nephthys, Jesus and Horus, Mary and Martha all wept over the inert Lord, El-Asar-us, and at the same place, Bethany. The weeping of Horus over his father, Osiris, was at Anu in Egypt. Translation to English changed the *u* to *y*, giving *Any*, to which the Hebrews prefixed their word for "house"—*beth*—making it *Bethany*. Thus the ancient people pictured the budding of spirituality in human consciousness as the coming of a beautiful radiant youth.

World history was sharpened by crisis when Alexander swept the two surging waves of Hellenism and Judaism into conflict. In this clash of the two great systems, the Greek and the Israelite concepts of Messianism also confronted one another. We have seen that the Greeks conceived the Messiah in impersonal abstract form, as a stage or level of divine consciousness. The Hebraic concept might be said to hover indecisively between the personal and impersonal. The Messiah was to come to the Jews, yes, in the person of that long-heralded scion of David who was to be exalted in Jerusalem and lead the nations back to God. He was to be a person, but at the same time the resplendent symbol of real might and majesty. The Messiah, therefore, was not mere man, but the world-radiance of the Israelite destiny, the people chosen by God to lead the nations of the world to the universal apotheosis. He would be the ruler of the world, to be sure, but only as the embodiment of world hegemony promised by Jehovah to Abraham and his progeny of Israel. To Abraham, the Israelite father, the Lord had promised that in him should all the nations of the world be blessed. That promise has enchanted the mind of every son of Jewry for some three thousand years.

It was a fateful day for the Hebrews when they came to the point of identifying themselves, as a tribal or a racial group, with those "children of Israel" whose history occupies so large a place in the Old Testament. The date of this event is lost in the dim past, but at some moment in remote Palestinian history they laid hold of three names used in the Mysteries to designate the highest grades of initiates and applied them to their ethnic group. These three names—*Israelites, Hebrews,* and *Jews*—each origi-

nally designated a grade of attainment in the religious life. In
much the same way, the religious elite of India appropriated to
themselves the title of *Brahmins,* signifying their status as em-
bodiments of Brahman, the universal Creator. Similarly, the
Greeks called themselves *Hellenes,* "the bright and shining ones,"
and referred to the rest of the world as barbarians. So the
Palestinians adopted for themselves these three names that had
connotations of the highest spirituality and called the rest of the
nations the "Gentiles," which means "born"—thus not "reborn"
in a spiritual sense. Names that might have denoted religious caste
distinction began to have simply a national or social reference.
The "children of Israel" were of "illustrious ancestry," as the gram-
marian Gesenius phrased it, meaning descended from the gods,
or God's chosen race.

Additional confirmation of the fact that the term *Israelites*
was not intended to refer to the Jews as a race or nation is to
be found in the *Introduction to the New Testament* by Theodor
Zahn. In part 2 of this work, when analyzing the Epistle of
James, Zahn discusses the apostle's motive for addressing the
readers of his letter and the identity and religious status of those
to whom it was ostensibly addressed: "the Twelve Tribes in the
Diaspora." This term, the *Diaspora,* refers to the Jews who did
not live in Palestine, but were scattered among the population of
other lands. "The Jews of the dispersion" is an equivalent term.
From the way James writes to these dispersed twelve tribes, Zahn
finds it a matter of some question as to precisely what groups are
meant—whether those thus designated as in the Diaspora were
the scattered Jews generally, or explicitly Jews who had become
Christians, or Christians generally, either former Jews or Gentiles
of various nationalities. His remarks confirm our contention as
to the meaning and reference of the key name *Israelites:*

> The object of this redemption is not the Jewish people,
> but nevertheless a people of God to whom the titles of

Israel are applied. . . . At that time no one could say that the Jewish nation as such was living in a diaspora, either as regards its condition or its location, nor is any such statement made. No matter how largely the Jews were living outside of Palestine, and no matter how widely they were scattered, the nation retained its fatherland. One is still at a loss to understand why he, James, makes Christians his readers also, and how he could have omitted to indicate by a word the religious condition which distinguished his readers from Israel as a whole.

And besides, this construction stands in absolute contradiction to the idea of the "Twelve Tribes" which indicates specifically the Jewish people, with special emphasis on their entirety. Here the contrast is not between individual Jews or single tribes of Israel and the remaining Jews or tribes, but between the "Twelve Tribes" which live in the diaspora, so constitute a homeless diaspora, and another "Twelve Tribes" of which this is not true. This phrase is replaced by one which, while on the one hand retaining the comparison with the Jewish people, on the other brings the object which it describes into sharp contrast with the Jewish people. Unlike the Twelve Tribes which have Palestine for their native land, Jerusalem for their capital and the temple as a center of their religious worship, the Twelve Tribes addressed in his letter have no earthly fatherland, nor any capital upon earth, but always, no matter where they have been settled, live scattered in a strange world, like the Jewish exiles in Mesopotamia and Egypt. It is no new doctrine concerning a twofold Israel which James develops here. The expression, "the Twelve Tribes in the diaspora" may mean *either* the entire body of Christians living at the time . . . or it may mean the Believing Israel, the entire body of the Jewish Christians.

Jesus spoke of this future fellowship as of another *ethnos* in contrast with the Jewish people led by the High Priests and the rabbis. There is, of course, no need for proof to show that he meant . . . not some other particular nation, the Greek, e.g. . . . but rather the same people of God whom he elsewhere called his church and represented as a house to be built by him (Matt. 16:18). The thought that the Christian Church, composed of men of various nationalities and based not on birth at all, but on faith in Jesus, was a new people of God, the true race of Abraham, or a spiritual Israel, was consequently implanted in his church from the beginning, and was developed by it in manifold directions. True followers of Christ would become Israelites by being grafted on to this spiritual Israel. The thought that the Christian Church, in contrast to the Jewish people, is the spiritual Israel is so usual with Paul that he only tacitly presupposes it and quite incidentally calls Jewish people with their culture "Israel according to the flesh" (I Cor. 10:18). This spiritual Israel also has its metropolis, which likewise can be termed Jerusalem. It lies, however, not in Palestine, but in heaven, where the ascended King of the spiritual Israel is enthroned (Gal 4:26; Heb. 12:22). There the members of the true Israel are enrolled even while still living on earth (Phil 4:3; Luke 10:20). There is the proper seat of the Commonwealth of which they are descendants even here (Phil 3:20). Paul likens their condition in the world to that of those Jews who were scattered abroad far from their native land. *Hermas* (*Similitudes* 9:17) in a manner quite characteristic of him and yet often misunderstood, applies the figure of the Twelve Tribes to all mankind as the field of mission work and the source of the materials for the building of the church. Hernias represents the church as the true Israel. If a Jew believes in Christ he becomes an Israelite (Romans 4:11 ff.).[2]

Zahn thus corroborates our contention that the racial group known for over two thousand years as Israelites, Hebrews, or Jews does not constitute the "Israelites" of the Bible. They are not the sons of the Father in any more special sense than that of *all* humans. St. Paul himself said that no one becomes an Israelite by virtue of birth in a Hebrew family or nationality, but by the birth within him of the Christ spirit. Bluntly stated, the Jewish appropriation of the term *Israelites* to themselves as an ethnic group, regarding themselves therefore as having been divinely chosen and set apart from all other groups for a special spiritual purpose, was as much a misconception as the Christian belief that Messiahship could be embodied in one single man, Jesus.

As we have mentioned, the Judaic tradition of the Messiah was not, like the Hellenic, entirely impersonal. The Messiah was expected to appear in the form of a great Personage, but this figure was rather a representative, a symbol of the real Messianic Power, than its complete embodiment. The Jewish concept was of epic proportions; it was the cosmic drama, embracing in its scope and perspective the whole of God's plan for human history. If the Israelite nation was indeed Jehovah's chosen agent for the consummation of the divine plan, its fate was inevitably full of significance. Every event could reveal the purposes of the divine Will. It is doubtful any people ever lived their own history more self-consciously, ever watchful for the hand of God to show itself in each turn and vicissitude of fortune. If adversity befell them, it was read as God's anger meting out punishment for their dereliction in his service; if success and happiness were their lot, God was rewarding them for their obedience. Perhaps more than any other nation in history, the Jews have lived, fought, prospered, and suffered defeat under the constant persuasion that God was giving his whole attention to their fortunes.

In defense of this belief, it could be said that the creative power does stand in conscious relation to the creatures whom it has endowed with intelligence. But that this dynamic, life-giving relation should operate under the same terms and at the same level as the human father-son relationship is anthropomorphic and foolishly naive. The ancient tradition rested on the principle that every living self in creation participated, according to his grade and capacity, in the One Life from whose infinitude he sprang. But at no time did it presume that the infinite Consciousness itself could be limited by special concern or favoritism for any of its creations. *All* selves are unique, and all are of unique value and relation to the Whole; this is their common inheritance, shared equally by every soul, whether the man be cultivated or simple, genius or peasant. But the value is intrinsic. The relation of each soul to the Oversoul is somewhat analogous to that of the cells in his body to the whole man. Each is important, even indispensable. Yet the man does not pay conscious attention to these cells; nor does he choose among them, saying, "The cell in my eye is more valuable than the cell in my hand." How the divine Mind maintains its ever-creative relationship to the multitude of conscious beings, of which it is the source, is a profound mystery. One may speculate that what we call the laws of nature are the operative results of the workings of God's conscious mind, but this is a speculation only.

Returning to the Hebrew concept of the Messiah, it was impossible for the Jews to accept the Christian interpretation. They did believe that a man, the scion of David, was to lead Israel to its glory. But the glory was not to be confined to him alone; Israel itself, in the consummation of its special mission, *was* the Messiah. So we see that just as the Greek concept of the

Messiah was spiritual and impersonal, so that of Judaism was theocratic and national, with a personal element ancillary and incidental to the main doctrinal axis.

But if Judaism could not countenance the idea of the Messianic advent in the person of Jesus or any one human being, how did it come about that this Christian concept took root and grew to power within Judaism itself? We have tried to show that in the beginning there was some sympathy between the two views, in that the Hebrew conception did include the figure of the Messiah as a human or mortal King of the Jews. The birth of David's son was to play a part in the drama of their history. It is probable that, had Jesus proclaimed his kingdom to be the rule of earthly power, he would have found Jewry far readier to support his bid for recognition. Many writers have stressed the point that his cause was in jeopardy the moment he declared that his kingdom was not of this world, but of the world of the spirit. Even in relatively recent times, the Jews have demonstrated that they would go along pretty far with the pretensions of personal claimants to the Messianic role if, as in the case of Sabbatai Zevy and Jacob Frank, the program was to develop as a force in world affairs. Even the great Rabbi Akiba supported the Messianic status of Simon bar Kochba, when the great military hero of the Zealots was waging successful resistance to Rome's armies. It is reasonable to surmise that if the fortunes of war under the drive of the Zealots had carried the Judean armies to wide success and brought the little Judean kingdom some prospect of world empire, as it appeared it might in the time of the Maccabees, the Jews might have been ready to hail the conquering leader of its armies as the long-expected Messiah. So considered, it is apparent that the expectation of a personalized Messiah was a deeply rooted element of the Jewish religious consciousness.

A statement that bears on this question is found in the work on the Messianic theme *He That Cometh,* by the Norwegian scholar, Sigmund Mowinckel: "The surprising thing," he writes, "is that the thought of the Messiah as a mortal held its ground so well" in the life of Judaism.[3] The author asserts that two fairly distinct forms of the Messianic hope manifested themselves in the Judean community. There was the traditional, national, political, or this-worldly concept centering in the appearance of the Davidic King, necessarily in human form, and there was a transcendental conception of the Son of man coming as a power that would restore the Torah and the reign of Levitical Law, establishing a higher and otherworldly spiritual order. Mowinckel holds that these two aspects alternated in influence from time to time. Furthermore, he brings forward a strong point that helps to clarify understanding of Israel's reluctance to follow the Christian movement. He refers to the fact that in the Christian concept, the Messiah was destined to achieve his glory through the endurance and the final conquest of suffering. The Christian view laid great—indeed, almost central—emphasis upon this aspect, grounding it in the Hebrews' own scriptures, most signally of course in the famous fifty-third chapter of Isaiah in which the Messianic personage, the Suffering Servant (so great a puzzle to all theology), is depicted as the god reduced to the status of the divine Lamb led to the sacrifice in order to atone with his own suffering for the sins of the unregenerate world. Christianity, with its legend of the temptation, trial, condemnation, crucifixion, and death of the Jesus figure in the Gospels, saw in the Isaiah portrait of "the man of sorrows and acquainted with grief" the antetype of which Jesus was made the historical fulfillment.

But this aspect of the tradition, as we have seen, was too negative and defeatist for acceptance by the Jews. It did not comport with the Israelite expectation of crowning victory. The Jewish theocratic view did include the chastening salutary influence of suffering, which it regarded as just punishment for Israel's faithlessness to Jehovah and as disciplinary training for its role as world leader. But suffering for no more ostensible purpose than a vicarious spiritual atonement was quite at odds with Jewish thought. Mowinckel points out that the Jewish ideal of Messiahship took the form of an immanent power, a symbol of the eternal progress of the human spirit or of a future perfection as the goal of evolution. In this form the Hebrew concept approached closer to that of Hellenistic philosophy. So we see that Judaism vacillated indecisively between the Greek and the Christian views of the Messiah.

This analysis has set the stage for another important observation. As the two wings of the Messianic concept, the Hebrew and the Christian, failed to beat in harmony, so the religious life of which it was so essential a part failed to soar freely and effortlessly into the spiritual light. As a result of the conflict, Jewry was to suffer an endless persecution, while Christianity was to suffer the fate of the persecutor—a loss of spiritual power. As for the Hellenic concept of the Messiah as the coming of spiritual insight, the Greek world was, in the course of several centuries, brought under the dominance first of Rome, later of Persia, and still later of Arabia and Islam. With the enthronement of Christianity in world power through the conversion of the Roman Empire, all Hellenistic concepts were forced to take refuge in Gnosticism, Essenism, and the mystico-occult societies, which had little world influence. The Hellenic ideal went underground in Europe, became a subdued mystical strain in Eastern or Greek Christianity, and is only now showing signs of a renaissance in the modern world through the recently awakened interest in metaphysics and the ancient tradition.

We have thus seen that the Jewish and Christian systems represent the crystallization of two divergent conceptions of the Messiah into two great religious movements. With this separation of the Christian offshoot from the parent root of Judaism, there came the first breach in the unity of Eastern subjectivity, the first indication of the objectivity that was to characterize

Western thought for the next two thousand years. Jung's analysis of the forces struggling for dominion over the human psyche is corroborated by the historical consequences of Christianity's shift of spiritual focus from the divine Self within all hearts to an external, transcendental God in heaven and the person of his hypostatized Son in Galilee. This event was the first schism between the subjectively oriented East and the objectively oriented West—a cleavage that was to widen and deepen with the centuries so as to become a well-nigh impassable barrier. This tendency toward emphasis upon external and objective reality was, of course, influenced and intensified by other forces—notably the rise of science in Europe. But it is fair to say that it was largely the extroversion of the hope and expectation of divine salvation that initiated the trend toward objectivity. Even as men became surer of themselves in the material world of nature, they lost confidence in their ability to find spiritual reality. This may have been one of the most critical junctures in world history. It was the point at which the psychic wholeness that characterized the ancient world was torn asunder.

Personification of the Christ spirit in the man Jesus imposed upon the age the necessity of transmuting the Messiah from a universal principle to a man. This involved the transfer of the meaning of the entire body of scriptures, comprising countless allegories, dramas, and ritual constructions, from a previous subjective spiritual sense to an objective personal sense, from mystical relevance to historical fact. The text of scripture had to read meaningfully as history, whereas previously it had been regarded as spiritual truth in allegorical dress. The Sun God, whose power was that of life and mind, became the saintly figure of Jesus; the twelve rays of divine light that streamed from the central radiance became the twelve "fishermen"; every town, lake, and river that figured in the allegory became a local village, the Sea of Galilee, the Jordan River; and the central focus of spiritual consciousness, long celebrated as the heavenly "city," now became Jerusalem. The church fathers, notably Clement, Origen, and the Alexandrian school following Philo, were well aware of this stream of allegory. But still few have understood how completely the whole volume of allegory, drama, and symbol was transformed into objective reality—an accomplishment that included changing the "cross of matter" into the cross of tangible wood, the Eternal Mother of all into the woman, Mary, the gradual assimilation of the Christ life and mind in the human personality into the partaking of Jesus' body and blood—converting the miracle of the healing power of the divine nature in man to transform and purify the human nature into the "miracles" wrought by Jesus.

When the subjective interpretation is intelligently applied to Biblical exegesis, it removes the contradictions and inconsistencies created when the scriptures are read as veridical history. All these inconsistencies have, over the ages, become so interwoven with the ethical and spiritual message of the Bible that they are often considered to be an essential religious ingredient—which they are not, since they are a mere excrescence or incrustation on the inner truth contained therein.

While medieval Europe lay under the spell of ecclesiastical pietism, the essence of much of the archaic science was preserved by Jewish, Arabian, and Moorish scholarship in the East, North Africa, and Spain. Maimonides and Avicebron kept the flame alight, largely through the elaboration of Aristotelian philosophy; it later erupted with sweeping force in the ebullience of the Italian Renaissance. Today, free scholarship, the modern scientific cast of mind, general education, and the spirit of individual creativeness in literature are combining to bring it back to common knowledge.

The ecclesiastical power that still dominates Western religion well knows the psychological strength and hence the danger of interest in esotericism. At the same time, it is well aware of the utility of such interest in the nurture of the divine spirit in man, especially when that spirit is already awakening. But the disastrous historical experiences of the Christian hierarchy with the movements of free thought have taught this controlling power the tactical advantage of readopting the esoteric policy of the ancients—the very measure it had repudiated in those first centuries. The church withholds from its following many of the truths it inherited from the Mysteries. Practical considerations have dictated the policy of secrecy, lest the debacle of the third century be repeated, with Christianity now the victim as it was then the perpetrator.

It might be said that the Catholic sector of Christianity includes a careful study of esoteric philosophy in the theological education of its priesthood, the better to guard this philosophy from the laity. It is, however, generally shunned or ignored by the Protestants.

Germane to the discussion, and indeed corroborative of the position taken here, are the ideas expressed by the eminent Jewish mystic and philosopher, Martin Buber. In his work, *The Origin and Meaning of Hasidism,* Buber discusses Judaism's attitude toward Messianism and the appearance of Jesus. To understand this attitude, he says, one must pierce deep into the inner core of the Hebrew faith, which does not state the doctrine in any formal creed, but reveals it in a living Messianic sense, as experienced by Hebrews individually and mystically and by the Hebrews collectively in the theocratic foundation of their national life. He asserts that Jesus was the first in a long series of self-proclaimed Messiahs arising in the course of Jewish history—the first, at any rate, to proclaim openly to the world his inner consciousness of his Messianic role.[4] However, many devout Jews before him had testified to the effective working within them of the spiritual power of Shekinah. We cannot ignore the great mystics among the Kabalists. It was the *Zohar,* the sacred treasure of the Kabalists, that inspired the movement of Hasidism. It would seem much nearer the truth to say that while Jesus was by no means the first to experience the inner afflatus, he may have been the first to proclaim it abroad, and in such a way as to identify his personal conviction of its presence in his mystical life with the expected historical figure of Davidic ancestry, the very element that brought him to the cross. Buber believes that Jesus felt the sacred mystery of the divine catharsis within himself so fully that he openly acknowledged it in word and deed.

But is Buber able to certify that the experience of Jesus was uniquely and exclusively God-consciousness, different in quality as well as degree from that of religious mystics the world over? He does go so far as to say that the announcement of this first in the "automessianic" series was incomparably the purest, the most authentic, legitimate, and real manifestation of the Messianic power, thereby implying that the professions of all the others were less real, less well defined, less truly evident of the presence of the divine charisma. This statement by the Jewish scholar is all the more remarkable, in that it comes from a non-Christian. His reflections upon the Messianic role of Jesus make one wonder all the more why the Jewish people should *not* have followed the Christians in their worship of this authentic Son of God. Yet Buber's analysis of the state of things that permitted the Christian ferment to grow to power in the Israelite community is admirable. He intimates that the Jews who launched the Christian upsurge did so because Jewry was distraught with suffering, eager to heed any sincere claim to Messiahship that would bring them relief and release. Always, he says, the people had resisted the automessianism of the self-proclaimed false Messiahs, but in this instance they yielded. In so doing they prepared the way for certain catastrophe and demonstrated the futility of a man's venturing to offer his subjective experience of spiritual visitation to the gaze of the worldly; even more, to risk the misunderstanding that would ensue upon his proclaiming himself *the* Messiah.

The modern prophet also speaks of two self-deceptions, one of a person as the Messiah, and one of a group as such. This coincides with our earlier characterization of the Christian concept of Messiahship (Jesus as a person) and that of the Jews (the Messiah as a group). Buber says that these were two transgressions of a real boundary, the line between personal self-realization of the God-presence, and the actual embodiment of God in a human person. He is frank in saying that the occurrence of these automessianic pretensions was a mishap, but only an internal one—a mishap between a real and a spurious ideation in individual minds. These, the lone man and the group, mistook the reality that related them mystically to God, for the historical fulfillment of the world tradition of the Coming. They should not have presumed to extrapolate thus from their own subjective experience.

Buber makes it beautifully clear that the true Hasidic conception of divine possession stands opposed to the concept of a single, unique embodiment of Messianic power. This view rejects the idea that one man alone can embody supreme holiness and claim differentiation from all other men; it rejects the claim that one period of time can be more sacred than all other time, or that one act can be uniquely sanctified among all other acts. One seems to hear the voice of Emerson in this passage. All mankind is given the Messianic potential, all time is pregnant with coming divine birth, all action directed to God is Messianic action. And, be it said, this pronouncement of Martin Buber could become a clear directive to our times to bring all religionism back to a proper evaluation of the true sense of the Messianic hope.

PRE-CHRISTIAN
CHRISTIANITY

W e have averred that the new and true catalyst for the resolution of the vastly complicated problems of Biblical exegesis is available in the allegorical interpretation. If this key can introduce harmony, consistency, and rationality into Biblical study and also illumine the hidden meanings of this literature (as is here claimed it can), the sacred scriptures must be accredited as allegory and not as history. And next, if it is demonstrated to be allegory, there flows from this determination one inescapable conclusion: the characters in this, as in all other allegories, are not real people; they never really lived and never did the things their story tells of. An allegory is a dramatization of a phenomenon that has its real existence only in the subjective world.

What, then, can it mean to Christianity if it be convincingly established that the four Gospels of the New Testament are spiritual allegories, and that therefore the characters in them were not living people but *dramatis personae* representing very real elements in the subjective life of man? Many honest, knowledgeable, and conscientious scholars have upheld the truth of this contention. They have been able to see Jesus as a dramatic typefigure, symbolic of man's divinity, akin to the other Messianic deities of the Mediterranean basin. How have they been able to take issue with the whole Christian world on such a momentous matter? The answer is simple. They can believe in the existence of no historical person until they have been shown *some evidence* that accredits the claim for such existence. And in regard to evidence in this case, they say there is none. The Christian may well be aghast at such a statement. But, these investigators rejoin, of authentic historical evidence, truly there is none. How then, it will be asked, can the scholars who have devoted two thousand years to the indefatigable study of the period of Biblical writing have been so flagrantly deceived? The answer recapitulates what we have already said: That which the sages of the ancient mysteries conceived of and wrote as spiritual allegory, the uncritical took for history. The early leaders of the church found it in time politic not to contradict this notion, until finally knowledge of the true origin of the sacred scripts was lost and the legend of their historicity dominated all conceptions. This is the answer; this is the history. But now, the habit of questioning that the rise of science has instilled in the Western mind is forcing scholars to look for factual evidence to support the claims of Christian historians. And finding none, many of these scholars hold that the case for the nonhistoricity of Jesus is growing stronger and stronger.

What is this evidence that must be so carefully weighed, in the face of the four canonical Gospels and Acts, some apocryphal literature, and much of what is called "pseude-pigrapha," constituting a veridical, if concededly not very substantial, biography of the man, Jesus? We have already made references to Gerald Massey's vast assemblage of material in the field of comparative religion, a work since corroborated in large part by later Egyptological researches. Massey's testimony indicates that the Gospels are first-century republications or redactions of very ancient scripts. Even if these statements are not fully ac-

cepted, they show that the life and work of Jesus is, to an astonishing degree, a repetition of the story of Horus and other god-
figures of antiquity.

However, it will be claimed that there must surely be a
world of evidence beyond the content of the Gospels themselves. Yet it is a matter of fact that the eye of scholarship has
searched the files of history to the last document in the last
monastic library, and all that has ever been written on the matter comprises some twenty-four lines of print. Purporting to
refer to Jesus is a passage of some dozen lines in Josephus' *History
of the Jews;* there is a short passage in the *Annals* of the Roman
historian, Suetonius, and an even shorter passage seeming to
refer to Jesus in Pliny's *History.* So brief and ambiguous are these
references, however, that a large majority of the schools of
scholarly study have agreed to dismiss their claims to historicity as fraudulent. They have been discredited as spurious inter-
polations inserted with the obvious purpose of introducing
these few scraps of "authentic" history into the Gospel legend.

Nowhere else does the field of history turn up any evidence
as to the existence of Jesus. During the lifetime of this "heavenly emissary" whose visit to earth was to save humanity, and for
close on to two hundred years thereafter, not one line appears
in the records of history that can be accepted as a true chronicle of his life story. These facts completely reverse the normal
procedure that gives us history. A man's record is known and
insofar as important, is registered during his lifetime; then it
begins to fade out and become haloed and legendary in later
years. In the case of Jesus, during his day and for some six generations after, history presents us with total silence. It is only
after this stretch of time that he emerges from obscurity and
becomes a center of controversy and an object of worship. To
emphasize the strangeness of this phenomenon, let us suppose
that George Washington had lived the life story assigned to
him, but that only now, some two centuries later, was his career

being chronicled in our books. The lack of printing in Jesus' time might be conceded to be a factor in such phenomenon, yet it is not adequate to constitute a real explanation. There were many historians in those days assiduously reporting current events, and there were scribes who made a profession of writing letters. Is it not extraordinary that, of the thousands of Judeans who, as the narrative has it, witnessed the marvels performed by Jesus (the miracle of the feeding of five thousand, for instance), not one letter has ever been found to have been written by an eye witness to some friend or relative, telling of the marvelous event? This is such a departure from normal human reaction in the circumstances that it strongly suggests the nonfactuality of those "miracles." (Again, it should be added that most of these works of wonder duplicated those to be found in old Egyptian manuscripts, always in the forms of allegories.) There is, in fact, no corroborative eyewitness evidence of any event in Jesus' life.

Gospel literature was obviously in existence centuries before Jesus' period. But it could bear no witness to his life as ostensibly lived during the years 1 to 33 AD until it had been brought out from obscurity in the latter part of the first century, when naturally the figure of the central character in the drama would become the subject of universal notice, wonder, and worship. The reasonable conclusion seems to be that the Gospels were not written as original documents by four separate recorders in that first century, shortly after Jesus' presumed life, but that they emerged from seclusion at that time. This is the crux of the story, the axis on which world history turned.

It is constantly to be regretted that the dearth of evidence for any positive conclusions in these matters prevents apodictic declarations. But some evidence is available, one item of which indicates that the Gospels and Epistles of the New Testament were in existence long before that pivotal first century. This evidence comes from the man who, with the Emperor Constantine, called the first church council and wrote the first history of Christianity—the bishop-historian Eusebius, who may be said to be the founder of Christian ecclesiasticism. In his famous *Ecclesiastical History* of the new faith, he discusses the Essenes, those religious figures whom the discovery of the Dead Sea Scrolls has made the subject of intense world interest. The Essenes were also referred to as the "Covenanters," or, especially in northern Egypt, as the *Therapeutae* or "Healers." In Book 2, chapter 17, Eusebius discusses the monastic life of these Therapeutae, making the following observation: "These ancient Therapeutae were Christians, and their writings are our Gospels and Epistles."[1]

This statement is not altogether unsupported by other authority, for Augustine, Justin, Marcion, and others openly aver, even protest, that the Christian faith was in no sense a new and unique system, a sharp departure from ancient cults, but was indeed the universal faith of all antiquity. Augustine, in a famous passage, asserts that it existed from the very beginning of the world, was indeed propagated by the patriarchs of the Old Testament, and in his day or a little before, "began to be called Christianity," picking up the wholly Greek term for the divinity in man, the *Christos*. If Eusebius' words represent the truth, they corroborate Gerald Massey's conclusions that the Gospels, the only literature purporting to support the historical existence of Jesus, were in existence as Essene scripts, before the first century of our era. Indeed, the bishop says that the books of the Christian canon were ancient documents that those same Therapeutae had treasured, copied, and recopied from still older parchments.

Similarly, Justin Martyr, the outstanding protagonist of the new faith in the second century, protested to those who charged that it was a heretical departure from the pagan religion that in no way was this charge true. He insisted that the Christian dogmas and beliefs were in every way in harmony with the mythical presentments of the pagans and that the advent of the

Christos fulfilled the prophecies of the sibyls. How closely this claim matches the similar one that the birth of Jesus in Bethlehem sealed the truth of Jewish Old Testament prophecy! Whether these early protestations may be taken as completely sincere or as uttered out of expediency, they nevertheless refute later claims.

It is evident that, like most events in human history, the Christian movement developed into something quite different from what was intended in the beginning. No one knows fully what forces propelled it, what its prime motivations and incitements were, or what the influences were that tended to give it form, content, and direction. However much the product of its original milieu, Christianity early generated the dogma that it was of divine origin, the result of a specific divine revelation, having no relation to, much less dependence upon, contemporary faiths.

Eusebius penned a lengthy statement asserting that while the name *Christian* is new and "of late," the principles of the faith are by no means new, but were promulgated by ancient men renowned for piety, such as the patriarchs of the Old Testament, who were described as being no less Christian than those of his day. Augustine, companion founder with Eusebius of the Christian construction, who gave to Christian theology its first distinctive formulation, wrote in similar vein:

> That which is called the Christian religion existed among the ancients and never did not exist; from the very beginning of the human race until the time when the Christ came in the flesh, at which time the true religion which already existed began to be called Christianity.[2]

In confirmation of Justin Martyr's statement, a work by Robert Taylor called *Diegesis* quotes the famous founder of the school of Neoplatonic philosophy, Ammonias Saccas, to the effect that Christianity and paganism differ in no essential points.[3] Augustine himself had been a Manichaean and was associated with Plotinus in the school over which Saccas presided, and the great saint of the church almost certainly drew his doctrine of the deific Trinity from the Neoplatonic formulae expounded by Plotinus in his *Enneads* at least a century before it was incorporated in formal Christian doctrine by the Council of Nicea. It may be assumed that this, one of the most distinctive doctrinal features of Christianity, was unquestionably a pagan derivative.

In Bellamy's translation of Justin Martyr's work (*Apol.* 2) we find Celsus, the Jew with whom Origen waged his famous debate, saying that "the Christian religion contains nothing but what Christians hold in common with the heathen; nothing new." Thus confronted, the Christians fell back on the "argument from diabolism" stated as follows:

> It having reaching the devil's ears that the prophets had foretold that Christ would come . . . he [the devil] set the heathen poets to bring forward a great many who should be called sons of Jove [that is, the sons of God]; the devil laying his scheme in this to get men to imagine that the true history of Christ was of the same character as the prodigious fables and poetic stories . . .[4]

Justin Martyr was the most outstanding exponent of Christianity in the second century, (along with Irenaeus); this citation registers his confession that the alleged "true history of Christ" was almost the same in character and content as the stories of the many mythical saviors and solar deities. Christianity must take serious cognizance of the studies in comparative religion that demonstrate that the Gospel narrative represents a fresh statement of the universal myth of the birth, baptism, temptation, life, trial, condemnation, death, burial, resurrection, and ascension of the Christos-Messiah, whether under the "vegetation myth" of the autumn death and vernal resurrection of the god or goddess of grain, or the death and resurrection of the pilgrim soul in the Mystery dramas. There is almost no limit to the body of data that establishes the presence of numberless features of the Sun-God myth in the context of the Christian structure. In the earliest Christian community, prayers were even addressed to "Our Lord, the Sun."

The Christian festivals were all originally dated in relation to the solstices and equinoxes. In 345 AD, an encyclical issued by Pope Julius I decreed the shifting of the date of Christmas from March 25 to December 25, with the express statement that it was done in order to align the Christian celebration of the birth of the Savior with the custom of the followers of Bacchus and of Mithra, "who commemorate the birth of the Deity at the winter solstice." The tradition of Christianity, in short, is shot through and through with features of the Sun-God myths of antiquity. Some dozen ancient pagan Sun-God saviors, including Mithra, Osiris, Bacchus, Adonis, and Attis, were also born on December 25.

Lest it be contended that the statement of Eusebius as to the Essene source of New Testament books is almost too slender a testimony on which to rest decisive judgments, let us consider the substantial report of yet another early historian of Christianity, Epiphanius. He, too, when speaking of the Essenes, says:

> It is very likely that the commentaries [scriptures] which were among them were the Gospels and the works of the Apostles and certain expositors of the ancient prophets, such as partly that Epistle unto the Hebrews, and also what the other Epistles of Paul do contain.[5]

Again, as quoted in Doane's *Bible Myths,* the fourth century Epiphanius has this to say concerning these Essenes:

> They who believed in Christ were called Jessasi [Essenes] before they were called Christians. They derived their constitution from the signification of the name "Jesus," which in Hebrew signifies the same as Therapeutae, that is, a savior or physician.[6]

Since the discovery of the Dead Sea Scrolls, liberal-minded scholars have been speculating freely upon what connection there may have been between these Qumran Covenanters and the founder of the Christian movement, Jesus. Evidence supplied by Epiphanius may be a telling item. What could have been more likely than that, first taking the name of *Jessasi* or *Jesusites,* they later picked up the name *Christians* as that Greek term began to be applied widely to these brethren?

Notable here also is a citation from a writer, De Quincey, who says:

> If the Essenes were not the early Christians in disguise, then was Christianity, *as a knowledge,* taught independently of Christ—nay, in opposition to Christ?[7]

Godfrey Higgins is another scholar who speaks authoritatively on this subject in *Anacalypsis.*

> The Essenes were called physicians of the soul or Therapeutae; being resident both in Judaea and Egypt, they probably spoke of or had their sacred books in Chaldea. They were Pythagoreans, as is proved by all their forms and ceremonies and doctrines, and they called themselves sons of Jesse. . . . If the Pythagoreans

or Cosnobites, as they were called by Iamblichus, were Buddhists, the Essenes were Buddhists. The Essenes were Koinobii, lived in Egypt on the lake of Parembole or Maris in monasteries. These are the very places in which were formerly found the Gymnosophists or Samaneans or Buddhist priests. Gymnosophists are also placed by Ptolemy in northeastern India.[8] Their [the Essene] parishes, churches, bishops, priests, deacons, festivals are all identically the same [as the Christians]. They had apostolic founders, the manners which distinguished the immediate apostles of Christ, Scriptures divinely inspired, *the same allegorical mode of interpreting* them which has since obtained among Christians, and the same order of performing public worship. They had missionary stations or colonies of their community established in Rome, Corinth, Galatia, Ephesus, Philippi, Colossae and Thessalonica, precisely such and in the same circumstances as were those to whom St. Paul addressed his letters in those places. All the fine moral doctrines attributed to the Samaritan Nazarite are to be found in the doctrines of the ascetics.[9]

Might it not be significant that, while Jesus vehemently denounced the Pharisees and scribes and the strict legalistic orthodoxy of his day in Judea, he never spoke against the Essenes? Writers have speculated as to whether he may not have been actually a member of the Qumran or other monastic community of these devout practitioners of the sanctified life. His teaching, his attitudes, and the general tone of his life offer no reason why he would not have been in closest sympathy with their beliefs and practices.

Another apposite paragraph is from Gibbon's *Decline and Fall of the Roman Empire:*

It is to be confessed that the ministers of the Catholic Church imitated the profane model which they were impotent to destroy. The most respectable bishops had persuaded themselves that the ignorant rustics would more cheerfully renounce the superstitions of Paganism if they found some resemblance, some compensation in the bosom of Christianity. The religion of Constantine achieved in less than a century the final conquest of the Roman Empire; but the victors themselves were insensibly subdued by the arts of their vanquished rivals.[10]

Rome had conquered Greece, but there is hardly a historian who has not said that it was Greece that conquered Rome.

We again remind the reader that the Jewish scholar, Joseph Klausner, states categorically that Christianity is the result of a combination of Jewish religion and Greek philosophy, and that it cannot be understood without a knowledge of the literature of the Jewish-Greek academy of Christian teaching established at Alexandria and a study of contemporary Graeco-Roman culture.

A modern authority in exegesis confirms Massey's assertion that the Judaic-Greek-Christian corpus of religion was derived from ancient Egypt. In his *History of New Testament Times,* Robert H. Pfeiffer of the Harvard Divinity School states that as early as the third millenium in Egypt, wisdom was held to be the highest pursuit and *summum bonum* "through which man attains happiness and success." But after the Israelites had adopted this body of teachings, they tended more and more to regard their legacy from Mother Egypt as a product of their own genius and came finally to identify it with their own religious ethic, associating it with the law of Moses and the Pentateuch. After Baruch and Sirach, Pfeiffer says, no Jewish book of wisdom except Ecclesiastes "fails to regard the Law of Moses as Israel's wisdom and as the divine norm of human conduct." Commenting on the Testament of the Twelve Patriarchs, he says that its "noble moral teaching is in the best tradition of orthodox Judaism" and that it is abstracted from the letter of the scriptures "by the subtle allegorical and analogical interpretation of scribes and rabbis."[11]

The eminent modern expositor, Charles Guignebert of the Sorbonne, states frankly that the evangelists were not in the least concerned with the biography of Jesus; what they composed were manuals of spiritual edification and ritualistic indoctrination. His statement confirms the opinion of Alfred Loisy, whom we have previously cited. It is notable that one of the ancients, Polybius, who was a keen analyst of religious cultism, says that the miraculous prodigies woven into the story of the nativity of Jesus were added in order to produce a striking effect upon their hearers, and perhaps in the end they are more significant than the main incidents they ornament. Pfeiffer observes that the early Christian writers advisedly cast the esoteric teaching of the central figure of the scriptures within the framework of a historical series, *fictitious but plausible,* since the concrete is always more arresting and gripping than truth in the abstract. This scholar also says that the book of Tobit combines the strictest Jewish practices and tenets with Oriental folklore. He adduces a point that we commend to attention, namely, that the efforts often necessary to prove the historicity of what are really allegories can be even more fantastic and grotesque than those that are sometimes necessary to prove alleged history to be allegory. He states that Jerome was the first to discover the allegory in the book of Judith. It tells an interesting story "which uncritical readers might regard as history." In commenting on the story of Jesus and the Syro-Phoenician woman, Guignebert says, "it is probably only an allegory." He declares that the writers of the Gospels were interested not in recording history but only in proving a doctrinal system. And in order to interpret an allegory, he says, one must possess the proper keys; one must be "initiated." He quotes

St. Augustine as saying that while parables are accessible to all, they are understandable in truth to few. (For example, the statement that Daniel was cast into the den with seven lions and remained there six days is obviously allegorical.) In dealing with much apocryphal material, Pfeiffer believes that we may safely dismiss these tales as samples of popular Jewish fiction, of little literary and no religious significance. Numerous stories of similar character could be assembled to augment the thesis of biblical spiritual allegory.

Chapter Fifteen

FOUR EVANGELS

The special aims of this work pose the problem of evaluating more closely the Gospels of the New Testament in respect to the evidence they present on the question of the historicity of Jesus. The discussion thus far has stressed the thesis that the central character of the Gospels was a dramatic type-figure of the divine nature in the constitution of man. But from an objective point of view, the very existence of the Gospels, which contain so much that seems to pertain to the biography of a living person, must be accounted for. Likewise, it must be determined, if all this material is spiritual allegory, how the narrative came to take the form of a biography—a form that has led to its unquestioned acceptance as an historical narrative since at least the third century.

It seems obvious that the life story of Jesus was presented in this form by the authors of the scriptures in the firm belief that they were veridical history. The very word *gospel* has become associated with truth; we say, "It is the gospel truth." Yet, as the Gospels are unquestionably interlarded with material of undeniably poetic, legendary, prophetic, and allegorical nature, the investigation is confronted with the problem of how actual history, and biography of history's greatest personage, came to be written in a setting of traditional and nonhistorical elements. To put this in as graphic a form as possible, the problem is that of determining the literary motive that dictated the writing of the life, acts, and sayings of this Son of God in the form and setting of a corpus of legendary literature already extant in the stories of other gods and heroes antecedent to the time of Jesus. It must be explained how Jesus' biography came to be composed of the elements widely present in the structure of a universal archaic tradition. The question is, How did the life of one mortal come to be written as the life of a god?

Our inquiry now faces the problem of determining into which of three categories the Gospels, along with much of the Apocrypha and pseudepigrapha, fall: first (as we have averred), books of spiritual allegory; second, the biography of a historical man, Jesus, to which some of the traditional legends were affixed; third, an historical account faithful, in the main, to the facts. The first hypothesis has long been negated by religious orthodoxy, theology, and exegesis. The third has been as steadfastly upheld, but with fair concession to the allegorical element in the account. But on the whole, the second position—that the history of an actual Jesus was set in an environment of Old Testament "prophecy" and legendary embellishment—has been the one that permitted the ecclesiastical hegemony to hold its dominance over the religious world of the West.

It is contended here that the force of the massive evidence supporting the allegorical thesis warrants a judgment for that side. The unfailing synthesis, unity, and organic solidarity of this evidence, as said before, can only be seen through extensive study and reflection; it does not register immediately, or on first inspection.

There is another point that must be seriously taken into account. If the allegorical view gains ground and becomes more widely accepted than heretofore, will it be a serious threat to

Christianity itself? Should this trend be permitted to corrode the rock of historical fact on which the whole edifice of Christianity has been erected? There is little doubt that this fear will cause orthodoxy to defend its position and firmly reject the ever-accumulating new evidence. The danger in which orthodoxy stands can be illustrated by comparing the situation with that of the Old Testament. To take one example, it is now impossible to deny that the words *Red Sea* do not belong in the Bible, whether Hebrew or Christian. The Moffatt translation indeed renders the Hebrew words *Iam suph* as what they indeed mean: "Reed Sea," and not "Red Sea." The Red Sea, geographically and symbolically, has disappeared from the Bible; ergo, the Israelites fleeing Pharoah's wrath did not cross it, as indeed, no other document in existence ever said they did. If the Israelites did not cross this sea, what becomes of the story? It vanishes as history and can retain its significance only as allegory. With the whole of that central portion of the Exodus narrative disqualified as history, the rest is also fatally weakened *as history.*

But it should appear that, in proportion as this narrative loses its power as history, it gains meaning as allegory. The history could little profit mankind, for such prodigies of God's whimsicality have no relevance for ordinary men. But in the spiritual reference of that Crossing—that the soul of man can pass over the ocean of life safely with the aid of the divine power that never fails to guide us if we rely upon it—there is enlightenment, reassurance, and courage to face life's struggle.

Does the New Testament stand in similar jeopardy? Perhaps there is not in sight any one item that is as significant as is this Red Sea reference from the Old Testament. But there are hundreds of matters of greater or less consequence that have been brought to light, which do cast doubt upon the historicity of the New Testament. Many writers, including such well-known names as Warschauer, Guignebert, Schweitzer, Weiss, Bauer,

Van Paassen, and others, have shown the legendary character of incident after incident in the Gospels. For example, John's Gospel is the only one that relates the raising of Lazarus by Jesus. How could the three synoptists have omitted such an important event, if it actually occurred? Again, many scholars have questioned the incident wherein Jesus wrathfully drove the moneychangers from the outer precincts of the temple, where, as a matter of fact, they had a right to be, under the regulations governing the sale of doves for sacrifice. Such questionable occurrences abound in the narrative.

As things stand at present, the question of how much is history and how much allegory is beyond definite determination. The two elements are so interwoven as to be well-nigh inseparable. So remote is the period in time, so equivocal the material, that we may never be able to determine, once and for all, what in the Gospels is true history and what is spiritual truth simulating history. The reader who is well versed in allegorical literature obviously perceives much more of this element than the unlearned.

Yet even the scholar finds enough apparently well-grounded fact to withhold him from any categorical conclusion that the scriptures are solely allegory. He is driven to conclude that a modicum of actual history has been woven into the content of the great universal tradition. This is something that has rarely occurred before. Portions of the narrative read with such authenticity that it is difficult to believe they are not reports of actual happenings. It would be over-rash and foolish to think that all the history can be swept out with one gesture.

It is therefore pertinent to ask what motive dictated the writing of books in which allegory and history were so inextricably interwoven. A satisfactory answer can only be obtained through careful sifting of the evidence. Beside the few uncertain references to Jesus in the historical works of Josephus, Pliny, and Suetonius, it is contended that there is a considerable record of the life of Jesus in the Talmud, the Midrash, and other haggadic literature of the Jews, written during the two centuries after he lived. The mere fact that the man Yeshu (Jeshu, Jesus) does appear in these chronicles in itself supports the existence of the Gospel character. But when one reads *what* is said about him in this Jewish record, the impression grows that it is of little value as certification of the Gospel narrative. A rereading of this body of "evidence" in the Talmud, Midrash, and the Toldoth Yeshu, as rehearsed in Joseph Klausner's *Jesus of Nazareth,* confirms this statement. This learned Jewish exegete himself inclines to credit the scant references of the Jewish books to "Jeshu" as verifying the historical Jesus. But he quotes other scholars, notably Friedländer, who differ, and who disqualify it as history. It is worth recording Friedländer's remarks: "Every Talmudist worthy of the name knows that the few Talmudic passages which speak of Jesus are a late edition." He ends with the statement that "the Talmudic sources of the first century and the first quarter of the second afford not the slightest evidence of the existence of Jesus or Christianity."[1] Many scholars, however, disagree with this conclusion.

For the sake of its generally sobering effect, it may be worthwhile to present some of the material that has been claimed to refer to Jesus and therefore to constitute the ground in support of his existence in Judea in the first century AD. Instead of one figure clearly referred to as Jesus in the Talmudic literature, there are three or four names with which an effort has been made to identify him. Three of the most prominent are Jeshu ben Stada, Jeshu ben Perachia (Perachya), and Jehoshua ben Pandera, along with another probable one, Pappus ben Yehuda. These names appear in writings of the Tanaim and Amoraim, scholars and scribes of Jewish religious literature in the first and succeeding centuries of the Christian era. Their literary activities were concerned with the origin, interpretation, commentary, and elucidation of the Torah, the Talmud, the Mishna, and Halakhic and

Midrashic formulations of the books of the scriptures and the Law. This body of literature is ponderous, and Jewish rabbis have spent their lives studying it.

The figure with whom Jesus has been chiefly identified is Jehoshua ben Pandera. In brief, he was a Jew who went to Egypt, became proficient in the magical arts of the Egyptians, returned to Judea, went about healing many people, and incurred the hostility of the Sanhedrim. He was stoned to death at Lud (or Lod), and his body was "hanged on a tree."

Klausner reviews this body of literature in his *Jesus of Nazareth*, his treatment being doubtless as authoritative as that of any other writer. He asks how the Tanaim could assert that "Jesus" was crucified in Lod if he had been crucified in Jerusalem. (The eighth verse of the eleventh chapter of Revelation says that "our Lord was crucified" in a city "spiritually called Sodom and Egypt.") So Jesus could not have been ben Stada, whom Klausner calls the "Egyptian pretender to Christhood," and who, he says, was a madman and a "beguiler" and "led the people to the wilderness." (The latter apparently was one of the many such "pretenders" who continually appeared, gathered a knot of credulous followers, and were summarily executed by the authorities as dangerous political agitators.) Klausner disqualifies the statements that seek to identify ben Stada with ben Pandera. He comments on the unreliability of the Amoraim as witnesses to the identity of ben Stada with Jesus, describing the ways in which they confuse Pappus ben Yehuda with the father of Jesus, and Miriam (Mary), the mother of Jesus, with M'gadd'la N'shaya (the women's hairdresser). He even makes the name *Stada* a pseudonym of *Miriam*. He gives *Stada* as derived from *S'tath'da*, meaning "she went astray," that is, proved faithless to her husband.[2]

However, the mystery deepens when we find that the Jewish scribes also confused this ben Stada with both Jesus and ben Pandera. A couple who are mentioned as Pappus ben Yehuda and his wife, Miriam M'gadd'la N'shaya, were confused with Joseph, the father, and Miriam, the mother, of Jesus. (And the connection of this Miriam's name with Mary Magdalene is not to be overlooked.) But, avers Klausner, neither this Pappus nor Miriam M'gadd'la has any connection with Jesus. And only the Amoraim made this connection between ben Stada and Jesus.[3]

As to ben Perachia, the references are so vague as to be, according to Klausner, not worth discussing. Some allusions, however, seem to imply that Jesus was a disciple of this ben Perachia, who was a contemporary of Shimeon ben Shetah and King Jannaeus, who reigned in Judea from 103 to 76 BC. This slight testimony has been made the basis of a claim taken up by some Theosophists, Rosicrucians, and others that the Gospel Jesus lived from 100 to 115 years before our first century. A very sound treatment of this theory is found in the study by G. R. S. Mead entitled, *Did Jesus Live 100 Years B.C.?*[4] However, in the opinion of Klausner, the evangelists in the Gospels confused this ben Perachia with one of the "false prophets" who caused a disturbance and was put to death at the time of Pontius Pilate. He affirms that this whole hypothesis is based solely on a single Talmudic passage of doubtful authenticity.[5]

If there were the slightest basis of reliability in this portion of the Talmudic material, the shifting of the date of Jesus' life to about 115 BC would at one stroke render obsolete virtually every "Life of Christ" written since the early centuries. It would sever any connection of the Jesus figure with Herod, whose dates are a matter of clear record, as well as with Pontius Pilate, St. Paul, and the entire setting of the Gospels. Yet Mead's analysis reveals considerable plausibility for the theory.

There is another passage in a Baraita (section of the Talmud) that Klausner holds to be of greater value. It runs as follows:

On the eve of Passover they hanged Yeshu [of Nazareth] and the herald went before him for forty days, saying "[Yeshu of Nazareth] is going forth to be stoned in that he hath practiced sorcery and beguiled and led astray Israel. Let anyone knowing aught in his defence come and plead for him." But they found naught in his defence and hanged him on the eve of Passover.[6]

Following this Baraita comes a significant comment of the Amora 'Ulla:

'Ulla said: "And do you suppose that for [Yeshu of Nazareth] there was any right of appeal? He was a beguiler, and the Merciful One hath said: Thou shalt not spare, neither shalt thou conceal him." It was otherwise with Yeshu, for he was near to the civil authorities.[7]

The Jewish scholar throws no light upon the inclusion of the name *Yeshu* in brackets. Much—indeed everything—could hang upon the origin of the name as here inserted and the legitimacy of the insertion. It could have been a bit of Christian tampering with texts of which there was admittedly much. Purely as the result of some scribe's whim or notion, we may be asked to take for the history of Jesus a story that had not the remotest connection with the Gospel Jesus. At the very least, the insertion is suspect, for this 'Ulla was a disciple of R. Yochanan and lived in Palestine at the end of the *third* century. The scholar, Friedländer, who places Jesus at 115 BC, evidently on the ben Perachya reference, thinks all these items in the Talmud are forgeries interpolated later.

Klausner further declares that the statement about the herald going before the condemned Jesus shows an "obvious tendency" which makes its historicity difficult to accept. A second Baraita gives Jesus few disciples, by name Mattai, Nagai, Netser, Buni, and Todah. This difference in names and numbers of disciples would seem to preclude all possibility of identifying this "Jesus" with the Gospel figure. Similar difficulties dog the whole inquiry.

Material related to the other figure, Yehoshua ben Pandera, seems of somewhat more credibility in its connection with the Jesus of the Gospels. It can be introduced by quoting a notation by Origen, greatest of the Christian theologians of the third and early fourth centuries. In his book, *Contra Celsum* (Against Celsus), he mentions a story Celsus said he had heard, to the effect that Miriam was divorced from her husband, a carpenter by trade, after it had been proved that she was an adulteress. Discarded by her husband and wandering about, she bore her son in secret, the father being a certain soldier Pantheras. To refute this tale, Origen himself says that James, the father of Jesus' father, Joseph, was called by the name of "Panther," apparently meaning to explain in this way why Jesus, son of Joseph, was called ben Pandera, or "ben Pantere" by the Jews, after the name of his grandfather.

Klausner speculates on this version of Jewish tradition along these lines: This part of the story of Jesus' ancestry may have resulted from the popular corruption of a deeper element of the Messianic allegorism; it is impossible for us to assume that there really was a Roman soldier by the name of Pandera, or Pantheras, who became the father of Jesus, since this entire canard of Jesus' birth had come from popular perversion of the legendary conviction of the Christians, from the time of St. Paul, that Jesus was born without a natural father. Klausner holds that we must seek elsewhere for the source of this name, Panthera, and he quickly finds a hint in a suggestion picked up from two scholars, Nietsch and Beck, to the effect that *Pantheras* is a corruption, exactly such as the common people were likely to make, of the Greek word for the "Virgin," *Parthenos* (*Parthena* feminized). The Jews constantly heard the Christians call Jesus "Son of the Virgin." If there was in Jewish social life of the time half as much propensity as there is in our day to catch at every opening for a clever and insidious remark, it is not at all unlikely that someone could have seen a chance for irreligious mockery of the much-disliked Christians, and made the leap from the sacred *Parthena* to the ribald *Panthera*. Klausner's solution of this conundrum, therefore, is by no means an unreasonable assumption.

There was, however, another story that Jesus was the son of Miriam and a Greek sailor, who bore the name ben Pandera, his father, Cleopas, having picked up the nickname of "Panther." Yehoshua ben Pandera means "Jesus, son of the Panther."[8] In certain of the mythologies, the *Christos* principle, being evolved out of man's animal nature, was called the lion's whelp, son of the wolf, saved and suckled by a wolf or lynx or other animal; in Egypt he was in one aspect Anup, symbolized as the dog, wolf, or jackal. Thus there is a plausible source of the story of the Christ's descent from an animal. Through popular debasement, this allegory could have tempted anyone inimical to the Christian movement to modify Jesus, son of the Virgin, to Jehoshua, son of the Panther, by the mere shifting of a letter. Pandera is not a Jewish name, and as a pure caricature it was assigned to a Roman soldier.

Klausner also cites a pointed similarity between the legendary flight of Jesus with his parents to Egypt from a cruel king, Herod, and the escape of this Yeshu with his master to Egypt because of a cruel king, Jannaeus. Another striking similarity is established between the two Jesus figures in that both were accused and condemned on the same charge, practicing sorcery, beguiling and leading Israel astray.

But what appears to be the portion of Jewish literature that comes closest to being a shadow of the Gospel construction is found in the document entitled *Tol'doth Yeshu*, or the "Generations of Yeshu." It will tend to clarify this discussion if the actual substance of the document is before us. Klausner's version is as follows:

A certain Yochanan, who was learned in the Law and who feared God, of the House of David (according to some versions it is Pappus ben Yahudah, following the *Talmud*), espoused to himself in Bethlehem, Miriam, the daughter of his widowed neighbor, a respectable and humble virgin. But Miriam attracted a handsome villain named Joseph Pandera (or Ben Pandera) who betrayed her at the close of a certain Sabbath. Miriam supposed that it was her espoused, Yochanan, and, submitting only against her will, marvelled at the act of her pious betrothed; and when he himself came, she mentioned her astonishment. He suspected Pandera and told his suspicions to Rabban Shimeon ben Shetah. When Miriam was with child and Yochanan knew that it was not by him, but that he could not prove who was the guilty party, he fled to Babylon. Miriam brought forth her son and called him Yehoshua after the name of her mother's brother, and his name was corrupted to Yeshu. The child learnt much Torah from an able teacher and distinguished scholar, but he proved "an impudent child" and on one occasion he passed in front of the Sages with uncovered head (and according to another version delivered an offensive exposition about Moses and Jethro), whereupon the Sages said that he was a bastard and a "son of uncleanness." Miriam confessed to this and Shimeon ben Shetah recalled what his disciple Yochanan had told him.

Yeshu then fled to Jerusalem and in the temple learnt the "Ineffable Name." In order that the brazen dogs who stood by the gate of the place of sacrifice and barked at all who learned the Name, and so made them forget the Name [this resembles the legend of the lions of Solomon's throne told in the "Second Targum"]—in order that they should not make him forget the Name, Yeshu wrote it on a piece of leather and sewed it in the flesh of his thigh. He gathered around him in Bethlehem a group of young Jews and proclaimed himself the Messiah and Son of God; and as a retort to those who rejected his claim he said that "they sought their own greatness and were minded to rule in Israel"; while to confirm his claims he healed a lame man and a leper by the power of the "Ineffable Name." He was brought before Queen Helena, the ruler of Israel, and she found him guilty of acts of sorcery and beguilement.

But Yeshu restored a dead man to life and the queen in her alarm began to believe on him. He went next to Upper Galilee where he continued his miracles and drew many people after him. The Sages of Israel then saw it was essential that one of their number, Yehuda Iskarioto, (some versions give R. Yehuda the Pious), should learn the "Ineffable Name" just as Yeshu did, and so rival him in signs and wonders. Yehuda and Yeshu came before the queen. Yeshu flew in the air, but Yehuda flew higher and defiled him so that he fell to earth. The queen condemned Yeshu to death and delivered him up to the Sages of Israel. They took him to Tiberias and imprisoned him there. But he had instilled into his disciples the belief that whatever happened to him had been prepared for the Messiah, the Son of God, from the day of Creation and that the Prophets had prophecied it all. So the disciples of Yeshu fought against the Sages of Israel, rescued Yeshu and fled with him to Antioch.

From Antioch Yeshu went to Egypt to fetch spells [as is recorded in the Talmud of Ben Stada], but Yehuda

(Iskarioto the "Pious") had mingled among his disciples and robbed him in the meantime of the "Name." Yeshu then went a second time to Jerusalem to learn the "Name." Yehuda reported this intended visit to the Sages of Israel in Jerusalem, and told them that when Yeshu should come to the Temple he, Yehuda, would bow before him and thus the Sages of Israel would be able to distinguish between Yeshu and his disciples, for he and his disciples all dressed in garments "of one color" (or, according to another version, because all his disciples had sworn never to say to him "This is he.")

And so it came to pass that the Sages of Israel recognized him and arrested him. They took and hanged him on the eve of Passover (as recorded in several of the Talmudic versions) on a cabbage stem—for no other tree would bear him, because Yeshu during his lifetime had adjured all trees by the "Ineffable Name" not to receive his body when he was hanged; but he failed so to adjure the cabbage stem, since this does not count as a tree. The body was taken down while it was yet the even of the Sabbath (in order not to violate the prohibition: "His body shall not remain there for the night") and at once buried. But Yehuda the gardener removed the body from the tomb and cast it into a water-channel in the garden, and let the water flow over it as usual.

When the disciples came and did not find the body in the tomb they announced to the queen that Yeshu had been restored to life. The queen believed this and was minded to put to death the Sages of Israel for having laid their hands on the Lord's Anointed. All the Jews mourned and wept and fasted because of this dire decree, until at last R. Tanchum (who lived four hundred years after Jesus!) found the corpse in Yehuda's garden by the help of the Holy Spirit. The Sages of Israel removed it, tied it to the tail of a horse and brought it before the queen in order that she might see how she had been deceived.

We are next told how the disciples of Yeshu fled and mingled among the nations. Among these disciples were twelve apostles who sorely distressed the Jews. One of the Sages of Israel, Shimeon Kepha (*Petros,* Peter, "rock" in Greek, of which the Aramaic equivalent is *Kepha*), thereupon undertook to separate the disciples of Yeshu from the Jews and give them religious laws of their own, so that they might no longer affect the Jews. After he had acted in such a way as to feign belief in Yeshu he went and lived by himself in a tower built in his honor [a reference to the Church of St. Peter in Rome] where he composed hymns and psalms full of devotion and piety which he sent to all scattered communities of Israel, by whom they are sung in the Synagogues to this day.[9]

There is ample justification for the republication of this bizarre document. The reader will doubtless have registered his own reflections in a wide variety of reactions. He will have been struck by the undeniable similarity with much in Gospel "history," and at the same time with the glaring differences. He will have been shocked at the scurrility that turned the virgin birth into a social scandal, and he must have realized how easy this conversion must have been to crude yokels and "rough fellows." If he chanced to be a student in this field, he would have recognized at once the purely allegorical nature of eight or ten items, while being willing to accredit about as many to possible history. On the side of allegory he would place certainly such items as the barking of the brazen dogs, the sewing of the Name in the thigh, the restoration of a dead man to life, the personal air flights, the cabbage stem. As possible history, but more likely allegory, he might list the caricature of the virgin birth, the self-proclamation of Messiahship, the miracles of healing by the "Ineffable Name," the predestined events of Yeshu's career, the dispersion among the nations, Peter's treachery, the empty tomb, and the opposition and betrayal by "Iskarioto"; and he would see Yeshu's "impudence" and flouting of the Sages as matching Jesus' defiance of the Sanhedrin.

It is obvious that the whole passage is a weird admixture of allegorical elements with a modicum of history, focused upon the life of one of the numerous hallucinated, or sincerely self-deceived, claimants to Messiahship, who appeared in numbers around that period. Klausner's comment that the account is a melange of bits of the universal legend of the Messianic tradition, inspired by Jewish desire to caricature the Christian pretensions as to the virgin birth, may well be the case.

A further observation is that the shrewd policy of Christian zealots has dictated a program of concealment of all such material and suppression of all that immense body of religious literature subsumed under the two terms, *apocrypha* and *pseudepigrapha*. The first term suggests "hidden from," and the second, "falsely written." Had the Gospels all along been studied in a wider context that included these two elements of religious writing, the consequences would have been a saner and more balanced interpretation of the scriptures.

One other fragment of apocryphal material may be referred to here, because it shows the obvious allegorical character of the ancient scripture. This is an entire chapter from the Protevangelium, or so-called Gospel of James. It dramatizes the winter solstice as the stasis in evolution when ascending organic development from the physical world below meets the descending spirituality from above. The relation is so analogous to the stasis of light and darkness at the solstice that it had to be kept out of the scriptural canon. The passage poetically express-es the cessation of movement in either direction when the two forces in man's nature, the human and the divine, are locked in polar equilibrium. Scripture was the loser by the exclusion of this fragment from the Bible. Here it is:

1. And leaving her [Mary] and his son in the cave, Joseph went forth to seek a Hebrew midwife in the village.

2. But as I was going [said Joseph] I looked up into the air and I saw clouds astonished, and the fowls of the air stopping in the midst of their flight.

3. And I looked down toward the earth and I saw a table spread, and working people sitting around it, but their hands were upon the table and they did not move to eat.

4. They that had meat in their mouths did not eat.

5. They who had lifted their hands up to their heads did not draw them back.

6. And they who lifted them up to their mouths did not put anything in.

7. But all their faces were fixed upwards.

8. And I beheld the sheep dispersed, and yet the sheep stood still.

9. And the shepherd lifted up his hand to smite them, and his hand continued up.

10. And I looked into a river and saw the kids with their mouths close to the water and touching it, but they did not drink.

This passage forcibly reminds us that if there be historical factuality at the basis of scripture, it has been presented in the guise of beautiful allegory.

In the Yeshu story, we have the contribution of Jewish testimony to the existence and career of Jesus. It is striking and challenging in a number of particulars. It carries the impression that it may have been some scribe's attempt to write down from memory, or from popular oral tradition, a summary or epitome of the Gospel narrative. The evidences of history in it are scant and precarious, yet they are there. It comes down again to the question of where allegory ends and history begins. Upon careful examination, every item in the story can be made intelligible as allegory, whereas as history much becomes improbable, strained, and unnatural. Klausner's final judgment on the Yeshu story is that it contains no history worthy of the name. The book reflects the folklore spirit and was evidently a sort of parody of the Gospel narrative, traduced to appear as a mixture of shameful human weakness and miracle. In sharp contrast to the Gospels that recount Jesus' birth as heralded and glorified by celestial fanfare, the Tol'doth Yeshu degrades the recital to a low level. It clearly expresses the attitude of disdain that Judaism held toward Christianity in the early period. Klausner explains that as the primitive Christian religious teaching was entirely oral, the first written accounts aimed merely to preserve from possible loss the language of the secret instruction and exposition; they had a theological, not an historical aim. We should therefore not expect from them any strict factuality. Their one discernible purpose seems to have been to portray the life of Jesus as the fulfillment of the age-old Messianic tradition.

This last statement expresses the dominant motive of Gospel writing. Book after book written on these documents and about Jesus' life expound the theses on which the Christian faith rests. The Gospel narrative reflects an objective predetermined by the narrators to reinforce the tradition inherited from antecedent religious lore. The editors merely picked up a body of traditional teaching with its interior significance already stamped upon it and redeployed it in the presentation. The

Gospels were such rescripts of old inheritances. In fact, the career of the Messiah was predestined to conform to a pattern already outlined in sacred texts and Old Testament prophecy. In Procrustean fashion, his acts and sayings had to be expressed under the limitations of the standard by which it was to be rendered significant. Jesus had, in fact, to walk down the *via dolorosa* that ancient scripts had marked out as the road to glory. His life expressed no free agency, but simply carried out God's plan of human salvation. He had to die in Jerusalem, not because the Jews hounded him to his fate, but because that was the condition for the fulfillment of Messianic prophecy. The evangelists Matthew, Mark, and Luke simply impose a Christological systematism upon the personality of the figure standing in the role of the Messiah. Many writers have stated that Mark first presented the crude outlines of the tradition and that Matthew and Luke added embellishment and detail for the sake of a more poetic statement. The form so developed came to be the foundation of Christianity.

This exegesis of New Testament documents as fulfillment of Old Testament prophecy has been accentuated in thousands of books. Few have discerned the implication for Christianity itself, an implication that Loisy expresses in this reference to the Gospels:

> From the very beginning it was a tradition of faith. In all strictness the Gospels are not historical documents. They are catechisms for use in common worship . . . that and no other is the content they announce; that and no other is the quality they claim.[10]

This being the case, the only defense of the historicity of the Jesus life in the Gospels is that in actual truth the life of this human Son of God did marvelously run in the very pattern prescribed for it in archaic writings, a life unique, of a kind never experienced before by any son of man. Yet scholarship now discerns this same life story had been in essence lived before by a score of personages whose only claim to historicity is founded on their appearance in allegorical tradition. Christianity rests, not upon the miracles allegedly performed by Jesus, but upon the greater miracle that his life recapitulated the traditional events in the lives of many gods who were also born on December 25, died, and rose again for the salvation of mankind. The only possible defense of this thesis would be positive evidence that Jesus did live the life set forth in the Gospels. As we have said, of such presumed evidence there is little, and that little is extremely precarious.

Most of what has been taken for authentic evidence can be proved to have been extant before the time of Jesus' period. In fact, the truth is that the world would have been in possession of the entire body of literature that posits the existence of Jesus, including the text of his discourses, even if he had never lived at all.

Some time ago, the *New York Times* carried an article announcing the discovery of a letter, found two years before, in a monastery of Mar Saba, twelve miles southeast of Jerusalem, by a Columbia University professor, Dr. Morton Smith.[11] This letter, which was addressed to an unknown "Theodore," was attributed to the great church father Clement of Alexandria, since it definitely appears to be in his well-known style. It seems to be a reply to a letter addressed to Clement by this "Theodore," who had written of the sect of Carpocratians and set forth his opposition to them, in respect to their knowledge of a "secret Gospel." Clement admonished Theodore on the necessity of keeping secret the knowledge of the Gospel, which included the story of the raising of Lazarus from the dead by Jesus, which evidently Clement had found in a second Gospel attributed to Mark. The Alexandrian father, speaking of this new document that he thinks is of Mark's authorship, says that Mark brought to Alexandria from Rome the notes of Peter, and from them incorporated in his first Gospel what he thought essential for progress toward knowledge. But Mark, he writes, did *not* include "the things which are not to be uttered," that is, "the hierophantic teaching of the Lord," but added to his Gospel other stories and sayings that, when interpreted, would "lead the hearers into the innermost sanctuary of that truth which is hidden behind seven veils." This composition was left by Mark with the Church of Alexandria and kept carefully guarded, "being read only to those who are being initiated into the great mysteries." The document adds a new witness, Salome, to the raising of Lazarus. Clement further states that Mark, while in Rome with Peter, had written "an account of the Lord's doings," but had not narrated all of them, nor "had he even hinted at the ones pertaining to the mysteries."

It has seemed desirable to cite this newspaper account, because it corroborates in a general way the position taken in this work. We have asserted that Christianity had at the start, and for two centuries more or less thereafter, an intimate relation to the pagan Mysteries, which it soon repudiated, and has denied ever since. But here is Clement's direct confirmation of the connection, and in addition, the great church father's reverent evaluation of them. The *Times* article also contributes the statement that Clement's writings once included "works that were considered scandalous" and that these have disappeared. From what one learns of Clement's Christian theology, it would not be rash to say that these "scandalous" writings of the head of the great Christian seminary at Alexandria, who is, with Augustine, the founder of Christian theology, were dissertations interpreting the Gospels allegorically and defining the *Christos* as the divine principle in man. For his work, and that of his great pupil, Origen, were in the main elaborate and ingenious interpretations of the scriptures as divine allegory, not as history. The article includes a prediction made by the discoverer of the letter, Morton Smith, that if the document is accredited as genuinely a writing of Clement, "opinions about the teachings of Jesus, the origin and character of the Gospels and the character and early history of the Christian Church would have to be reconsidered." It is our firm conviction that the direction in which such reconsideration will lead us is back to the Mystery tradition of the Ancients. From that source Christianity emerged, and back to that source it must inevitably return.

ARE THE
GOSPELS FICTITIOUS?

We have tried to show that Christian doctrine, having in the early centuries taken a misdirection, was pushed farther and farther from the truth by the force of its own momentum. Ceasing to rely upon cosmic law as a prime determinant of man's evolution, it substituted a special scheme of salvation, dependent upon Jesus' atonement for the sins of mankind.

All the great ancient religious systems posit a point in the normal evolution of man when the process of individuation would require the natural or instinctual propensities to be curbed, and, in the end, give way before more spiritualizing energies. Understood properly, this result might be considered as the end of one evolutionary cycle and the beginning of a new one—a transcendence, as it were, that yet occurs within the framework of natural order and in full harmony therewith. Through the operation of the law of polarity between the positive spiritual principle and the negative physical forces in the economy of man's nature, there was to come a time of crisis in evolution at which the further progress of the soul would be facilitated by the resolution of the tension between the two.

Out of the *agon,* the struggle of which St. Paul speaks so eloquently, was to be born a new and higher order of conscious being for the soul. But Christian theologians mistook the *beneficence* of the polar opposition between the natural and the spiritual law for the *evil* of nature's battle of the flesh with the spirit. This confusion impaled Christianity on a false concept of the true significance of human life on earth. As a result, Christians were persuaded into an attitude of hostility to the world, which was regarded as inherently sinful. They were at enmity with their environment, when that relationship should have been wholesome, delightful, and natural, as it was with the Greeks. Psychologically, a posture of distaste and rejection of the world can blight nature's power to sustain, nourish, and heal the soul. Christianity failed to grasp the beneficent role of *physis*—"nature"—in life's polarity. And, as John Dewey perceived, the false view split the soul of man and produced the tragic hostility of the spirit to the world, which has so great a need of that spiritual flowering.

The seventh chapter of St. Paul's Epistle to the Romans has disturbed and baffled theologians to this day because it lauds the law of the flesh that brings the soul into polar relation to physis, entailing for it the battle against "sin" and "death" and explaining that man could not know spiritual glory if his soul had not had to wrestle with and know the nature of "sin." This makes St. Paul's discourse a tribute to "sin." Yet this chapter, which reveals the salutary nature and office of the negative pole in the duality of life, is one of the most luminous expositions in all the scriptures. The polar tension in the heart of man can be fierce and take tragic forms, and the soul's battle in this arena can have its grim moments. The struggle is only complicated and, indeed, debased by the persuasion that the battle itself is a miscarriage of divine intent.

It has been a failure of Christian insight not to realize that all the potential needed for the implementation of man's self-evolution is there, within the arsenal of his own constitution. He has all the militant power of God that he can possibly appropriate and utilize within his own organism, available to him at every moment. God could do no more than plant the seed of his own nature in the tiny garden of man's physical life and let man have the thrilling adventure of nourishing it to growth and glory. As many a Christian thinker has said, "God could do nothing for man without man's own effort." The *Zohar* again and again declared that the "above" could or would not bestir itself on behalf of the "below" until it was awakened by the effort of the latter. Modern philosophers like Buber are saying that God needs man as much as man needs God. The natural extension of this view is the recognition that the Messiah God, the Christ Savior, comes to mankind, not as a gift from a benevolent Father in heaven, but in inevitable response to the compelling call from within the depths of man's own being. In that moment when the spiritual fire enters man's earthly tenement, the Christ child is born within his heart, progeny of the union of the two polar energies.

The spiritual evolution of man is grounded in this wedding of polar forces; *both* energies are required. The cross of matter alone can set the spirit free. How foolish, then, are those ascetics who try to force the issue by mortification of the body! The ancients were not merely ribald in their acknowledgment of the great god, Pan. With his goat horns, tail, and cleft feet, Pan has been identified with the devil; but there is no great world religion that has not represented polar forces such as Christ and Satan, or Horus and Sut, as twins—like Jacob and Esau. The ancient art of astrology pictured them in the sky as Castor and Pollux in the house of Gemini, the Twins. The error of Christianity was that it sundered this cosmic twinship, under the mistaken assumption that spirit could redeem man only by tearing itself away from its union with matter, when in truth, spirit can manifest on earth, materialize, only by marrying its powers of consciousness and creativeness with the energies within the heart of the atom of matter. (Indeed, we know from science that this heart is pure energy.) Ancient knowledge taught that if one of the twins is, or could be, dissociated from its brother, both would disappear; for they exist only by virtue of their mutual pull and tension.

The canons of the Christian faith, which held within them every truth important to man, ended by grievously misleading mankind when they transferred their frame of reference from the realm of man's spiritual consciousness to purported history. Everything that becomes false when misconstrued as our relation to an external deity, mediated through one human embodiment, is restored to its full truth, majesty, and saving power when its relation to the divinity that God has made innate in us is restored.

We have asserted that the Gospel writers possessed as basic material the substance of antecedent Messianic prophecy, but they had little authentic record of the actual life of Jesus. It now seems necessary and only fair to say clearly that there could have been a personage whose character, life, and piety did furnish to a group plausible ground for a reconstruction of the Messiah literature that incorporated him as the cardinal image of the Son of God. Such an admission, however, immediately injects into the exegetical problem scores of historical and dialectical dilemmas, impasses, contradictions, and situations virtually impossible to solve.

For example, if this Yehoshua-Yeshu lived at the time of King Jannaeus more than a century BC, scholarship is at once confronted with the task of picking up the whole body of expository theses that have been fitted into the time of Herod and readjusting it to the historical realities of the earlier period. As the wicked king dragon or serpent threatening the life of the infant god, Jannaeus must be substituted for Herod—and who is to substitute for Pilate? The problems would be similar to those confronting modern scholars in their task of finding veridical historical persons with whom to identify the central figures of the Dead Sea Scrolls—the Teacher of Righteousness and the Wicked Priest, the "man of truth" and the "man of the lie." But here, too, it seems self-evident that these two characters simply typify the divine and the elemental aspects of human nature. They are the Christos and his opposite twin, Satan.

Putting the date of Jesus' life story back a century would negate Paul's relations with the Roman officials Festus and Felix, who were officials in Judea-Syria fairly late in the first century AD. The shift of dates would even tear asunder by some hundred and fifty years the contemporaneity of Jesus and Paul. If Herod had John the Baptist in prison in the Machaeris fortress about the year 6-4 BC (Herod died in 4 BC), then to put Yeshu back one hundred years ahead of Herod's time would eliminate John's role of herald and baptizer of Jesus. How could John have baptized Jesus if Jesus (Yeshu) lived in 115 BC and John lived about 33 AD? To accredit the stories of Yeshu, either as Ben Stada, Ben Perachia, or Ben Pandera, as actual history, and base on them the acceptance of the historicity of Jesus of the Gospels, is to admit several major and a hundred lesser anachronisms. The difficulties, indeed, seem to rule out the earlier date.

Even as it stands, there still exist a number of unrecognized or unmentioned difficulties in fitting the history into the period of 1 to 33 AD. Here again we reiterate that these and other complications would fall away if the allegorical interpretation were adopted.

Yet, we are still faced with the question of how it is that the Hebrew Talmud and Midrash speak, though vaguely and inscrutably, of this Yeshu, or Jehoshua, or Ben This or Ben That. The evidence is substantial enough to induce a Jewish scholar like Joseph Klausner to credit the historical existence of the Gospel Jesus. Other noted scholars, however, do not regard the Talmudic evidence as sufficient ground for predicating the existence of Jesus. And, strangely enough, one finds a peculiar phenomenon in the attitude of Jewish scholars—indeed, of Jews generally—namely, a settled disposition to affirm Jesus' existence, despite the fact that proof of his nonhistoricity would automatically exculpate the Jews from the centuries-old onus of having slain the Christ. This universal Jewish attitude perhaps influenced Klausner, for in some passages he hints that the Talmud's evidence is not very strong.

But how did the Yeshu stories get into the Talmud? What is the origin of the book Tol'doth Yeshu? Here there is no ground for anything more solid than speculation: to wit, that the scriptures are beyond doubt allegorical, but center around a nucleus of historical fact. Yet this does not rule out the conjecture that the whole thing may be a great traditional body of allegory that has been so reworked as to appear to be actual history. The reworking of the documents of scripture is indeed a recorded fact of history, and it was done with the intent of obliterating the evidence for allegory, and strengthening the evidence for history. We again refer the reader to Gerald Massey.

To reiterate an important point, there could and may have been a man named Jehoshua, Yeshu, or Jesus, one of the many who came forward to voice his inner conviction that he was the Messiah. He may have advanced his cause by preaching in the region of Galilee and thereby gathered, as others did, an earnest and numerous following. Some or many of the political zealots of the time may have accepted him as a possible leader of revolt against Rome; and he may have ventured to seek popular endorsement at the Jerusalem Passover of a given year, only to be seized and executed by the Roman power at the instigation of the jealous Sanhedrin. This is roughly an outline of the most probable historical events underlying the biblical narrative of Jesus' final week, as drawn by many modern exegetes, such as Van Paassen in his *Why Jesus Died*. Van Paassen thinks that the "triumphal entry" into Jerusalem was the planned demonstration of a party of Zealots, designed to arouse popular support for a general revolt, or at least to test the feeling of the people for such a move. Its failure to produce a strong response is an understandable reason why the mob that cried "Hosanna" one day was howling for the death of Jesus the next.[1] It should be mentioned here that Van Paassen's thesis agrees in many respects with the position taken by Klausner and others. With any number of possible variations, something of this sort must have happened if, indeed, the scriptures are founded on actual history.

It is certain, also, that Jesus was indeed a man of extraordinary intelligence and piety, a person of the loftiest spiritual aspiration, who had made a profound study of esoteric religious literature. No doubt he believed he had a truth to give and a significant mission to fulfill, and he manifested such intense consecration to his task that he became conspicuous in the countryside—for some as an eccentric, for others as a truly sanctified and holy man. Since the untutored *am ha'arets* of the rural districts were in fact looking for the coming of the Messiah in human form, a certain number of pious folk would have taken him seriously. He would have appeared so different from the ordinary man he would have come to be marked as one possessed either of a *daemon,* in the Socratic sense, or of a demon in the churchly sense. This is the very impression of him that is recorded in the Gospels. Even his mother and members of his family thought that he was mad; the scribes and Pharisees likewise put to him the nature of his obsession. One can all too easily picture a group of scoffers rallying about his great mission, jibing at him with questions as to which of the old prophets he thought he was, and generally making mockery of his seriousness. It is likely that he did speak with an eloquence that would impress as "one having authority, and not as the scribes and Pharisees."

We are free to suppose that he was a truly great soul, innately gifted with spiritual genius and holiness, such a man as the

Hindu scriptures describe as an avatar or divine embodiment—one of the great ones who come to earth periodically to teach men spiritual truth. Gautama Buddha, Sri Krishna—all these are regarded as such avatars. If Jesus was in actuality a man of such extraordinary character, we have in this fact an answer to the question of why, out of the numerous company of aspirants to the Messianic mantle, this one alone succeeded in founding one of the world's great faiths, while the pretensions of all the others ended with their deaths. If Jesus was in truth a man thus divinely overshadowed, it is no more difficult to understand how he came to establish a great religion than it is in the case of Confucius, Gautama Buddha, or Mohammed.

It is, however, astonishing that the whole Christian world has, for centuries, been oblivious of the existence, career, and significance of another figure born in the year 1 (or 2) AD, who also lived a life of extraordinary saintliness. This man, Apollonius of Tyana, preached, taught, and worked wonders bordering on the miraculous; he traveled over the greater part of the known world and left a name of such universal repute as a master of divine wisdom that the emperor Severus placed his statue in his palace next to that of Jesus. *The Life of Apollonius of Tyana,* written by Philostratus at the urgent behest of the empress Julia Donna, wife of Severus, is the biography of this great figure; it reveals in its teachings, theurgic power, and saintliness so many close parallels to that of the Gospel Jesus that the Christian hierarchy has been inclined to keep it in as much obscurity as possible. There would seem to be far more solid ground for thinking that a great religion could have sprung from foundations laid by Apollonius than by Jesus, for Apollonius was a renowned and venerated figure, his works were as marvelous as those reported of Jesus, and he was exactly contemporaneous with him. It is very unlikely that Jesus could have been Apollonius, yet it is possible that some of the latter's following, among them the empress Julia Donna, considered him the true Messiah.

Oddly enough, there is even more reason to identify the other great personage who rates with Jesus as the cofounder of Christianity—St. Paul—with Apollonius. The names of both are derived from Apollo; both were educated at about the same time in the same center of Hellenic culture, Tarsus; both had a secretary and travel companion named Demas (Damis); both traveled widely and founded esoteric societies in much the same cities and at about the same time; and both preached much the same gospel. It seems improbable that two such men should have founded groups and taught the same spiritual philosophy at the same time in the same cities; yet that is what the record seems to say.

There is, however, historical testimony that these two "Pauls" did, in fact, know each other and work together in the same evangelical cause. Acts 18: 24-26 states that "a certain Jew named Apollos, born at Alexandria, an eloquent man and mighty in the scriptures, came to Ephesus. This man was instructed in the way of the Lord; and being fervent in the spirit, he spake and taught diligently." This characterization of an evangelist of high rank and great ability for spiritual crusading could be a description of Apollonius. The surprising similarity of names inclines one to ask if this Apollos might not have been Apollonius. Paul calls him in one place (I Cor. 16:12) "our brother Apollos" and commends him to the brethren. Then there is Paul's mysterious reference, where he says, "I have planted, Apollos watered; but God gave the increase" (I Cor. 3:6). This would indicate that Apollos was commissioned to follow Paul's pioneering with more durable, stabilizing work. The whole matter opens up a wide and intriguing range of speculation.

Yet what a mystery faces us when we ask why, if this Apollos's work was so highly regarded among Christians as to be linked with Paul's mission, there was not much more to be said about him. Did their paths cross only at a few points? The church hierarchy early reacted quite negatively toward the historical Apollonius, and it could have been that in handling the Acts document and Paul's Epistles, the scribes were not above deleting references to Apollonius, perhaps even changing his name to Apollos. Paul's mention of Apollos in I Cor. 3:22, "Whether Paul or Apollos, or Cephas, or the world, or life, or death, or things present, or things to come; all are yours," appears to put Apollos in a category with himself, with Peter, and indeed with many verities, as outstanding elements in the movement that was engaging their life interest. It is unfortunate that the church savants have given no consideration to these matters, consigning them to silence as unworthy of notice, for they raise questions that need answers.

At first glance it seems hardly possible that allegory could have been worked into the events of Jesus' final week in Jerusalem. The writer would have had to be very skillful to be able to cast the allegorical theme into the form of an historical account, using the occasion of the Passover festival, the rulers, the religious hierarchy, and the political alignment of the times as the setting for the consummation of the spiritual drama. Yet we must remember that devices of the kind were frequent in the literary artistry of that day. Also, we know that the greatest events in history have been used again and again as source material in literature. In this case, while daring in conception, it would not have represented too violent a break with the literary usage of the day. The movement and characters could have been used as a typograph and parable, so to say, of the Mystery representation of the great universal spiritual ritual. Speculation in this case, as in others, is only of value if it takes place within the range of the realities and the possibilities. The chief reality that should govern judgment here—and the one that Christian writers have consistently ignored until quite lately—is that in the sphere of religion the prime literary motive was always allegorical and symbolic. In all the extant literature of the Essenes and in the scriptures generally, there are few if any human characters, and what characters there are can be assumed to be typal figures of spiritual elements in man's constitution.

As we have said, if the evangelist redactors of the ancient drama did take a bit of Judean history and weave it into the traditional drama, this was not strange in an age in which all kinds of mysteries and indeed, the hand of God, seemed to hover close to men's lives. In those days, almost every religious and national group represented its history and its geography as integral elements in the divine drama of creation and redemption. Geographical features were named, kings' titles copied from the divine names; history was so interpreted as to make it dramatize the celestial allegory. It is not mere speculation to say that the Gospels show an extraordinary conjunction of allegory and veridical history. The true explanation must take this fact into account. No one can say whether it is allegory woven into the historical woof, or history embellished, colored, and shaped to express the divine allegory. The most crucial question is whether the compilers made a known Jesus personage into the epic hero-martyr of the crucifixion drama. If so, why was it thought necessary to project into the dramatic story an actual living man? The mythical figure of the Sun God *Christos* was never wanting. What is more, why choose just *this* one out of the many who had come forward in the role of the Messiah? To this query, orthodoxy will protest that he alone *proved* his claim by his miracles, if by nothing else. But what becomes of such "evidence" if the scholars are now tending to explain away these "miracles" as themselves allegorical constructions?

Many exegetes have dealt elaborately with the sharp contrast between the attitude taken toward Jesus by two different portions of the New Testament scriptures, the three synoptic Gospels on the one side, and the rest of the New Testament—embracing chiefly John's fourth Gospel, Paul's Epistles, Hebrews, the Pastoral Epistles, and Revelation—on the other. In the synoptic Gospels, the historical theme and interest seems to predominate and to have preceded the theological interpretation. But in the others it seems that the theological interpretation not only preceded the historical events, but did not even depend upon them, and seemed to render them unnecessary and supernumerary. The narrative itself seems to have been preadapted to express the theological principles allegedly derived from the events that compose the recital. This has been accounted for by some who say the original history may have been conditioned so that the theology would seem to grow naturally out of it. If so, this strengthens the case for the allegorical thesis.

Other analysts ask frankly whether this other New Testament material bears any real testimony to the existence of Jesus and whether the Christ character mentioned is the same Jesus found in the Synoptics. They admit the authors of this latter portion of the New Testament were little concerned to give evidence that the "Lord Jesus Christ" was actually Jesus of Nazareth. None of these writings set forth in any detail the events that had ostensibly taken place in Palestine. They bear, in fact, scant reference to these events. No scholar ventures to state confidently that the fourth Gospel, that of John, is truly another narrative of the life of Jesus, for, if so, why does it stand apart—so sharply distinguished from its three predecessors? And is there categorical proof that the three others did precede it? John seems to be interpreting his own subjective spiritual experience in terms of the history of Jesus.

Even more do we find this the case in regard to the Epistle to the Hebrews. Here, we are told that the author (agreed by most contemporary scholars not to have been Paul) wrote this epistle "under an obsession with allegory" that was cast upon his thinking by his contact with the Greek element in some branches of Judaism and that led him to expatiate upon the mystical and supernatural substance of inner spiritual experience. Herein the actual history becomes secondary, more or less inconsequential. *Hebrews* implies that the historical figure of Jesus is of very little importance in comparison with the personal baptism of the "Christ spirit" the primitive Christians are alleged to have experienced.

Some works declare that in the fourth Gospel the history of Jesus is simply symbolic of the new "life hid with Christ" and that this deep mystical experience is not even made to flow from the "life lived by Jesus"; no causal connection is shown. In short, it cannot be claimed on any dialectical ground laid down in John's Gospel that the Christian experience rests upon the bedrock of the Christian religion—that is, in Jesus' exemplary life and death in Judea.

Many authorities in the field of exegesis strongly emphasize the principle that the inner experience of the presence and power of the mystical Christ within the individual consciousness is a better proof of the authenticity of Christianity than the events in the life of Jesus. The Pentecostal flood tide of the divine spirit bears its own witness. The overpowering reality of the inner illumination reduces the value of the history of Jesus. Once the living waters have been tasted and their dynamic refreshment experienced, the mechanism of their efficacy becomes comparatively inconsequential. The point of ultimate significance is that intrinsic assurance arises from the self-certification of the experience of reality, not from any authority, which requires a constant effort of faith and demands an irrational loyalty to a mere tradition to maintain its validity. Johannes Weiss says that the certitude needed to reinforce the Christian faith must be found in the field of inner exaltations, since the Gospel narrative is too weak a foundation to rest it upon. Anyone might ask what psychological value a collection of stories of unnatural events of the long past might have, if the significance of these strange events is not certified in the conscious life.

Chapter Seventeen

JESUS AND
THE CHRISTOS

Earlier this book made passing mention of the twofold concept of the Christ Jesus character. In many books of Christian doctrine or exegesis, the reader is in doubt as to whether reference is being made to Jesus the man, or Christ the spirit; for Christian theology has given to the names *Jesus* and *Christ* the double connotation of man and principle: Jesus Christ. One school of theological thought has specified that *Jesus* refers to the man of flesh, while *Christ* denotes the divine power that took possession of him at his baptism by John. But is one really warranted in thinking that when a churchly person speaks of the Lord Jesus Christ he does not refer to the Gospel Jesus, the man?

The fact is that Christianity has entified two Christs—one the man, the other the spirit of God—and has been interchanging them frequently according to the convictions of different periods of its history. Sometimes it is suggested that the two are identical; sometimes they are discriminated. In the broad historical view, it might be said that Peter, or his party, gave currency to the Jesus story and that the concept of the spiritual Christ emanated from St. Paul. Two factions in the early church were at odds with each other over this issue: the Petrine and the Pauline. The concept attributed to Peter was the product of the apostolic group in Judea; that of Paul clearly embraced the teaching of Hellenic philosophy. The religion as a whole has succeeded in fusing the two into one entity, the man Christ.

Pierre Van Paassen in *Why Jesus Died* discusses this dichotomy of the Christ figure in terms others have also advanced. He says that if we can extricate the actual person, Jesus, from the mass of legend, poetry, and tradition in which he has been almost smothered in the Gospels, we shall be able to see that he has been made to appear as an enemy of Judaism, not by anything he said, but by what the Greek philosophers and the formulators of the Christian doctrine managed to utter through his lips a hundred years after his death. Van Paassen goes so far as to say that these writers created a myth, in which Jesus was the central figure and the symbol of man's divinity. The tragedy, he asserts, is that the symbol has so largely obscured the original as to blot it out almost entirely. The Greek ideal of the spiritual Christos has obliterated the man.[1]

But this writer must be aware that there is a growing tendency among exegetes to adopt an opposite point of view: that the vital inner experience of the Christos principle has been obscured by the figure of the man of Galilee. It was undeniable at any rate that the Christian transmutation of the spiritual Christos into the man-Christ resulted in the blending of the two characters, one historical, the other mystical, into a single figure which has been, down the centuries, neither dominantly one character nor the other.

It is well to look more closely at the picture Van Paassen draws of this situation. He states that the Gospel writers made a human being out of St. Paul's Christ-God, admittedly reversing the commonly advanced thesis that the Christians made a God out of Jesus the merely human. God—St. Paul's God—

already existed in Hellenic systematization. The authors of the Gospel gave to this God the name of Jesus of Nazareth. True Christianity, the religion of the Christos, is far older than the Christian church, Van Paassen reminds us (as did Augustine), saying, "The two, the human being, Jesus, and the metaphysical personage, Christ, were blended into one."

The fact of the blending, or the metamorphosis of the one figure into the other, is not to be denied, but in the confusion of dogmas and doctrines advanced by Christianity over the centuries, one can scarcely be blamed for failing to discern exactly in which direction the change tended. But there is still a third way of explaining the phenomenon. The first thesis is that Christianity took the human Jesus and made him to be very God; the second is that it took the Hellenic spiritual Christos and personified it into a human being, Jesus. A third solution is that the spiritual nonhuman Christos could have been humanized even if there had been no living figure of Jesus. The absence of authentic historical evidence of Jesus' existence argues strongly for this third suggestion. It was felt that the abstract Christ was too remote; that the essence of this divine saving principle needed to be brought nearer to man; that it should be personalized. Most of the evidence seems to point to the humanizing of the Divine, rather than the reverse. This whole question remains in grave doubt. Whether the mantle was specifically proffered to a living man—Jesus—or whether it was worn by a supposititious hypostatized man whose name had to be Jesus or Christ or even Lord is very questionable. Certainly some men have felt that others deserved the title. Akiba wanted it for bar Kochba, and many learned scholars have been searching the records of the first and second centuries BC for the King of Righteousness named in the Dead Sea Scrolls, believing that he was some actual man living then, but unable to identify him. Could not the man have been equally unidentifiable in "Christ's" day? If the evangelists or the little sanctified group that was attracted to the Galilean carpenter felt sure it was he, we simply have the answer they gave to the great question. Can history be said to have proved them right? A definite affirmative is possible only to those who are deeply rooted in age-old traditions of pietism and who admit no evidence into their minds.

Some of this evidence has already been given here. More is to be found in the words of the beloved theologian-physician-musician-humanitarian, Albert Schweitzer. Schweitzer spent years in the most searching and conscientious study of Christian history. In the end, he summed up his conclusions in one sententious paragraph that can be found in his work, *The Quest of the Historical Jesus.* This Jesus, he says—who came forward, as others did, with the announcement that he was the Messiah; who proclaimed the near coming of the Kingdom of God, and urged men to repent that they might be prepared; and who sealed and consecrated his message by his death—this Jesus never existed. He stands to the world as a character conceived by liberal theological doctrinism and projected into historicity by the heads of the Christian religion.[2] This is the essence of Schweitzer's statement, but he elaborates its substance in subsequent pages. He says that the historical foundations of the Christian faith, as these have been laid down by theological thinking, ancient, medieval, and modern, no longer exist. The mistake was to think that Jesus could effectuate the redemption of our time if he was converted into a being like us. A Jesus of that description never existed. Man's true sense of history forced him to question the theological interpretation, which Schweitzer calls artificial history. Facts themselves have become the strongest critics of this supposititious history. It is not the Jesus of the Gospels who can be meaningful for our time, says Schweitzer, but the Christ that can be known within the arena of man's inner experience. The theologians had been sure mankind could be saved and brought to the glorification of the inner life by the propagation of faith in the Nazarene biography authenticated as history. But this tactic has failed, according to Schweitzer. It was bound to fail, as will all doctrine that looks to a source other than man's own innate, divine potential—which is one with, part of, the true Christ, the divine ground of all. We thought, Schweitzer says, that we could use the Jesus of history to lead the world to the mystic Jesus who is the living, spiritual power today. But the road leading through the historical Christ to the brooding Christ-spirit proved too forbidding and never brought the pilgrims to the longed-for Mecca. What is more, this detour has now been closed by genuine history.

Schweitzer enlarges upon how, with so little authentic data of Jesus' life to guide them, the theologians have given free rein to their imaginations in the effort to bring his image into conformity with the ideals set up for the figure of the Christ Savior in orthodox religion. In the process, they have weakened much of Jesus' moral teaching that demanded rigorous discipline, impossible purity, and unblemished spirituality. Jesus has been remolded so that he can fittingly represent the church ideal, while the ethical-spiritual principles he laid down in the Sermon on the Mount and other discourses are passed over as impractical for our society.

What is more, Schweitzer says, knowledge of the personal life of Jesus is not a help to the religionist. What is really of value in his life is those elements in him that are absolutely independent of our knowledge of his personality or career—that is, the eternal spirit of his Christliness. He is pictured for us as comely in feature according to the style of Italian art, divine in speech and action, pure, serene, inscrutably wise, sanctified by grace and holiness, aureoled by the halo of celestial radiance, a divine being. When this figure is shown, on closer view, to be a person not unlike ourselves, many find this aspect a shock, even repellent; the two aspects, divine and actual, seem most unnatural in proximity. Schweitzer's thesis, that the stratagem of bringing the world to Christ through Jesus has failed and must be abandoned, is in accord with the views of the eminent Johannes Weiss, of Guignebert, and of many others who agree with Schweitzer.

We must make it clear, however, that while Schweitzer asserts that the Jesus figure created by the theologians never existed, he does not negate the actual historical existence of the Galilean, nor deny in any way the nobility of his teachings. His position is that in essence Christianity took up the Galilean and straightway made a God out of him. What needs to be affirmed immediately in the wake of that statement is that Christianity has demonstrated the inadequacy, the irrationality, and the unseemly incongruity of its thinking in not seeing that the merely human villager of Galilee could not be expected to carry the world-load of the Christos, much less the Logos. For that was an office, a dignity, that no human being could encompass—a cosmic role beyond the scope of mortal flesh and blood. It was not to be supposed that men would not ultimately be sharply sensible of the incongruity. The ancient mind would not have made such a mistake, for it was keenly sensitive to the unseemliness of attempting to incorporate Deity in a gross body. If the Egyptians did put animal heads on their gods, it served a symbolic purpose. There was no ancient philosopher or student of the Mysteries who did not know that divinity in germinal form was innate in every mortal. But to claim that the infinite God, who endows all the worlds with life and truth and beauty, could be brought down to the human level was a denigration of the highest spirituality to the mundane level. It would have been a sacrilege and abhorrent to a Hellenist. We have been so indoctrinated with this age-old heresy that it does not shock us. But let us try to imagine how we would feel if we were to find ourselves in the personal presence of Jesus without knowing his historical role. What would we see? A man of certain height, weight, features, and dress. He might be unusually striking, even beautiful—calm, benign in manner, with mild eyes and a gentle

sweetness of demeanor. Perhaps he would excite our admira-
tion, respect, and even awe. But, whatever the impression of his
personality or beauty of soul in speech and countenance, he is,
finally, just a man. Is there the least sign whereby the beholder
may know that in addition to and infinitely beyond his humanity he is the Lord of the universe? How could there be? The sublime character of such a role is numinous, ineffable, beyond
description or logical analysis. In truth, no man standing before
us in his full humanity could furnish the credential for his claim
that he was the cosmic Christ.

To return to Schweitzer, this reverent and religious thinker
does not seem to doubt that Jesus was actually there at the time,
in Galilee. What he declares is that this man was not the supernatural being, the celestial cosmocrator, who is hypostatized by
Christianity and worshipped by Christians. With nothing authentic about Jesus in the histories of the period, with no mention
of him even by St. Paul or any of the missionary associates of
the Apostle, with the "beloved disciple" John speaking in his
Gospel rather of the Christ as spirit than as a man and referring
to Christ as the spiritual aeon in Revelation, the assumption of
Jesus' mortal life on earth is precarious, to say the least.

The use of allegory in the interpretation of the Gospel figure introduces, at every step, a parallelism between the image
and the reality behind it, between the two Jesus figures, the
assumed living man and the mythical Christos. It is as though
the two accounts ran side by side like two roads that lead in the
same direction but never meet. One path carries us through the
events and amid the characters of the factual world; the other
takes us into a world of lofty concepts, sublime beauty and ideal
perfection. Yet the two can never meet, because the relevance of
the one lies in the objective world and the other wholly in the
subjective. They can only mirror each other; their identity can
only be seen by reflection. In fact, one might say that the two
Jesus personages are as different and unidentifiable as the mirror

and the image reflected within it. One could affirm that the object and its mirror reflection are exactly similar and serve all the purposes of identity. But they are still in two separate worlds, and what is more, the mirror image reverses the lineaments of reality. Christianity has asserted that the actual Jesus and the allegorical reflection of the Christos are one and the same. But no matter how close may be the resemblance, they remain in two different realms. Hermes of Egypt, long ago, identified this subtle distinction. "That which is above is as that which is below; and that which is below is as that which is above, for the performance of the miracle of the One thing." Note carefully that he says they are *as* each other, not that they *are* each other. Jesus may be *like* the Christos, that is, he may be as nearly a human reflection as was or is possible, but he is not the Christos, which remains undiminished, eternal, inviolate.

Anyone who has deeply thought upon the spiritual significance of the Hellenic concept of the Christos feels a certain distaste for such phrases as "Christ healed a leper" or "Christ tarried at Cana" or even "at the time of Christ," for they seem to limit and thus degrade the concept of a sublime and universal spiritual principle. *All* time is the time of the Christos. Any ground on which the Christ consciousness is imprinted is "the Holy Land." *All* life is a miracle of spiritual sacrifice. Men consecrate particular places to commemorate high moments in human history, or to show their veneration of those who attained such moments. This veneration of the special shrines must take care lest it fall into the error of holding other places to be less holy. Sanctification of the few spots where Shekinah and the Holy Spirit manifested their presence should not reduce for any soul the light of divine beneficence that broods undiminished over the whole earth. No, an abstract principle of spiritual consciousness cannot be a concrete being of flesh, no matter how closely the two are conjoined. It is as though we were to take one statue by Praxiteles and say, "This is beauty—

all other representations are false." Or, as Plato pointed out, as though the concept of "twoness" could be derived from just one pair of objects.

However, if the concrete symbol and the abstract quality can never be completely identified, there is still a way in which they can be unified in *relationship*. That way is through the conceptual power of the human mind. In the depths of our awareness, the man Jesus may attach to himself the essence of the quality known as Christliness. His life, his actions, his speech, and his graciousness may lead us to an appreciation of what Christliness can mean—its ability to transform the human heart. But even so, the theophany shining through his soul and body must be within the range of what a human being may become, albeit a human being of the most exalted order. He will not transcend what we conceive to be the human spiritual potential, or he would be so far beyond us that he could not reach us at all. If Jesus was very God, it was in no way other than is the one open to any man who has generated within him the attributes of Christliness. Christian adoration of Jesus as Supreme Deity has carried theology to the point of assuming that he represents Deity absolute and unconditioned. But human nature is obviously but one stage or level of development in the grand scheme of cosmic evolution. Even if a very important stage, it is only a small portion of the infinite energy and being that is God. What can be expressed through a human being could never be absolute divinity; it is only that degree and quality, that aspect of the divine Being that the human order can express. Is it not said that when God incarnated in man he took on man's limitations, he circumscribed his infinitude within the tiny capacity of human nature? He took on himself *our nature.*

The efforts that have been made to proclaim the absoluteness of Jesus' divinity have only succeeded in demeaning the very Christliness we are urged to cultivate. Christianity has maintained that if a man pour out his heart in love, compassion, graciousness, and charity, his gift still falls infinitely short of the perfection of Jesus' divine love. When the communion address to God reminds us that we are not worthy so much as to pick up the crumbs that fall from the banquet table, we are being denied our human birthright. God does not ask us to be perfect at the level of divinity, but only at the level of human capacity for divinity. It is by no means sacrilegious to assert that there have probably been many men and women of consecrated lives who have expressed the human capability of divine expression in their own way, as did Jesus in his—if, indeed, he was the human being theology declares him to have been. If it is retorted that this cannot be so, because Jesus had the potentiality of all deity within his humanity, whereas common men have only their own small share, the answer is that the divine potentiality is ever the same—it is only the expression that varies in degree or kind. And again, it must be said that the Christian identification of the divine attribute of Christliness with Jesus alone has deprived all other men of the hope of its flowering in their own lives.

Man's highest goal, his ultimate objective, is to achieve such a flowering of Christly attribute. It demands that a man cultivate the garden of his soul and body with supreme intent and unswerving fidelity. It requires the development and exercise of every power and faculty potential in his nature. The aspirant must study the play of the two polar forces, spirit and matter, the Christos and the human, in his own life. And here we have a paradox, for the two paths, the outer and the inner, which we have said never meet, do finally join in man's life. Those two "antagonists" that, as positive and negative forces, created the whole manifested world meet and merge in their return to primal unity. But this ultimate is achieved only at the cost of the disappearance of both into the nonbeing of absolute unity.

There is another consequence of the transferral of the spiritual Christos to "Christ," the man of Galilee, that must be mentioned. All theology has, as its ultimate concern, the descent of soul into matter, its imprisonment in the "flesh," and its resurrection out of that "death" to the beginning of a new cycle of ongoing life. This death was that of the *soul,* not that of the *body.* But when this soul, which epitomizes the spirit in mankind, was identified with Jesus, men lost sight of the wide significance of "death" as it pertained to the soul's confinement and obscuration in the material world, and instead transferred the reference to the death of the body of Jesus. And so the religion foisted on the world the ghastly picture of the Galilean drooping in agony on the wooden cross, believing that only through bodily death could the soul be freed. The "death" might rather be said to have taken place at "birth," and the "resurrection" at man's awakening to the spiritual life.

For earlier esoteric philosophy, all this lower world of matter and incarnation was the realm of Pluto and of "death." That which was spoken of as the "underworld," the "nether earth," was not some postmortem limbo of the astral world or some subterranean region, neither Hades nor hell, but instead, our own good earth itself. The "death," from which all spirit buried in body must be resurrected, is just that comatose, unaware, not-fully-alive condition that the slower frequencies and longer wave lengths of the life energies impose upon souls when they are born into the confines of a human body, thus losing the freedom that was theirs. St. Paul states all this clearly when he says that when the command to incarnate "came home to me, sin sprang to life and I died. The command that meant life proved death to me" (Romans 7:9-10). In the cryptic language of the ancients, incarnation of the spirit in fleshly body was its "death." When the Easter bells ring with the joyous news that Jesus' death and resurrection conquered death for all believers, sober reflection tells us that bodily death has not been conquered. The *body* has no resurrection, as we well know; nor would we wish it. All that a man really is lies in his soul and spirit, and it is this that must needs be resurrected. When the soul wakens and begins to exercise its powers, the true meaning of "bursting the bars of death and opening wide the gates of immortality" will flood the being with some foretaste of that immortality itself.

Further scrutiny of this cardinal word *death* discloses that there are two variant connotations in which St. Paul uses it, even besides its common meaning. In the seventh chapter of Romans he employs it to denote the soul's torpidity in its "wintertime hibernation" in mortal incarnation; but he also makes poetic use of it to denote the soul's "dying away from" the interests of the flesh. To awaken the soul from its dormancy one must "die" to the attractions of the flesh; Paul says that he thus "dies daily." But application of the term *death* to the soul rather than to the body was implicit in all the dialectical construction of Greek thought. In the cyclical progress of evolution, the two opposing forces, life and death, alternated in the eternal succession of manifestation and obscuration, of activity and quiescence. As one became active, the other retired into latency; as one visibly increased, the other proportionately diminished. Like Horus and Set of the Egyptian construction, each in turn conquers and "slays" the other. This thought is clearly present in the scriptures when John the Baptist, the natural forerunner of the spiritual Lord, says, "I must decrease, but he must increase." Hence Paul, who was educated in the Hellenic center of Tarsus and perhaps was even an initiate of the Mysteries, knew well that the life of the body was generated by the "death" of the soul; that while the life energy was expressing itself most fully and positively in the body, the spirit lay dormant as in a chrysalis, but when that energy ebbed and the body sank into physical death, the spirit would arise and ascend to freedom and glory in discarnate life.

The Greeks denominated the physical body as the tomb or sepulcher of the soul; the word for "body" was *soma* and for "tomb," *sema*. The images of the open tomb, the rent veil of the temple ("Know ye not that your *body* is the temple of the living God?"), and the stone rolled away were freely employed in ancient times. The usual interpretation of St. Paul's declaration that "since by man came death, by man comes also the resurrection of the dead" has been that total man, being Adamic and sinful by nature, had brought death, and that therefore the one man who was divine, Jesus, would bring resurrection. Paul's concept, however, was that the Adamic natural-man element in man's dual constitution having inflicted spiritual "death" upon the soul, the resurrection from that "death" would be achieved by the Christos potentially accessible in man's own nature. Christian doctrine condemned generic man as depraved and lost in sin, hence it could not conceive of the presence within man of a divine element that could resurrect his fallen nature. But Paul's loftier conception held that the "earthly, sensual, devilish" part of man's nature may drag him down to "death," but the seraphic, spiritual part of man can redeem and raise him up. The Adamic man and the Christly man are the two nodes of the polarity in man's constitution.

In St. Paul's Epistle to the Philippians 3:20, the apostle makes a striking statement. He says that "we are a colony of heaven [Moffatt's translation of what the King James version renders "our conversation is in heaven"], whence we look for the Savior, the Lord Jesus Christ," who shall change our vile bodies into the likeness of his own glorious presence. What are the implications of this statement made by the very founder of the Christian church? He seems to be saying that men are looking for the Savior, the Lord Christ, to come from heaven when that very same Savior and Lord Christ had been but recently present on earth. There is an implication that Paul did not consider Jesus as "our Savior the Lord Christ." In spite of the fact that Paul says (Galatians I) that he spent two weeks with Peter and with James, the "Lord's brother," on the occasion of his visit to

Jerusalem, and surely had every opportunity to become acquainted with the personal knowledge they had of Jesus, he remains completely silent about Jesus. This and other evidence indicates that Paul did not think the religion he spent all the tremendous energies of his life in propagating was based on the man Jesus. With the Lord Jesus Christ, yes, but not with the man. Likewise, does it not seem strange that James, in an epistle that was considered worthy of a place in the sanctified canon, never considered it a matter of even biographical interest to introduce an occasional reference to "my brother"? Why would he, as he long survived Jesus and became the spiritual head of the Christian community at Jerusalem, not have regarded it as extremely important to report intimate details of the life of his sublime brother? Benjamin Bacon, formerly head of the Yale Divinity School, in his book, *Jesus and Paul,* says: "It is never of a Jesus after the flesh that Paul is found speaking." The New Testament documents lack the usual elements and hallmarks of historical narrative and, indeed, do not convey a sense of history. St. Paul never once mentioned a single personal item about his contact with the disciples, about what Peter and James told him, or about meeting anyone in Jerusalem or elsewhere who had seen the tragic events of Jesus' last week. Paul says only that the risen wraith of the Master had appeared to him—an incident now assumed to have been of the same mystical-vision character as the appearance to him of the blinding light on the road to Damascus. When, finally, Paul writes that "we" are looking for a Savior from heaven (that very Savior having just left his people), we cannot but infer that he had no knowledge of a movement based on the claim that his Greek *Christos* had appeared in the mortal flesh of this man Jesus in Palestine. As Paul was then still looking for the appearance of the redeeming power of the spiritual Christ, so it may be said that the world today is looking for the "Logos" in the form of a rational answer to this and many other baffling episodes, the result of mistaking allegory for history.

Many Christian authors affirm that Paul's preachment bore no relation to the Mystery teachings; they declare that Paul focused all his theology upon the historical Jesus. But research has shown that many of the idioms and phraseology of the Mystery cult ceremonials and literature can be found in Paul's Epistles, and when Paul speaks of the "Lord Jesus Christ" he obviously refers to the Christos principle. When he says, "This Jesus whom we have seen," internal evidence indicates that he is referring to the spiritual figure or the radiant light that appeared to him in his visions. It must not be forgotten that Paul is recorded as having earlier in his career persecuted the Christians, witnessing, if not abetting, the stoning of Stephen. The conjecture has been advanced that he thus stood out against the rabid fanatics who proclaimed the man Jesus to be the Christ. Paul was a high-minded Jew, and, as a student of the great Rabbi Gamaliel, he would have condemned and opposed the religious Zealots who swung so extravagantly into the Jesus cult, the Ebionites, and others. It seems possible that his conversion, instead of being a transition from Judaism to apostolic Christianity, in which he does not seem to fit with any degree of compatibility, was a shift from legalistic Judaism to Hellenic Christology, in which the figure of no personal Savior centered, all being spiritually conceived. This would, at least rationally, account for his silence regarding the man Jesus and two alleged appearances of the corporeal Jesus to his inner vision. That Paul was more intensely concerned with the purely spiritual aspects of his religious life than with outward events is borne out by a sentence in the first verse of Second Corinthians 12: "I will come to visions and revelations of the Lord." He also states that some fourteen years before he knew a man in Christ—whether the experience was consciously in the body or out of it he cannot say—who was caught up to the third heaven (which, in a following verse, he equates with paradise) and there did hear words that it is irreverent to speak about. His observation that "of such a one will I give glory" is strong indication that Paul believed in such mystical experiences. Does he not say that after his conversion he knows Christ no longer after the flesh, but spiritually? Does he not cry out, "Know ye not your own selves that Jesus Christ is within you?" And he also testifies that henceforth he regarded people no longer as Jews, Greeks, or barbarians, but all alike as men needing the baptism of Christliness.

We believe that such verses in the Bible as "The soul that sinneth it shall die" and "The wages of sin is death" are obvious references, not to the death of the physical body, but to the death-in-life that comes to the soul subdued by too active passions and desires. It is true that confusion in interpretation of these statements has arisen from the fact that they seem to attribute *death* to the one element in man that never dies—the soul. But just as the fervent belief in immortality is based on the realization that nothing in man's experience really ends, but only changes and flows into some other condition, so the ancients held that death is not a finality, but only a kind of sleep. The soul, entombed in flesh, is awaiting the moment of rebirth, whether it come through physical death, or through the awakening of man to the spiritual life.

Chapter Eighteen

THE WITNESS OF ALLEGORY

W e have earlier in this book offered a few examples of the allegorical materials universally present in all great world traditions, religious and cultural. We have no intention of burdening the reader with a voluminous account. Yet the statements about the allegorical nature of the Gospel narrative need some evidential support that we will try to furnish here.

First, let us offer a paragraph from Oliver Wendell Holmes's review of the first edition of Sir Edwin Arnold's famous poetic account of the life of the Lord Buddha, *The Light of Asia.* Here is the paragraph:

> If one were told that many centuries ago a celestial ray shone into the body of a sleeping woman, as it seemed to her in her dream, that thereupon the advent of a wondrous child was predicted by the soothsayers; that angels appeared at this child's birth; that merchants came from afar bearing gifts to him; that an ancient saint recognized the babe as divine and fell at his feet to worship him; that in his eighth year the child confounded his teachers with the amount of his knowledge,

still showing them due reverence; that he grew up full of compassionate tenderness to all that lived and suffered; that to help his fellow-creatures he sacrificed every worldly prospect and enjoyment; that he went through the ordeal of a terrible temptation in which all the power and evil were let loose upon him, and came out conqueror of them all; that he preached holiness and practiced charity; that he gathered disciples and sent out apostles to spread his doctrine over many lands and peoples; that this "Helper of the Worlds" could claim a more than earthly lineage and a life that dated long before Abraham was—of whom would he think the wonderful tale was told? Would he not say that this must be another version of the story of the One who came upon our earth in a Syrian village during the reign of Augustus Caesar and died by violence during the reign of Tiberius? What would he say if he were told that the narrative was between five and six centuries older than that of the Founder of Christianity? Such is the story of this person. Such is the date assigned to the personage of whom it is told. The religion he taught is reckoned by many to be the most widely prevalent of all beliefs.[1]

It is startling enough that Holmes, living in New England about the 1830's, could draw this close parallel. What seems more startling is that his words had little or no effect upon the prevailing climate of thought among Christians at that time.

At the very heart of its most sacred rite, the sacrament of the Eucharist, Christian blindness to its allegorical implications has resulted in a failure to grasp one of the cardinal principles of ancient theology. This is the doctrine of the "dismemberment" of the bodies of the gods because of their incarnation in mortal flesh. Their descent from higher planes of being into the physi-

cal world necessitated a progressive fragmentation of their primal unitary power into lesser units at each successive downward
step, since the weaker vessels could contain only a small fraction
of the heavenly fire. Hence, in every mythology the bodies of the
gods were represented as being cut to pieces so that all creatures
might be endowed with physical life. Generally the pieces were
scattered over the land and buried—emblematic of the sacrificial
"death" to which godhood submitted for mortals. There are
many tales of gods mutilating their bodies or shedding their
blood for mankind. Great significance was attached to the number of pieces into which the divine nature was divided, the most
common number being twelve, as man is said to be destined to
bring to perfection twelve aspects of divinity.

But, as every descent of deity into humanity was to be followed by its reascent to heaven, completion of the poetic image
demanded that the pieces be gathered together, reassembled
in their original unity, and "reconstituted whole and entire."
Christian scholarship seems to remain unaware that this drama
was enacted right at the heart of Jesus' institution of the
Eucharist. It is stated that he took a loaf and, having given
thanks to God, he brake it, giving a morsel to each of his disciples and admonishing them to eat it that they might obtain
immortal life. Having completed the distribution, the dismemberment, he concluded the sacramental rite by the reminder
that it was their duty to effect his rememberment. "Do this in
remembrance of me" he said. The translation of *rememberment*
as "remembrance" has lost to Christians the intrinsic meaning
of this passage, together with the spiritual unction of the sacrament, replacing its cathartic efficacy with a mere memorial
gesture. The worshipper's sacramental offering became one of
reverence to the person of Jesus, whereas by the injunction to
reunify in human society the dismembered body of the *Christos,*
the rite really symbolized the obligation of the believer to con-
tribute his own spiritual energy to the rememberment. By this

and similar historization of the divine allegories, both Judaism and Christianity have turned into mere memorial occasions a number of their most potent spiritual festivals. Christianity has turned even its great festivals of Christmas and Easter into "anniversaries" of the birth and death of the man of Nazareth. But, in fact, both the winter solstice date of December 25, and the Sabbath following the full moon after the vernal equinox, had been celebrated for centuries before the time of Jesus as symbolizing the birth and death of the Christ principle in the life of humankind.

Reference has previously been made to the conversion (which must have been deliberate) of the phrase "dense sea" (of matter), which is found in ancient formulas for the world into which souls descended for incarnation, into the figure of the Roman procurator Pontius Pilate. "Sea" in Greek is *pontos,* and "densified" is a Latinized Greek participle, *piletos. Herut* was an Egypto-Syrian word for the serpentdragon monster fabled to devour the infant sons of gods when born. The alleged "historical" Slaughter of the Innocents by the Roman Tetrarch can hardly be other than an allegorization of the danger of destruction that threatens the infant deific principle in man on its first entry into the body, because of the fleshly instincts. And its appearance in the New Testament could be seen as but a repetition of the analogous situation that occurs in Exodus in connection with the birth of Moses: Pharoah ordered the midwives attending the Hebrew women to destroy *by drowning* all the male Hebrew children as soon as born. The field of antiquity is strewn plentifully with legends of the exposure of divine infants to perils and their salvation by shepherds, cowherds, or wild animals. These all typify the real peril in which the soul stands when first it embarks on earthly life.

It is instructive to note how a symbol or its interpretation can at times almost reverse its role in an allegory. In the case of the Old Testament deific character, Moses, the danger menacing the newborn child came from Egypt. On the contrary, in the case of Jesus, Egypt was the land of escape from the danger. The apparent contradiction is resolved only by insight into the esoteric meaning of the myth. "Egypt," of course, is not a real country, but the Amenta-underworld, this mother earth of ours, in which, to be sure, the menace of carnality besets the soul from its first moment of entry, but which, in the end, gives to the soul its deification and its release back to heaven. This is clearly outlined in Revelation 12, where it is recounted how the woman clothed with the sun is in danger from the great red dragon with seven heads and ten horns that threatens to devour her man-child about to be delivered, and how she "fled into the wilderness, where she hath a place prepared of God, that they should feed her there a thousand two hundred and threescore days." The dragon, also cast out of heaven, pursued the woman on earth and let loose a water flood to sweep her away with her Christ child. But "the earth helped the woman" and swallowed up the flood of waters. Therefore, the earth is both the peril of the soul and its eventual salvation. Otherwise, why should the soul come to earth at all? The ancient drama represented souls as gladly abandoning the bliss of heaven for the greater reality of life on earth. It is even suggested that they fled heaven and came to earth as a place of refuge. Heaven afforded no opportunity for bright spirits to exercise their creative potential against the inertia of matter. It is only through the challenge and struggle of the battle of life on earth that the Christ child can be "born of the woman clothed with the sun, with twelve stars in her diadem and the moon under her feet." This is Mother Nature, and it is only here in the "wilderness" that she can bring forth her child. This was all prefigured for the New Testament evangelists in the story of Hagar in Genesis, for she, too, was driven out into the wilderness with her child (Gen: 17).

The symbol of the wilderness recurs again and again in the scriptures, in connection with at least four characters. In addition to the woman in Revelation and Hagar, the two others were Esau and John the Baptist. Both of these characters lived in the wilds, dressed in hunter's shaggy garments, and ate rough, raw food. The manner of life of both marked them as figures typifying the first and natural stage of human evolution: the first man Adam, of the earth, who precedes and prepares for the coming of the second Adam, the spiritual Christ. John specifically announces this as his role in the drama; it is more enigmatical in the case of Esau. St. Paul also states that the natural man must precede the spiritual. The wilderness was the apt and expressive symbol used to convey the truth that man is part of, lives in, and is nurtured by nature and only later becomes fit and able to implement the radiance of the spirit.

So even the Christ himself, since he is brought by his own wish and desire to descend into the life of the natural body of man, must also plunge into this wilderness and brave its challenge. Straight into it he is led by Satan, his polar twin, to undergo the testing of his powers against the opposition of the "world, the flesh, and the devil." Here again, the New Testament reflects the Old, for it repeats in essence the temptation of Adam and Eve in the garden. Misunderstanding of the allegorical meaning of this, too, has misled Christendom, for this "temptation" is in no way designed to be rendered as an attempt on the part of God to lure man to his fall. It is, instead, an allegorical account of the experience that must be undergone by the Christ soul if it is to develop its faculties and powers against polar opposition. In a sense, it might be considered as a testing, but it is more philosophically understood as a training.

Because allegory offered poetic imagination a wide variety of tropes and images, we find the wilderness supplanted by, if not equated with, another most suggestive symbol, over which, once more, biblical interpretation has stumbled and fallen. In one Gospel, Satan leads Jesus into the wilderness for the temptation; in another, he leads him up onto a high mountain, from which all the kingdoms of the world are in view. Nothing is more certain than that the young soul is going to be tempted by the sensual delights of the material world; its great achievement is to keep unswervingly to its spiritual objective. Much that is significant for Christianity arose out of Jewish history. It was on Mount Sinai that God and man met for the harmonization of their relationship. Man came up to the mount by means of the upward path of evolution, and God, via his expression through involution, came down to meet him. According to Gerald Massey, the word *Sinai* derives from an Egyptian hiero-glyphic root *sheni* (*shenai*), which, through the identity of *s* and *sh,* can as well be *seni* (*senai*), meaning "point of turning to return." The vowels in the Egyptian language, and even in the Hebrew, were so loosely distinguished that it is entirely legiti-mate to spell the word with an *i* in place of an *e,* thus making it *Sinai.* This word was one of pivotal importance in Egyptian religion, for it denoted the nadir of the arc of the soul's descent into matter and the body—the points at which its downward plunge was arrested and it entered into a period of quiescence exactly counterbalanced with the inertia of matter, during which it slowly swung round on a swivel or pivot and began its return journey on the upward arc of evolution, back to its celes-tial origin. One of the basic festivals of the ancient world, now lost in the mists of antiquity, was called the *Hag* (present Hebrew *chag,* meaning "holiday"—one consecrated by a religious pil-grimage). It probably fell into disuse because it was supposed to be celebrated by a pilgrimage to the boundary of the land, which was always a stream or body of water, at which point the pilgrim was to cross this water and then turn back to return home. This festival was obviously intended to dramatize the migration of the soul from its heavenly home out to the limits of a country bounded by water. The human body is itself born in, and of, water (its content is seven-eighths water); hence, the water boundary at which the soul stops and begins its return represents this physical house in which we live. So the pilgrimage of the Hag represents the soul's journey out into incarnation in a watery body on earth.

In this light, we see how wrong pietistic religionists have been in vilifying and mortifying the body as the evil enemy of the spirit. For where else can God and man meet for communion than in the human body? St. Paul has done the excellent service of reminding us that our fleshly body is verily the temple in which we worship the God who has consecrated it with his presence. If Mount Sinai is, in the allegory, the holy hill on which we meet with God, then it also stands for our physical body.

As the divine soul that is incarnate in the human body is virtually of the essence of solar light and power, the daily and yearly cycles of the sun in relation to the earth were made by the ancients the basic symbols of the cycles of the soul as it was immersed in incarnation and then returned to its spiritual abode. The sun reached its nadir of descent on December 22 and, pivoting about on the hinge of the solstice symbolically estimated at seven days, on December 25 began its return toward summer. Many of the pre-Christian sun gods were "born" on this date, the winter solstice, when sunlight is temporarily obscured by darkness. It is at the solstice that the sun slowly swings around on a "hinge" and "turns to return." Similarly, the sunlight of the soul, temporarily obscured in human nature, also is swinging slowly around as on a cosmic hinge and is beginning its return to the world of spirit. Long ago, at a Christmas midnight mass, the writer heard what was described as the oldest known Christian Christmas carol, dating from the fifth century, printed and sung in Latin. It spoke simply of the Christos, Son of God, through his mother Mary, the Virgin. But in it occurred a startling phrase: *a solis natus cardine,* "born from the hinge of the sun." Here was the ancient image: the Christ is born at the solstice of evolution, at the point of the soul's turning away from darkness to light.

The cardinal symbol of the hinge, which represents the period of stasis, introduces us to another important symbol, the "stable." The Christian legend held true enough to paganism to retain the ancient allegory of the birth of Christos in a stable. As in all symbolic language, relevance and meaning are to be found by transfer from the objective world to the subjective. *Stable* is therefore to be read as "stability" or "stabilization." The Christ is born in the *stable,* or stabilized, relation between body and soul. The two polar forces of spirit and matter are "stabled," stalled, in a stasis or stationary standstill or point of stabilization, and in that state in evolution they are wedded together and give birth to their Son.

Further significance is revealed if one takes the stable as the building itself and draws the obvious parallels. A stable is a tenement provided for man to house and shelter animals, mainly during the winter. The incarnation period was always described as the soul's period of "hibernation"—its wintertime, its night. In keeping with this figure, legend had the divine Child born in winter and at night. "At midnight came the cry: the bridegroom cometh." The "Heilige Nacht, Stille Nacht" of the German carol depicts the silence and mystery of the moment. "While shepherds watched their flocks *by night,*" Christ came as the immortal Light in the darkness.

The symbolism of the captivities and exiles undergone by God's Israelite children is also important enough to be mentioned. The legends of all ancient religions describe the soul's expulsion from heaven for incarnation on earth as an "exile," an expatriation, a lonely pilgrimage to a "far country" (as in the Prodigal Son allegory); the soul's incarceration in the body they liken to a "captivity" or even a "death." St. Paul says that we are a "colony from heaven." In the Old Testament it is a "bondage in Egypt," this land being selected to designate the dark underworld, Amenta, Sheol, Hades, and Hell, because it chanced to lie immediately southwest of the land, Palestine, in which the reformulators of the religious epic of the soul happened to live. As the sun at eve sets in the west, and in the autumn moves south, the southwest direction symbolized the path of souls on their way to incarnation. So "Egypt" was the house of bondage, "that slave pen," as Moffatt translates it. Later, when the kings of Assyria and Babylon moved in and carried off a few thousand of the people calling themselves Israelites, the literalists called those minor episodes the fulfillment of the prophecy that God's children of Israel were to be scattered among the nations and held captive to *ha go'im,* the heathen nations of the world, until the great day of their recall to supremacy in Jerusalem.

In this connection we might mention that, in his dissertation on the apocryphal book of Jeremy, Robert H. Pfeiffer of the Harvard Divinity School says that the long diatribes of the prophet against the heathen worship of idols is utterly absurd, as it certainly can be shown that his charges are wholly without foundation. He asserts that Jeremy's elaboration of the Babylonian scene is artificially built up to give allegory the appearance of historical veracity. The whole tirade against idol worship is quite likely the prophet's literalization of the allegory of the soul's bent, in incarnation, to mistake the natural images of noumenal ideas for the reality of being, instead of its outer symbols—"For all the gods of the people are idols."[2]

This brief description of some of the symbolism to be found in the Bible is offered to show how indispensable allegorical interpretation is in reading the scriptures. Christianity has suffered from its own indifference to the significance of comparative religion and symbolism generally.

We have previously mentioned two common modes of human knowing, the *Logos* and the *mythos.* The former is the pattern structure of the divine archai, or first creative principle, over which the mind of God formed the universe. The mythos is man's own expression of truth, the dynamic and living vesture he fashions to clothe the archetypal noumena and thus make them accessible to all men. The primary language devised for this purpose was imagery drawn from nature, since nature itself was the living embodiment of the divine ideation, the epiphany of the Logos. As Patanjali, the Hindu sage, says: "The universe is wholly pervaded by the Supreme Being. There is therefore no aspect of the universe which can not be used as a means for attaining realization of the divine."

Ancient thought had cultivated and sometimes achieved a kind of genius that could intuitively perceive the relationship between nature and divine mind. It had developed the art of representative ideography to a high degree of subtlety. The great Egyptian, Greek, Persian, Indian, and even biblical myths and allegories remain inscrutable to the modern mind; the Mysteries of old are still mysteries. The scriptures are mostly great tomes of undiscovered wisdom and hidden truth.

There was a prospect of some awakening to the true nature and value of myth and symbol when modern psychology discovered what it calls the "unconscious" area of the psyche; C. G. Jung especially showed the possibility of communication between an inner self hidden in this unconscious region and the outer conscious personality. Psychoanalysis revealed the fact that this hidden side of the individual conveyed its messages to the conscious mind by means of the same general but multifarious code of symbols and images that had been used by the authors of the scriptures and the myths of antiquity.

Mircea Eliade, in his *Patterns in Comparative Religion,* begins his concluding remarks with the idea that "we moderns" believe that myth and mystic religious experience seemingly abolish history. But, far from being detached from history and objective reality, myths constitute in themselves an *"exemplar history."*[3] This revealing term indicates that the noumenal genius of humanity has divined the structure, design, import, and significance of all history and has represented its constituent archetypal ideas in the construction of the mythos. The meaning-essence of history, gathered up and epitomized in typal forms and figures, constitutes a true body of mythology, wherein the leading characters are the replicas in nature of the original divine archetype. St. Paul states categorically that the invisible realities of God are not unrevealed, but are clearly manifest and may be seen by looking at "those things which are made," that is, the natural world. As this world is but the projection of the divine ideation, it can offer a potent talisman to bestir the mind's latent powers of intuition. This is just the principium of all knowledge, which Plato expounded in his doctrine of the soul's oblivion to the memory of her precarnate acquaintance with the divine ideas in the heavenly sphere, and the possibility of her reminiscence or recovery of those lost recognitions through contemplation of their earthly counterparts that she meets here in this world.

Eliade sees that myth and symbol present hierographs of the noumenal realities that lie implicit in the visible world, that they stand as a summary or paraphrase of the content, substance, and mind-essence of history itself. The myth would come near to being the dramatization of what Aristotle predicated as the conclusion or consummation of manifestation in the entelechy, or end product, which the whole time-and-evolution process is unfolding. The myth can be thought of, then, as a preconception of what evolution is intended to unfold on the screen of history and also what that unfoldment may be in universal and ideational terms.

But while myth is "exemplar history," Eliade reminds us that it is not at all "history" in the ordinary sense of the word, that being, the record of particular happenings. It is rather the paradigm of something that, as principle and truth, is happening all the time. It can be enacted in living history again and again, whose events manifest and illustrate the eternal *archai*.

Eliade also points to the phenomenon that always conditions the transmission of truth, that is, the dismal fact that the myth inevitably undergoes a sorry transformation as it passes from hand to hand down the ages. It suffers a blurring of its original clarity of meaning and a loss of the interrelation of its elements. It may even suffer mutilation at ignorant hands. This fate has obscured the luminous quality of myth as a revelation of truth, so that it has ended, in our day, by being stamped as a fancied concoction of meaningless chimerical "events" that are impossible to identify with reality. The myths have thus been labeled the bizarre imaginings of primitive people, whose ignorance led them to fantastic explanations for natural phenomena. The *am h'arets,* the countryside folk, who in piety and ignorance converted the mythical constructions of the Mysteries and the Gnostics into ostensible history, are shown to have been guilty of "infantilism." Eliade thus identifies as a universal phenomenon the tendency that we have been noting in the treatment of the Gospel story.

Jung, however, states that in spite of the fact that myths have become mere jargon, they nevertheless still exercise the symbolic power to awaken feelings and intuitions of their hidden meaning. Since they are graphs of truth and reality, the symbols cannot totally fail to point the mind toward an apprehension of verity. Jung has elaborated this thesis, averring that this universal symbolism is the source or ground of power that, in particular, Roman Catholicism exercises over the collective consciousness of its millions of devotees.

Both Eliade and Jung seem to applaud this naive intuition of the deep power of symbols and to feel that fostering it has been a good service rendered by ecclesiasticism. In-so-far as it is a universal impulse in man, it is natural and therefore presumably "good." But when one sees it as the unhappy result of general ignorance, it is difficult to be as complacent with the results as these two analysts seem to be. B. A. G. Fuller, in his *History of Philosophy,* takes a more serious view of this matter.[4] He concludes a discussion of this very theme with the observation that no image of truth could ever be less dynamic for human good by being understood. Surely, what is intellectually meaningful to a man is a more potent influence than what is incomprehensible. How can one argue that it is better to have vague and nebulous feelings than clear comprehension? If we do so argue, it is because we have little confidence in man's ability to know the truth and act upon it. Such an attitude exalts ignorance over knowledge. The Buddha did not make this mistake when he declared that the cause of all suffering is ignorance. Nor did Hermes, when he said: "The vice of a soul is ignorance; the virtue of a soul is knowledge." Nor did the writer of Proverbs when he exhorted us: "With all thy getting, get wisdom, get understanding" (Prov: 4:5), the most precious of all things. Nor did the Upanishad that runs: "By sharp and subtle intellect is He beheld." What is valid about the position taken by Jung and Eliade in this connection is that the potency of a symbol is so great that it can stir some dim intimation of truth by its very presence. What must also be true, however, is that the same symbol would be tenfold more productive of good if its subtle but profound meaning were understood.

It has sadly to be said that a lack of comprehension of the truth behind the magnificent symbolism of the scriptures has led to gross distortions of the truth in the Christian world, which is still dominated by what Eliade calls "infantilism." He says that the images generate in the soul a "nostalgia" for recovery of its lost paradise of divine knowledge and the "intellectual love of God" that is enjoyed in heaven. Mind is the power that has raised human life above that of the lower orders. John Dewey has boldly said that the discovery of symbols has been the greatest single achievement in world history. We are all aware that language and all conceptualization is symbolic, and such intellectual advances are the only real signs we have that man has advanced much beyond his fellow animals. Man must know what is good before he can successfully perform it.

Eliade makes frequent use of two words, *hierophany* and *kratophany*, both of which hold a wealth of meaning. They refer respectively to the awareness of the presence of sacredness and of power. Religion has also always had its *epiphany*, which, in the large, signifies the appearance of the Divine as an invisible presence that haunts the visible world. When an object, a place, or a phenomenon in life affects the mind with, as Wordsworth phrases it, "a sense sublime of something far more deeply inter-fused," it is a hierophany, an appearance of the divine in some objective situation. The heights of poetic beauty, the deepest insights into truth, the most ecstatic mystical experience, can trace their origins to the power of a symbol. A symbol furnish-es a link between the Logos of God that created it and the human mind that experiences it. A symbol carries in its form every clue to its identity with the divine thought that projected it. Thus, the symbols of the tree, stream, snake, bee, cow, lamb, seed, fruit, earth, water, air, fire, sun, moon, star, horizon, dawn, eve, night, and, above all, light and darkness have each been a medium of most profound and potent spiritual force for men.

It seems to us in this connection, however, that Eliade gives too much credit to "primitives" in their conception of myths and the efficacy of symbols. He asserts that the primitive mind was able to formulate a coherent symbolism and a prodigious mythology. He also asserts that infantilism does not impair the validity of the symbolism, since a symbol does not depend upon being understood; it holds the truth in spite of every corruption and maintains its structure even when long forgotten. It is true that we do find primitive peoples now or in the past who have made great use of myths and of symbols, sometimes as talismans. But can we assume that these recondite constructions were orig-inated by primitives? Were they not, perhaps, originated by others and handed on? The primitive mind could not avoid see-ing the symbols, since all nature, as Thales said, "is full of gods" and carries the epiphany of the divine cogitation. But naive infantilism can never do more than receive, then misconstrue and misinterpret the myths. It dimly senses the symbols in nature without recognizing their significance. If primitives possessed the constructions and ritualized the use of symbols, it is because the wisdom and subtle intellect of sages had produced these works of genius long before. The great legacy of myth, symbolism, and ritualism came not from primitive intuition, but from the gods or "holy men of old." The legend still holds that the tomes of ancient wisdom emanated from "God," that is, from men wise enough to appreciate the divine archetypes after which the material world is patterned. Today we preserve in our traditions and rituals many symbolic elements we no longer understand. It is questionable whether many practicing Christians could explain the significance of the yule tree, or the red and green colors emblematic of Christmas, or many other familiar symbols. Are we, then, primitives?

Eliade also says that a symbol "carr[ies] further the dialectic of the hierophany"[5]; it prods the mind to grasp its significance. It is a mnemonic, tending to initiate the recognition of the divine image it reflects. It carries on the process of "hierophanization," because it discloses a sacred or cosmological reality not otherwise to be revealed. "It is in the actual symbol itself that we must seek the reason."[6] This is indeed a truth that should be widely noted and remembered.

But even more important for our purposes, Eliade states that Christ himself can "be held to be a 'symbol' of the miracle of divinity incarnate in man."[7] This certainly bears out our thesis, if, of course, it is made clear whether by "Christ" he means Jesus of Nazareth, or the imaginatively hypostatized Christ-Logos, the creation of the theologians. If symbolism, as Eliade says, is an autonomous form of revelation, any man can symbolize the divinity in man.

The only thing that matters in religion, Eliade asserts, is the fact that all the myths and rituals comprise a coherent, consis-

THE WITNESS OF ALLEGORY

tent system that predates them all. This warrants us in speaking of a "logic of symbols," as is now conspicuously demonstrated by the symbolism expressed in the unconscious mind, or the "transconscious." Symbols are enduring because they are so pliable; they are capable of reflecting the widest range of meaning. For example, light and darkness can symbolize any and all pairs of opposites, as white and black, life and death, good and evil, male and female, and so on. Symbols thus constitute a language and, be it added, the only ultimately true and competent one. And there is, or should be, no break in continuity between the spontaneous "figments of the unconscious" and the logical nature of the mental processes of the waking state.

What may be called "symbolic thought" makes it possible for the mind to feel the relevance of a truth grasped by the aid of symbol at every level of reality. For the symbol hints at universals and generalities. This is why thinking in the language of symbols gives the mind such a luminous, buoyant sense of expansion, a feeling that all things are unified in one all-encompassing revelation of relatedness, balance, and synthesis. This is a large part of the afflation experienced by Plotinus, Spinoza, and the other great mystics, such as Tauler, Boehme, Ruysbroeck, and the rest. It must be closely allied to Kant's "synthetic unity of apperception."

One final point Eliade makes is extremely interesting: He holds that the individual who cultivates the art of thinking in the language of poetic symbolism arrives ultimately at the recognition that he himself is the central symbol of all. He realizes that he is not an entity standing apart and aloof from his objective world, but that he is integral with it, a living part of the universal synthesis. He senses that in fact he is a "living cosmos" in himself, brother to all things large or small, the solar system or the atom.[8] And so he recovers for himself the knowledge and the self-recognition attained by the initiates and the Gnostics, that he is himself the universe in miniature, the cosmos *ab initio,* the microcosm. And the function of the myth, as man's echo of the Logos, is to impress upon his consciousness the self-realization of the fact that he is himself the way, the truth, and the life, and potentially the heir of God.

With this experience, the world at large is no longer something outside him, foreign and alien. On the contrary, everything calls him home to himself, by revealing to him his own nature and destiny. The myths, rites, and symbols beat upon his consciousness with suggestions and reminders, stimuli and incitement, to awaken his deeply buried memory of the cosmic universal realities of being, the potential of which was implanted in him at the inception of his life. It is even suggested that, owing to primitive man's closeness to the eternal symbols omnipresent in nature, he lived an existence less broken and alienated from reality than does civilized man today.

One outcome of this revelation is to sanctify the whole world with the presence of the logoic archetypes, so that the distinction between sacred and profane largely vanishes. This does not mean that the previously limited area of the sacred is reduced to the level of the commonplace, but that the aura of sanctity is spread over the whole ground. The preachment of men like Martin Buber is that the truly holy life is achieved by the power of the self to hallow the daily life, to metamorphose the commonplace and the so-called profane. The gap between sacred and secular, holy and profane, becomes merely relative and expands or contracts with the flux of mood and insight.

Reference to man as a microcosm brings the ancient traditions to mind. But this concept also finds an important place in Jung's analysis of the process of man's attainment of individuation. In this process, there comes a point at which the individual arrives, even as Eliade suggested, at the consciousness that he is himself the microcosm of the universe. Consciously or unconsciously, but with tenfold more psychic dynamism if consciously, he feels that his life and being correspond to that of the cosmos, and that the same evolutionary process that is bringing the cosmic creation to birth is, within the compass of his smaller universe, bringing his soul to birth. And he senses that the self in him is the same as the Self in the Cosmos, one unit among an infinite total of such selves, homogeneous and essentially one with all, and all one with the Whole. He can think of himself as a star among the numberless stars of the firmament. He sees himself as the center of all being, so that no other center is to be rated as more sacred than he. In *The Origin and Meaning of Hasidism,* we find Martin Buber saying that the real path to the Absolute is seen only in the relation of man to himself.[9] The ancient sages declare with unanimity that a man should never worship any power outside himself. And the apex of Hindu thought is perhaps reached in the *tat tvam asi:* "Thou art That." If a man truly learns to worship the life within himself, he is worshipping the God whom he conceives to be the Whole. The criterion of the righteousness of his worship would be whether he worships himself in narrow isolation, or associates himself in terms of love with all others who also participate in the universal essence. This would constitute the basis of the first and second great commandments of the Christian system, that one should love the divine within himself first, and then the divine in the universe exterior to himself. For the individual will disrupt the harmony and the unity if he withdraws from the community. The disintegration of the cells of an organism is the process of decay and corruption; love is the force that holds these together in health and felicity. And so with man. Each and every soul is an essential and integral component of that corpus we call God.

HISTORY ROBBED
OF MEANING

T he efforts of both Judaism and Christianity to transform
the tradition of Messiahship into actual history have had
an unforeseen result: they have reduced the significance of history, except for that fragment to which it is affirmed that *all* history must look for its meaning.

The Christians have based the whole history of the Western
world upon a series of alleged events recorded in an ancient document of dubious authenticity, failing to see that this action
leaves all other history bleak, bare, and destitute of meaning. In
the events that took place in Judea, according to this view, all
the past race of Adam, all the numberless streams of human
activity in the past thousands of years, converged and found
their raison d'etre. And from these events a new impulse was
engendered for the future, bearing all the fortunes of mankind
in a new direction.

As for the Hebrews, their formulation likewise focused the
essence of all previous history into another series of events
alleged to have occurred chiefly in ancient Egypt and Palestine,
events that, they asserted, would lead to the culmination of
the historic process at a time not too far in the future. The

persuasion that this denouement did indeed take place about the first century of the Christian era led certain elements among the Jews into the ferment that produced Christianity as a Jewish product. They steadfastly proclaimed their belief that the expected convergence of the forces of the past *had,* in effect, come to pass about the year 1 AD.

As we have said, the expectation of the Messiah's coming was never far below the surface of the Hebrew consciousness, for it was an integral part of the theocratic constitution of the nation. In all Jewish religious thought, the Israelite nation was divinely commissioned to deliver Jehovah's righteous will to the nations of the world, to establish the Kingdom of God on earth under its own headship and thus to bring history to its consummation. Then, as now, groups of people of uncritical minds and unstable emotional susceptibilities, brooding over biblical "prophecies," let themselves be swept away by the conviction that the great climax of history was approaching. Christianity could have originated in no other way. Irrational as the agitation may have been, it is certainly true that a religious ferment among a rural population in a small district took hold and eventually grew to be the religious faith of a third of the human family.

Both Christianity and Judaism have always held that their systems provide the key theses that rationalize history. But another view may be taken of the same events, namely, that on the terms of their systematization, both constructions have nullified history. For both faiths have circumscribed their vision by the narrow limits of their own special points of view, which in both cases were clearly distortions of the truth.

Let us consider what Martin Buber writes in *The Origin and Meaning of Hasidism.* Here he expounds four kinds of exile and redemption, referring to the soul's incarnation on earth as its exile from heaven, and its regaining of the lost paradise and return to God as its redemption. Under these terms, Buber is dealing with the axial elements in religion and its scriptures, and his handling of these principles shows great discernment and understanding. The four he cites are:

1. the exile of the "holy sparks" and their return

2. the exile and return of the individual soul in its pilgrimage through the stages of organic evolution to its high goal

3. the exile of the national soul of a people

4. the exile of the Shekinah and its redemption[1]

These four are closely related through their interconnections; for instance, a national exile would obviously include that of its component individuals. Then, if the Shekinah and the "holy sparks" are accorded their proper definition, the close connection of these with the others is at once apparent.

But what is also apparent is that the Jewish theologian is sufficiently uncertain with regard to the proper identification of these sparks—or their relationship to the Shekinah and of it to the individual and the nation—that he treads the ground with caution. What are these "holy sparks"? Hasidism is really a modern revival of the ancient Jewish Kabalism, exploiting the wisdom of the great Kabalist work, the *Zohar*. Both the sparks and the Shekinah are designations used powerfully in this work. The former are the individualized units of the fiery spiritual essence of God's creative mind, represented in religions under a wide variety of names. They are sparks from God's eternal flame of spirit (spirit is always symbolized by fire). The soul in Egyptian books says: "I come from the sea of fire, from the lake of flame, and I live." There can be no dispute that the holy sparks are our divine souls here in our human bodies.

The *Shekinah* is a term referring more generally to the presence of the spiritmind of the divine nature ubiquitously throughout the universe of consciousness. When it is used to refer to the presence of its divine ray in the psyche of humanity, it becomes identical with the sparks. And as regards the exile of the individual (and the nation as an aggregate of such), since the Shekinah-spark in each man is just his inner core of individual being, we reach the surprising conclusion that all four of Buber's entities, which suffer exile and must be redeemed, are one and the same. This being so, the problem of the redemption of all elements in exile is simply a matter of the redemption of the one thing, which might be called the Shekinah-spark incarnate in every individual and nation. If a man reawakens his divine soul from earthly "pollution" to divine purity, he is redeemed, and if all men accomplish this task, the world is redeemed.

But Buber is held by the Jewish purview, and conditioned by the Torah, with its divine promise that the seed of Abraham is destined to implement the redemption of man; he therefore concludes that there can be no redemption of the individual, the Shekinah, and the sparks until one nation has consummated its redemption so as to become God's instrument for the redemption of the rest of the human race. It is because he has diversified the one divine fire into four flames that he can thus save the Jewish theocracy and religion, by making the redemption of all the rest contingent upon the redemption of "one nation." All that need be said is that the redemption of man comes with the redemption of all individual souls (Shekinahs, sparks); and that souls redeem themselves, never lacking God's help because they are themselves rooted in God and embody the potential of God himself. The only exiles in the scriptures are souls expatriated from heaven for their schooling in life, whose discipline teaches them how to achieve self-mastery. Their redemption is in their own hands, and the experience of mingled joy and suffering they undergo on this cross of matter is itself designed to forward their growth.

So Martin Buber subtly invokes the thesis that has laid upon the Hebrew race the task of spiritualizing the world. He affirms that the redemption of the Shekinah is described in the same terms as the redemption of "Knesset Israel," the "congregation of Israel." Of course this is so, if one reads these designations in their esoteric reference to *spiritual* Israel and not *physical* Israel. Those who first used these terms never dreamed there would be men who would mistake a spiritual host in the heavens for their own human selves.

Buber states that the exile and redemption of this one nation play an important part in the destiny of the world. He says they are connected with God's deepest sorrow in witnessing the wreckage of his first cherished plans for the creation of mankind. This duplicates Christianity's postulation of the "fall" of man from Paradise into sin, evidently thought of by Buber as the error that has penetrated to the very roots of creation. The Israelite national exile is central to Hasidic theory, he states, only because it is central in all exile and redemption; God made Israel's incarnation and resurrection the axis of his scheme for the world. Just as the Roman Catholic Church holds that souls cannot be saved without its good offices, so Jewish theology holds that souls cannot be saved without Israel's achievement of its allotted task. Religion has an important place and function in the life of man, but when religions become formalized and feel their power as an instrument of man's salvation, they inevitably assume that they are a necessity in the divine plan. So, for the Hasidists, the history of this favored nation, Israel, looms up between the world and the individual. Christians, Buber argues, become such by entering a covenant with God as individuals; but Jewry stands related to God through God's own commitments to Israel as a nation. Therefore, in Jewish theocracy, salvation must be implemented by the achievement of Israel's national theophany. The redemption of the community of nations cannot come until one nation, designated specifically for this role and mission, shall redeem itself in its own way of life and thus implement the will of God for the redemption of humanity.

This is why Hasidism holds faithfully to the Hebrew theological dream that Israel (not spiritual Israel but Palestinian Israel) is the heart of humanity, the heart of the world, and that without the redemption of Eretz Israel, the ultimate redemption will not take place. But we must emphasize here that the modern Israelis *are not* the Israelites of the Bible. Those Israelites are God's mind-born Sons, here in incarnation as the souls of *all* human beings. It would not be amiss to say that they are the *malakim*, the angels of God, the messengers of his word and will.

It does something—yet in the end not enough—to testify to the fidelity, the devotion, the fortitude, and the heroic obduracy with which the Jewish people have sealed their conviction of their divine choice and mission. Little could surpass this demonstration of the tenacity of purpose of the human spirit. Yet even the greatest piety, sincerity, loyalty, and consecration cannot transform a mistaken object of devotion into a good cause. No amount of noble self-sacrifice can change the fact that the Jewish people have set themselves apart from the rest of humanity by accepting the special role as the world redeemer. Jewry can clasp hands with all people in brotherhood when and only when it has abandoned its age-old illusion that it has a different relation to deity from other people. Did not St. Paul exhort them to remember that one does not attain the status of an Israelite by the mere accident of birth in a Hebrew household? When the Jewish people are firmly united with the rest of humanity, they can rejoice in the privilege granted to all mortals of aspiring to membership in the glorious company of God's spiritual Israel. If Judaism could make this correction of its fundamental position, it could constitute a turning point in world history.

In point of fact, no nation or race of people in the world, now or ever, has a world role to play superior to that of any other. Just as the Greeks had no intrinsic right to take to themselves the illustrious name of *Hellas* and *Hellenes* (the bright and shining ones); and the high caste of the Babylonians no right to the name *Chaldeans, Chaldees,* or *Chaladim* (the Archangels); and, in a lesser sense, the Germans no right to the name of *Herrenvolk* and the Latter Day Saints no right to their self-designation of the Children of Israel (attributing to the Jews the title Children of Judah)—in the same way the Hebrews had no right to the name of *Israel* and *Israelites.* All such names appertain to the awakened spiritual man that every religion has cherished as its ideal—to the perfected and idealized race, not to the actual, frail, and very imperfect peoples themselves.

Hence, it seems high time that Christianity ended the double implication of the name *Christ.* All references should clearly state whether the term is being used to mean the man Jesus himself or the Christos spirit that may have overshadowed and manifested in him. Both positions, however, are in the long run unsatisfactory. The Christos is too mighty, too universal a term to be associated with just one person or one manifestation; it signifies the spiritual nexus that is the potential source of enlightenment for every man. No man's potential Christhood was ever obliged to wait for its implementation or awakening upon any other than himself. Thousands of souls in the pagan world were on fire with the pure flame of divine passion and Christly love centuries before Jesus ever lived. Now that so much about the real stature of non-Christian religions is known, Christians should have enough humility to acknowledge that individual spiritual growth is not entirely dependent on belief in Jesus, or in membership in the Christian church.

This questioning of the dogma that the divinity that flowered in Jesus' life is necessary for the salvation of all mortals on earth brings us to a consideration of the Christian doctrines of "the vicarious atonement" and "the forgiveness of sins."

Chapter Twenty

GODS DIE
FOR MEN

W e have noted that Christianity divested the sequence
of world history of much of its significance when it
attributed such overpowering historical meaning to events in
the narrative recounted in the Gospels. These events were so
interpreted that they furnished the ground and determinants of
human destiny; in this process, as we have seen, the controlling
influences of human life were allocated to a realm completely
external to man. Because of this, the principle of vicariousness
was almost de facto introduced into the Christian system. The
nature and meaning of that short period of time in Judea was
made the turning point in history, the dawn of a new era, the
beginning of man's true life. Indeed, the documents composing
the record of the occurrences of that time have been called the
Book of Life. It is Christianity's basic text on religion, philosophy, psychology, and ethics. Christianity calls upon people to
orient their lives to the life of the world primarily in terms of
those scriptures.

One of the central doctrines arising out of this interpretation of history is that if Jesus of Nazareth had not suffered death
on a cross two thousand years ago, no human being could be

saved from eternal damnation. That single death proffered to all men the gift of salvation—a gift that had but to be accepted in order to win a blessedness that, otherwise, could never be attained—and released a power that could be appropriated by the simple process of opening mind and heart to its beneficence.

It is hardly necessary to say again that this doctrine is a distortion of one of the ancient principles of spiritual understanding, a principle holding that the potential divinity in man's nature would, in the course of evolution, transmute, transfigure, and thus eventually "save" his lower animal self.

The Christian definition of exactly what man must be saved from has always been vague. The threat of evil condition has most commonly been designated as the life of sin and its consequences. God had offered the bliss of Eden, but "man's first disobedience" caused him the loss of that happy state and committed him to a wretched existence under God's curse. Being left no resources whereby he could save himself, he could win salvation only vicariously through the death of Jesus. The fifty-third chapter of Isaiah provided warrant for the doctrine: "He suffered for our sins." Jesus took our sinful nature upon himself and wrestled with death in order to overcome the curse upon mankind.

The beauty and truth of this doctrine can be seen only if it is regarded as allegory. It was a cardinal principle of the Mystery teaching that the animal-human nature could not elevate itself in the stream of evolution beyond the ring-pass-not of the animal nature without the good offices of a higher and potentially divine principle that was inherently one with God. By that agency its instinctive tendencies would be gradually subdued by reason, and its vague yearning for goodness and love would grow into an upsurge of spiritual aspiration. Man is, in many ways, an animal like all others, a product of nature's evolutionary drive; but he has something that sets him apart from all other living creatures. Within him is the seed of fully self-conscious, self-responsible life. This seed is the divine potential, infinitely creative, infinitely loving.

The ancient tradition taught that an outpouring of the divine Christos principle into man's heart can effect a sublimation or transfiguration of the carnal nature that could not be accomplished without such help. This is the only "oblation for sin," the only vicarious atonement that should be envisaged. The historization process attributed to Jesus this universal dynamic for man's growth. It gave into one man's hands the infinite power for redemption that is the divine birthright of every human being.

There is little more to be said about the doctrine of the vicarious atonement save to point out that it has had unfortunate consequences for the Christian world. It should be obvious that if a man believes his salvation will be won for him by a being whose efforts have already been crowned with success, he will not struggle to win the goal for himself. Thus the aspirant is robbed of his own divine initiative and reduced to spiritual beggary.

It is important to note that the principle of vicariousness has been prominent only in Christianity. Judaism makes room for the principle of the mercy of God, but this hardly diminishes its insistence on the role of both natural and divine law. It permits a certain latitude in Jehovah's dealings with his people Israel, but the doctrine, nevertheless, does not imply vicarious atonement. Hindu systems adhere closely to the reign of universal law and teach that a man must suffer the consequences of the karma generated by his own actions, both good and bad. Christianity alone permits a man to evade the results of his mistakes through divine intervention.

But whatever comfort might be drawn from the prospect of successful escape from the consequences of our sins is infinitely more than counterbalanced by the shattering of human confidence in the reign of law, both physical and spiritual. Both the

doctrine of vicarious salvation and forgiveness of sins substitute
for immutable law the capricious will of a Deity who is not
above whimsicality, if Old Testament history is to be taken as
gauge. Man, of course, in the end must ascribe all things to the
will of God. But one thing we can be sure he has willed is that
his children should develop intelligent responsiveness to his
edicts, rather than blind obedience, and employ reason the better to promote his creative work. If God has given men these
faculties of mind and spirit, he must wish them to be used for
the purpose of seeking the causes and operations of all processes, to the end of obeying that supreme Will. Yet throughout
centuries of history, if not still today, the best answer the church
could give to its people's cries of distress in adversity and suffering was *Dieu le vault*—"God willed it." Even though thinkers
like Thomas, Scotus, Abelard, and others tried to throw some
philosophic light on the problem of evil, the church had no
satisfactory or practical answer to give its followers. In fact,
because the principle of vicariousness risks putting the universal rule of law in jeopardy, there are grounds for believing it pro-
motes lawlessness. A man who believes he stands a good chance
that his transgressions will be forgiven is not likely to be pas-
sionately concerned with observance of law; he is not likely to
cry with the Psalmist: "O how I love thy law, O God," or "My
delight is in the law of the Lord, and in his law do I meditate
day and night." It is certainly a historical and social fact that
lawlessness is common in those countries called Christian.

The difference between the literal and the metaphorical
interpretation of Christian texts can be illustrated by reference
to the doctrine of salvation by the shed blood of Christ. This is,
of course, a statement of the ancient concept that deity pours
out its life-giving powers that man might live. "Blood" must be
thought of as the life-essence of the gods, generator of their
power. In the creation glyphs, God was described as originating
the world by projecting his seminal essence into the womb of

matter, the Mother. The figure is significant, for blood in itself is not creative, but blood in the form of seminal concentrate is the generator of life.

Many modern scholars have virtually abandoned the physical form of the resurrection. Christ is risen; we, too, shall rise, is the Easter paean of the churches. But St. Paul declares that if Christ be not risen, then is our faith vain. If by this is meant spiritual resurrection, one must ask how it could be that the God of Gods, the Lord of creation, could need spiritual resurrection. Does it not seem rather to imply that if the Christ spirit be not resurrected—quickened—in man, all his faith will avail him nothing?

One of humanity's tragedies has been the failure of religions to free man from the obstacles to salvation that lie within his own nature. Christians hoped and believed that the coming of Jesus would infuse fresh spiritual dynamism into the life of sin-thwarted man, bring divine grace to earth, burn the barriers of enmity between man and God, set aside the former reign of rigid, sterile law, make love the power to set men free, and thus inaugurate the golden age of the Kingdom of God. Yet the Christian movement seemed itself to release a storm of ferocity in the religious life of the West such as had never swept the earth before. "There is no wild beast like an angry theologian," observed the Roman Emperor Julian, once the head of the Christian church. Paganism had never bred such sectarian antipathies, such bigotry or superstition. In the name of divine love and mercy, a reign of terror and cruelty held sway over Christians for centuries. Human charity was so overshadowed that a man could remorselessly burn a fellow man at the stake for a mere technical difference in theology, perhaps in phraseology or translation.

Christians assert that Jesus' life, mission, and death brought men relief from sin, taught us how to conquer death and gain immortality, and showed the way to loving fellowship in Christ.

Unfortunately, history shows no evidence whatever that men have been less sinful, less afraid of death, or more loving and generous in life since the advent of Christianity. In fact, as the sociologist Pitirim Sorokin has shown, the incidence of war and violence in Christian lands is far greater than in non-Christian lands during a comparable period.

However, it must be reasserted that the Gospels were not written at the level or in the aura of mundane history, but that they aimed merely at setting a few events in a frame of theological doctrinism or catechetical instruction, as Loisy puts it. Some also declare that the dynamic message embodied in the Gospels is not to be deduced from the contents by human reason and judgment, since their meaning is numinous and not to be apprehended by rational processes. They must be accepted as pure acts of God; it is not for us to evaluate them. They are not to be understood, but only to be believed. This is a position other religions have also taken with regard to their most sublime concepts. It is certainly true that the nature of Deity—infinite, and yet finite in manifestation, boundless and partless, everywhere and nowhere—is full of paradoxes to the literal and analytical mind; all the terms by which man has tried to describe the Godhead are contradictory. One can only say that Deity is a fullness that cannot be comprehended in human terms; it is therefore nonrational or superrational. If belief were required of Christians on these grounds alone, no one could take exception. Instead, matters of supposed mundane fact that are contrary to natural law and the course of known history are what we are asked to accept unquestioningly.

The thesis of this book is that if the features of the Gospel story are taken to be the outward signs of inner and invisible reality of spiritual experience and eternal truth, they become luminous with meaning and value for every man's life. In this context, the move of the Roman Catholic Church hierarchy to open the door to the mythico-allegorical interpretation of the

scriptures is most encouraging. The poetry of angels and shepherds on Christmas, of stars and Magi, cave or stable, Herut
threat, flight to Egypt—this and more can now be restored to
its proper place in the whole beautiful allegory. All the drama of
temptation, crucifixion, and resurrection can be elevated from
Passover realism to the true significance of human experience,
of the souls of all men. The legend that all the events of Christ-
history fell into exact patterns fulfilling Old Testament prophecy can be illuminated by the understanding that those events
and prophecies were archetypal forms of universal events. Thus
there is hardly a character in the narrative that had not already
a dramatic prototype. Allegorical figures were brought to life as
persons in Judean history. Jesus was destined to choose twelve
disciples because every Sun-God figure of ancient times had
twelve companions. December 25th was fixed as Jesus' birthday
long before he was born; his resurrection was certain to coincide
with the Jewish Passover at the vernal equinox. He was destined
to fast in the wilderness and be tempted forty days. By zodiacal
symbolism he had to be born six months after John the Baptist,
his precursor. Since Gospel narrative fulfills ancient prophecy so
closely, the implication is fully warranted that it was written
designedly to fulfill such prophecy. Such a task was not at all
beyond the capability of the great minds of that age. Abundant
material was at hand, ready to be cast into shape to form an
ideal life of the Son of God.

The recent undertaking to exploit the gold of spiritual
truth that lies buried in ancient scriptures has been, in effect, a
project aiming to reorient the meaning of those scriptures to
modern thought. But this task, though worthy, is not without
its dangers. There is a wide and deep gulf between the ancient
and the modern mind; the scientific and materialistic cast of
thought today is temperamentally foreign to symbolism and
unlikely to appreciate the meaning of divine archetypes and the
ways they can image truth and relate consciousness to reality.

Still, any interpretation that attempts to render the ancient ideographs less opaque will be a gain after so many centuries during which they were considered sacrosanct—when it was almost sacrilege to venture to bring the events they pictured into the sunlight of rational evaluation.

Religion has been the area of human experience traditionally beyond the reach of that principle of reason that normally relates man's life to his environment. It has been governed by "higher" influences emanating from a superior Source. Depth and existential psychology today is willing to admit that mystical religious experience may be nonrational, but not that its fruits should be *anti*rational. At no level of its manifestation or apprehension should truth contravene reason. What is more, man is above all else a rational being whose nature is to know, to seek truth and understanding of the enigmas that confront him. Mysticism may deliver suprarational ecstasies and experiences of atonement that are strange to our particular everyday existence, but the reality thus revealed is substantiated by thoughtful study of the unity that lies behind diversity. The numinous, ineffable, direct perception of divine Being, when worked out in daily experience, yields greater, not lesser, understanding of that experience.

Any study of the kind we are pursuing should not neglect to mention the emphasis that has been laid upon the separation of the holy from the mundane in Western life, resulting in the traditional separation of church and state. This has come about as ecclesiasticism has gradually circumscribed religion, formalizing devotion and worship and setting them apart and aloof from secular existence. Thus has been established a great gulf between the sacred and the secular, which John Dewey described as the most disastrous of enmities. It was primarily encouraged by the religious hierarchy because it surrounded religious practices with an aura of awe and mystery, and at the same time it kept off interference from princely or secular power. For similar reasons, the separation seemed good to the early framers of democratic political systems, who feared ecclesiastical domination. But it unquestionably has had serious consequences for true religion, because it segregated God from common life and confined true worship to the churches. It set the secular and the sacred in opposition to each other. It also perpetuated the idea that man must have a church to mediate between himself and God. This statement should not be taken as in any sense denigrating the power of a true experience of transcendental values in religion. The criticism is directed rather at the orthodoxy that holds any and all religious activities automatically sanctified and holy just because they are church oriented and also holds that normal life—no matter how good, how loving and benevolent—is nevertheless profane. Christianity has tended to rob human life of its inner significance by insisting that the individual must leave his own sphere and come into a totally different realm if he is to partake of the religious life. Here again the source of the practice lies in the symbolism teaching that a person must leave behind the things of the flesh when he enters the house of God. But that house, that temple, should be his own body and soul, not a building, however noble and beautiful. Ironically, because Christianity has taught that man is unworthy, he has behaved unworthily. Had he considered himself potentially godlike, he might have been constrained to act divinely.

Religion should shed its influence upon all times and places, sanctifying the high festivals and the daily round of life. The special occasions are not beneficent if their celebration disparages the sacredness of the ordinary. Drama and ritual are necessary to generate the power of spiritual catharsis. But the benefaction should spread from the exalted moment to all moments. Sincere religious worship can dissolve the wall of partition, as St. Paul calls it, between the human and the divine, cementing them in "one new man, so making peace."

The doctrine of the opposition of the mundane and the divine has led to the belief that man must discard his humanity before he can inherit his divinity. He has been called a rebel, who has to put down his rebellious self. It was out of this conviction that the belief arose in the efficacy of asceticism—that is, that by tormenting and subduing the flesh, the spirit would be freed. It would have been far better to recognize that the enlightenment and beneficence destined to arise out of the tension and struggle between the two poles of good and evil could never be won if the force of the one pole was crippled or extinguished.

C h a p t e r   T w e n t y - O n e

DEATH THROES AND BIRTH PANGS

O ur challenge to Christianity has been primarily that it has abstracted the divine element from man's nature and externalized it, leaving him nothing but his grosser self. Christianity's failure to transform mankind for the better stems largely from this mistake.

We have said that when it allocated to Jesus alone the divinity that was the heritage of all, Christianity dismembered integral man. Deprived of the power to redeem himself, man was left to grovel, ashamed and afraid to stand on his feet and demand his birthright as heir to the kingdom of blessedness. He thus abrogated his title to Sonship of the Father and joint heir of his omnipotence. This reduced man to the level of pitiful supplicant. Under such an influence, people enter the race of life without self-confidence and so are defeated from the start. Therefore, the Christian has not been encouraged to face the battle of life with a stout heart. Like Arjuna facing the battle of Kurukshetra in the Hindu scripture, The Bhagavad Gita, he shrinks from the conflict. His philosophy has never instructed him that the struggle itself sets the conditions for victory. Instead, martyrdom was made the chief crown of glory. A key word in Christian psychology has always been *surrender.* Assured that Jesus has paid the debt of all mankind, the Christian has no basis for rationalizing the need for his own temptation and his own Gethsemane. Christianity has thus wrenched from its people's hands the sword of the spirit and sent them into the battle of life unarmed and helpless. It can truly be said that European man lived deprived of any sense of the value of his intrinsic self until the fourteenth-century Renaissance rediscovered and reaffirmed his innate nobility and resources.

The human spirit has perhaps never suffered a greater burden than under Christianity's insistence on the power of "sin." No doubt a soul struggling upward out of what the Hindus call *avidya,* or "ignorance," must along the way often realize poignantly its failures in knowledge and right action. But such recognition should serve as the spur to endeavor. Souls advance only as imagination, quickened by intuition, can anticipate the future with yearning and hope. Forgetting those things which are past," says the great Apostle, "I press on to the mark of the high calling of God in Christ Jesus" (Phil. 4:13-14).

In the pagan world, sin never carried the heavy implications that Christian theology injected into it. The Mount of Sin was a term used in virtual equivalence with the "Mount of the Moon." Ancient doctrine, according to Plutarch, derived man's lower bodily nature from an evolution long ago on the moon. It therefore refers to the "natural man" of Pauline theology, who had to precede and prepare the ground for the advent of spiritual man. As it was the negative side of the polarity in man of spirit and matter or energy, it became colored in religious thought with the dark hues of evil, as opposed to spirit or good. It was thus that the concept of the deadly and inevitable nature of sin originated.

No one will question that the struggle of the soul with its polarized opposite is a strenuous ordeal, often tragic and crucial. But, in the long run, this struggle is salutary, for it strengthens the soul's capacity to come to grips with life in action. Without temptation, without the long fight, there is no victory. St. Paul, in that luminous seventh chapter of the Epistle to the Romans, to which we have made previous reference, stated that if the command to incarnate had not brought him under the law that virtually killed him, he could have missed knowing sin. His implication is that he would not have known the blessedness that can be generated only out of one's combat with this enemy. He regards sin as the leverage by which man attains salvation, praising it as "holy, just, and for our good," and urging us to "make use of this good thing."

But in the Christian misconception of the meaning of a doctrinal term, sin came to mean any disposition on the part of the soul to find delight in the expression of its powers through the body. Christianity thus comes under the stricture of having aroused men to fear and abhor a necessary and strategic element in the economy of spiritual evolution. Man must learn a balanced, sane, and happy integration of soul and body, if he is to lead the good life on earth intended for him. The attribution of evil to the sensual side of human nature has not been fully considered by Christian thinkers in the light of the damage it can cause to the psychic life. Yet it should be obvious that if human consciousness is taught to look with contempt and revulsion upon the instrument through which it has access and relation to life, the result must be injurious feelings of guilt and resentment. If the influence of sensed life on the soul is doctrinally catalogued as evil, then it must be conceded that evil is not to be excluded from the constitution of good. The balance—the tension between mind and matter, light and dark, drive and resistance, outgoing and return—is the ground of all good. To laud spirit alone and condemn matter is to render the spirit impotent in action and to condemn man to self-deprecation, doubt, and fear. Such a position saps the will to joy, to adventure, to victory.

Christianity felt it a great victory, when, freed from persecution and entrenched in power, it sent up the cry "Great Pan is dead!" This message seemed to indicate that the spiritual element, typified by Jesus, had conquered nature. Paganism (from *paganus,* Latin for "the countryside") had received its coup de grâce from the Nazarene. Not only was the human soul henceforth freed from its subservience to sense; the sway of nature's immutable law was thought to be terminated. With their eyes fixed upon the goal of heavenly life, Christians did not realize that the kingdom of Great Pan extended from sunny hills, bosky dells, and rippling brooks right into the constitution of man, ruling that half of his life shared with God's other creatures. Christianity taught that man was separated from nature— a special creation. But the long record of history has taught differently, and today the scientific proof of evolution has made it fully evident that man is a part of nature, even if a unique development. Therefore, it is impossible to kill Pan—he will exert his dominion over the realm of what the Greeks call *physis,* or "nature," until his menial but beneficent service is completed. And the natural joy of the soul in the free exercise of its prerogative of creative activity in cooperation with God will finally dissipate the gloomy cloud of evil that religion has attached to the human body.

A grave charge against Christianity is that, through centuries of tradition, it has given form to many crude beliefs and has since done little to remove them from the popular mind. High on the list of such primitive misconceptions is the personalization of evil in the mythical character of the devil. In medieval times, the mere suggestion that the devil might be active in the person of one's enemy was justification for removing him. Witchcraft and sorcery were charged against innocent people in the name of Christianity.

We may deplore and condemn such cruelty today, but are we yet free from the yoke of fear and superstition that impels it?

Thousands still pray to images of saints for personal favors; heads of state invoke the Deity in their contests with other powers, whose leaders similarly ask divine forces to join their side.

Another pernicious doctrine is that of hellfire, damnation, and purgatorial ordeal. Hell (*Hades, Sheol, Amenta*) is here on earth—is earth, in fact. The figure was intended to portray the fierce flames of carnal passion and the smoky exhalations of dark ignorance the soul experienced in its bodily life until it turned these forces into the pure flame of love. The usual literalism changed these figurative images into a physical fire localized in a particular nether world; through association with the soul's "death" while in the body, this region was placed in the life beyond (physical) death. This confusion over the Greek usage of the word *death* has often been deceptive. As we have tried to show, both the trial of "hellfire" and "purgation" are the experience of the soul while living here in the tomb (*sema*) of the body (*soma*). Earth (and human incarnation) is the lowest of the hells into which souls can descend; anything lower would be birth in the bodies of animals. (The doctrine of metempsychosis, or rebirth in lower forms of life, is restricted to the less metaphysical religions, as it is logically inadmissible.) Earth is that fabled underworld of all mythologies. All gods descend into it to find their *shaktis,* the Hindu word for the physical instrument for the implementation of their powers in creation. Souls will never burn in any fiercer fire than those of the passions, desires, cruelties, and selfishness to which they are subjected when in the body and prisoners of the instinctual, psychic life.

A corollary of this doctrine of damnation and hellfire is the supposition that the ordeal of God's judgment awaits the soul in the heaven world at the end of earthly life. The truth is that souls are on trial every moment of their lives on earth, and the only valid postmortem judgment is that which in a higher dimension of consciousness they themselves pronounce on their past life as they review it from that higher plane.

Another cause of censure of the Christian movement is the hierarchy's failure to raise the popular conception of the term *God* above the level of anthropomorphism. It is shameful that any mind should have reached the modern era while still holding the crude belief that universal Being and divine Intelligence could be so debased as to assume even a semipersonalized form. This leads to the question of the right of any religious group to assume domination and to proclaim itself as the sole mediator with God and the sole arbiter of morality. No group of mere human beings can know the mind of God, or claim the right to exercise the function of God's vice-regent over the religious life of the world's people.

Today, the world faces the necessity of effecting something like a new eclecticism. A new and universal religion is possibly the solution, based upon the ever-closer association of the peoples of the earth and the dissolution of the barriers of separation and prejudice formerly causing men to consider other religions to be "heathen." As the growth of brotherhood and love moves humanity forward into that second dispensation and works its inevitable leaven into the consciousness of mankind, an amalgamation of religions must take place.

Another item in this critique of Christianity concerns its conception of prayer. Man, conceiving himself to be the child of the common Father, has always been disposed, as are all children, to look up to this heavenly Parent for help in all contingencies. Prayer is not, therefore, peculiar to Christianity; it has been a universal expression in all religions.

But the word *prayer* has been made to cover two quite different things, and, as our remarks apply to only one of these, we must sharply distinguish between the two. Under the most common definition, prayer means simply asking God for help and for blessing; under its second meaning, which is variously termed communion with God or contemplation of the divine Nature or Being, it represents an effort to merge individual consciousness with the Divine, or achieve union with the Absolute. In this second aspect, prayer takes many forms of spiritual or mystical devotion, which are all aimed at putting the individual into rapport with the "wisdom and spirit of the universe," as Wordsworth calls it. With the sole reservation that mystical experience needs the balance of a clear reason and an obedience to truth, one can only pay tribute to the selfless quest for a higher Reality embodied in this form of prayer.

It is to the first kind of prayer, the prayer that looks for special favor and divine benefaction, that we take strong exception. First, the prayer that asks God for favors presupposes God's complete disregard of the inviolability of the laws he has ordained for his universe. It asks him to bestow blessings by special favor and with total indifference to the question of the supplicant's worthiness or right to what he pleads for. He begs forgiveness for sins he knows he should not have committed, asks help though it may hurt another, pleads for help in evading punishment for his just deserts. And this pleading goes on in spite of the scripture's own categorical warning: "Be not deceived, God is not mocked: whatsoever a man soweth that shall he also reap." This kind of begging for mercy and for favors has demeaned the human spirit and reduced its courage and self-reliance. And it likewise demeans God, since it is based on the presumption that he is a willful, capricious, arbitrary despot, capable of being persuaded and cajoled by flattery, attention, and praise. It is obviously directed to an anthropomorphic deity who is willing to be propitiated and eager to heed the desires of supplicants, even though he is bombarded with millions of simultaneous and contradictory pleas at once! Does all this seem compatible with the Lord of the universe, whose infinitely vast yet delicately subtle workings—from galaxies to atoms—reveal in every particular the operation of immutable and universal law?

Prayer really is, however, an act of reflection. It is a kind of talking to oneself, and in the sense that every man is essentially a divine spark, this inward voice can perhaps be said to speak to God. Prayer can be efficacious if it is understood to be in truth our appeal to the higher and divine self, the fragment of God that we truly are. It is thus that most of the great mystics have interpreted prayer. If prayer is really heard and answered, it is the response of that seed-spark of God's being he has bequeathed to every man.

The spiritual science of every age has attempted to set forth the rationale of man's approach to God and God's availability to man. A causal chain proceeds from the transcendent being of God through the complex orders of principalities and powers, archangels and angels, to man. As the symbolism has it, the bodies of higher gods suffer dismemberment so that the fragments of their power may nourish the beings on the planes below. This is the true Eucharist, the true bread broken for all souls. The lesser gods are fragmentary beings in comparison with the fullness beyond, but their nature is nonetheless part of, and in immediate touch with, its source. It is only in this way that the infinite power of God can be said to be available to any soul's petition. It is in these terms that it can be said: "I will write my laws in their hearts, and in their minds will I write them. I shall be with them, I shall be their God and they shall be my people"; "the sheep also shall hear my voice." The presence of this divine potential in each human life is man's link with and path of access to God. It is all that the human can accommodate, appropriate, and assimilate of the Divinity that is infinitely greater than the sum total of all existence.

The preceding discussion leads into the heart of the debate between theism and humanism. Both these views are to be reckoned with, since they concern the two halves of the human problem. The arguments for both sides are strong and valid, for each represents a reality in the polarity of man's life. Human and divine powers are equilibrated in the human constitution; therefore, they must be equilibrated in philosophy and psychology.

The emphasis in Christianity would fall naturally on the side of theism, which has held that the source of power and inspiration lies beyond man, in God's will. Humanist theory has rejected the externality of the spiritual impulse and has sought the source of man's strength within his own nature. But it, too, has its weaknesses, the principal one being that it does not recognize the spiritual side of man's nature. Placing its emphasis on the secular rather than the religious, humanism's concern is for existential man. This concern has had wide repercussions upon all the departments of knowledge that impinge on man's psychology, philosophy, and even religion. Theism today is beginning to acknowledge a greater place to human initiative, conscience, and responsibility. On the other hand, humanism itself must become less agnostic, less influenced by behaviorism and positivism, and more willing to acknowledge that man's creativity is an indication of his inner link with the universal creative element we call God.

With the reconstitution of integral human nature, the world, both West and East, can turn to face the dawn of a new day of enlightened humanistic science—a new anthropology, in which the *conscious* human genius can study the art of releasing the divine forces latent within its unconscious depths. Such a study could inaugurate a new religious life for man, consecrated to the God who is everinstant to bless, a God who is within reach of acquaintance and fellowship. When the powers of enlightened intelligence and increased knowledge are brought to bear, finally, on the most important problem of all—the study of the whole man—we shall find man's inner resources will help him to the truth within himself. For the first time in the modern era, human beings can reawaken to the consciousness of their royal character as rulers of their own evolution, coworkers with God in weaving the patterns of world destiny.

If this is to take place, Christianity must become what it never was, the Science of Man. It has heretofore had no claim, with Protagoras the Sophist of Athens, to declare that "man is the measure of all things." Yet the discovery of ancient scrolls, the honest and sharper higher criticism, the recovered knowledge of the presence of spiritual power in the great world unconscious, the recognition of the allegorical nature of the scriptures, and the transfiguration of the message of those scriptures by the radiance of their hidden significance—all give hope of a new and far more radical Reformation than that which Luther, Calvin, Zwingli, Melanchthon, and Erasmus engineered in the sixteenth century.

The shimmering mirage Christianity set before its followers is in a process of dissolution. It was a mirage of transcendent imagery, but empty and unreal. The age-old emphasis of Christianity has been in the heavens; it has exhorted its millions of faithful to turn their backs on earthly interests and to look for their salvation in the skies. Now these millions are beginning to bring their gaze nearer to home, recognizing the values and virtues to be won in the world of human nature, the importance of human relationships, and the search for self-knowledge. This will seem a calamity to many. But it will lead to an important recognition: that a new transcendence in evolution is to be won here on earth. Christianity must turn its gaze back to earth, for earth is that Mount Sinai whereon God stands in immediate relation of fellowship with his children.

Man must know that he is himself the universe in miniature, the microcosm, identical with the macrocosm that is the garment of God. The soul is dispatched by the Father to earth expressly to become the ruler of that universe that is the human organism.

If Christianity will now recognize that the time has come to join with the other great living religious traditions and to direct its vision to the reawakening of the divine spirit, the Christos in man, it may vindicate its right to call its message the true religion of humanity. As the ancient science discerned, nature is the mirror of God's thought, and man's reflection upon the divine ideas as mirrored in nature will project the image and the power of their truth upon the thinking human mind. For as we behold this glory of the Lord in the mirror of nature, says St. Paul, we are changed into the same likeness of the divine mind, from glory unto glory.

NOTES

D r. Alvin Boyd Kuhn completed this work just before his death in 1963. In the form it had reached, his manuscript did not cite all the sources he had used for quotations and references. For the reader's convenience, the Quest staff has made every effort to supply the missing information, but it has not been possible to do so in every case.

Foreword

1. Gershom G. Scholem, *Major Trends in Jewish Mysticism* (London: Thames and Hudson, 1955), 19-20.

Chapter 1. Relighting an Ancient Lamp

1. Robert H. Pfeiffer, *The History of New Testament Times* (New York: Harper and Brothers, 1949), 334.

2. Gerald Massey, *The Natural Genesis* (London: Williams and Northgate, 1883), 1: 13-14.

3. Ibid., 2: 379.

4. Godfrey Higgins, *Anacalypsis* (New York: University Books, 1965). The quoted passage was not found, but similar passages appear on the following pages: 1: 281, 366 ff.; 2: 309 ff., 334, 340-42, 616 ff., 620-21.

5. Gerald Massey, *Gerald Massey's Lectures* (New York: Samuel Weiser, 1974), 132.

6. George Santayana, *The Life of Reason* (New York: C. Scribner's Sons, 1905).

7. Pfeiffer, *History*, 385.

Chapter 2. Egypt's Wayward Offspring

1. Frederick L. Moriarty, *Introducing the Old Testament* (Milwaukee: Bruce Publishing, 1960).

Chapter 5. Religion and the Illumination of Mind

1. Gerald Massey, *Ancient Egypt: The Light of the World* (London: Fisher Unwin, 1907), 2: 907 ff.

Chapter 6. Some Consequences of Esotercism

1. G. R. S. Mead, *Fragments of a Faith Forgotten* (London: Theosophical Publishing Society, 1906), 113.

Chapter 9. The Divine Archetype

1. C. G. Jung (1875-1961). Though the passage Dr. Kuhn is quoting has not been found, Jung elaborates on these ideas in *The Collected Works,* vol. 12, *Psychology and Alchemy* (Princeton, NJ: Bollingen Series XX / Pantheon Books, 1953), particularly 7-8.

Chapter 10. When Messiah Cometh

1. Pierre Van Paassen, *Why Jesus Died* (New York: Dial Press, 1949), 21.

2. Joseph Klausner, *Jesus of Nazareth* (New York: Macmillan, 1927), 384.

Chapter 11. Jesus—Man or Myth?

1. Angelus Silesius (1624-1677), *The Cheubinic Wanderer*, 1: 61-62.

Chapter 12. Peter's Jesus and Paul's Christ

1. Nils Wilhelm Lund, *Chiasmus in the New Testament* (Chapel Hill: University of North Carolina Press, 1942).

Chapter 13. The Triform Messiah

1. Though the particular translation that Dr. Kuhn is quoting is unattributed, the passage is from the *Lamentations of Isis and Nephthys.* One available translation can be found in E. A. Wallis

Budge's *Osiris & the Egyptian Resurrection* (New York: Dover, 1973), 2: 60.

2. Theodor Zahn, *Introduction to the New Testament* (New York: C. Scribner's Sons, 1909), 1: chapter 2.

3. Sigmund Mowinckel, *He That Cometh* (New York: Abingdon Press, 1956), 327.

4. Martin Buber, *The Origin and Meaning of Hasidism* (New York: Horizon Press, 1960), 109.

Chapter 14. Pre-Christian Christianity

1. While book 2, chapter 17 of Eusebius' *Ecclesiastical History* does claim that the sect known as Therapeutae were Christians, the passage quoted here is not in Eusebius. Dr. Kuhn appears to be quoting from T. W. Doane's *Bible Myths* (New Hyde Park: University Books, 1971), 424, which attributes this passage to Eusebius, but does not give a reference.

2. Augustine, *The Retractations* (Washington D.C.: Catholic University of America Press, 1968), book 1, chapter 12, paragraph 3. The particular translation Dr. Kuhn quotes is unknown.

3. Robert Taylor, *The Diegesis* (Boston: J.P. Mendum, 1873), 329.

4. Justin Martyr, *The Apologies of Justin Martyr* (New York: Harper & Brothers, 1877), 1: chapter 59.

5. Epiphanius, *The Panarion of St. Epiphanius, Bishop of Salami* (New York: Oxford University Press, 1990).

6. Epiphanius, as quoted in Doane, *Bible Myths*, 426. The passage is originally from *The Panarion of St. Epiphanius,* 29.4.9.

7. De Quincey, *Historical and Cultural Essays* (Boston: Ticknor and Fields, 1869), 116.

8. Godfrey Higgins, *Anacalypsis* (New York: University Books, 1965), 1: 747-48.

9. Ibid., 2: 43.

10. Edward Gibbon, *The History of the Decline and Fall of the Roman Empire* (Philadelphia: Claxton, Remsen & Hoffelfinger, 1876), 3: 163.

11. Robert H. Pfeiffer, *The History of New Testament Times* (New York: Harper and Brothers, 1949), 64.

Chapter 15. Four Evangels

1. Joseph Klausner, *Jesus of Nazareth* (New York: Macmillan, 1927), 38.
2. Ibid., 22.
3. Ibid., 23.
4. G. R. S. Mead, *Did Jesus Live 100 Years B.C.?* (New Hyde Park: University Books, 1968).
5. Klausner, *Jesus of Nazareth*, 26.
6. Ibid., 27.
7. Ibid.
8. Ibid., 23-24.
9. Ibid., 48-51.
10. Alfred F. Loisy, *The Birth of the Christian Religion and The Origins of the New Testament* (New Hyde Park: University Books, 1962).
11. Sanka Knox, "A New Gospel Ascribed to Mark," *New York Times*, December 30, 1960. For further discussion, see Shawn Ever, "The Strange Case of the Secret Gospel According to Mark," *Alexandria: The Journal for the Western Cosmological Tradition* 3, (1995):103-29.

Chapter 16. Are the Gospels Fictitious?

1. Pierre Van Paassen, *Why Jesus Died* (New York: Dial Press, 1949), 94 ff.

Chapter 17. Jesus and the Christos

1. Pierre Van Paassen, *Why Jesus Died* (New York: Dial Press, 1949), 75.
2. Albert Schweitzer, *The Quest of the Historical Jesus* (Baltimore and London: Johns Hopkins University Press, 1998), 398.

Chapter 18. The Witness of Allegory

1. Oliver Wendell Holmes, "Light of Asia: Review," *The International Review* 7 (1879): 345 ff. See Sir Edwin Arnold, *The Light of Asia* (Wheaton, Ill.: Theosophical Publishing House, 1969, 1982).
2. Robert H. Pfeiffer, *The History of New Testament Times* (New York: Harper and Brothers, 1949), 428-32.

3. Mircea Eliade, *Patterns in Comparative Religion* (New York: Meridian, 1974), 430.

4. B. A. G. Fuller, *A History of Philosophy* (New York: Holt, Rineheart and Winston, 1955).

5. Eliade, *Patterns in Comparative Religion*, 446.

6. Ibid., 447.

7. Ibid., 448.

8. Ibid., 455-56.

9. Martin Buber, *The Origin and Meaning of Hasidism* (New York: Horizon Press, 1960), 235.

Chapter 19. History Robbed of Meaning

1. Martin Buber, *The Origin and Meaning of Hasidism* (New York: Horizon Press, 1960), 203 ff.

INDEX

Philip of Macedon, 18
Philo Judaeus, 1, 2, 16, 25, 50
Philostratus, 178
Plato
    on allegorical doctrine, 5, 46
    on Atlantis, legend of, 67
    on concept of "twoness", 193
    The Cratylus, 61
    on man's mind, 38
    as son of Apollo, 14
    on the soul, 3, 212
Pliny, 103, 137, 152
Plotinus, 32, 141
prayer, 244–46
prophet, 102
Protestant Reformation, 51
Pseudepigrapha, 41, 136, 163
Pythagoras, 14, 61, 110

Quest of Historical Jesus, The (Schweitzer), 188, 254n. 2 (Ch. 17)

redemption, 100, 222–26, 229–33, 239–40
Red Sea, 151
Reformation, Protestant, 51
reincarnation, 118
religion
    ancient writings, influence on, 40–42, 45–47
    comparative, 63–64, 77, 109, 136–37, 141–42
    definition of, 39
    Hellenism, influence on, 43
    humanism, 246–47
    and man's mind, 38–39, 43–45, 236
    purpose of, 31–32, 225, 237–38
    separation of church and state, 236–37
    theism, 246–47
remembrance, 203
Retractions, The (Augustine), 253n. 2 (Ch. 14)
Roman Catholic Church
    and biblical interpretation, 33, 234–35, ix–x
    questioning of absolutism by, 57
    and redemption, 225
Rosetta Stone, 51

Quest Books

encourages open-minded inquiry into
world religions, philosophy, science, and the arts
in order to understand the wisdom of the ages,
respect the unity of all life, and help people explore
individual spiritual self-transformation.

Its publications are generously supported by
The Kern Foundation,
a trust committed to Theosophical education.

Quest Books is the imprint of
the Theosophical Publishing House,
a division of the Theosophical Society in America.
For information about programs, literature,
on-line study, membership benefits, and international centers,
see www.theosophical.org
or call 800-669-1571 or (outside the U.S.) 630-668-1571.

Related Quest Titles

The Hidden Wisdom in the Holy Bible, Geoffrey Hodson

The Genesis Meditations, Neil Douglas-Klotz

The Hidden Gospel, Neil Douglas-Klotz

The Cross and the Grail, Robert Ellwood

Jesus Christ, Sun of God, David Fideler

Yeshua Buddha, Jay Williams

Godseed, Jean Houston

To order books or a complete Quest catalog,
call 800-669-9425 or (outside the U.S.) 630-665-0130.

ſ